TRUE EDUCATION READER

SILENT, ORAL, MEMORY

FOURTH GRADE

By
SARAH ELIZABETH PECK

Published for the Department of Education of the
General Conference of Seventh-day Adventists

"So they read in the Book
In the law of God
Distinctly,
And gave the sense, and
Caused them to understand
The reading."
—*Bible (Nehemiah 8:8).*

TEACH Services, Inc.
PUBLISHING
www.TEACHServices.com • (800) 367-1844

World rights reserved. This book or any portion thereof may not be copied or reproduced in any form or manner whatever, except as provided by law, without the written permission of the publisher, except by a reviewer who may quote brief passages in a review.

The author assumes full responsibility for the accuracy of all facts and quotations as cited in this book. The opinions expressed in this book are the author's personal views and interpretations, and do not necessarily reflect those of the publisher.

This book is provided with the understanding that the publisher is not engaged in giving spiritual, legal, medical, or other professional advice. If authoritative advice is needed, the reader should seek the counsel of a competent professional.

Copyright © 2005 TEACH Services, Inc.
ISBNN-13: 978-1-57258-347-4 (Paperback)
Library of Congress Control Number: 2002103456

TEACH Services, Inc.
P U B L I S H I N G
www.TEACHServices.com ▪ (800) 367-1844

INTRODUCTION

Basic Principles of Reading

Reading is the key that unlocks the door to knowledge. Until children can get thought accurately and quickly from the printed page, they are handicapped in their progress in arithmetic, in language, and in every content subject.

But reading is more than the key to *knowledge*. It is a key to *character*. Nothing is more vitally important than the molding of the pupil's taste for that which is good and pure and true and noble. And in accomplishing this, reading is one of the most potent factors. To create in the child's own heart a distaste for the cheap, the trifling, the untrue, in language and thought, so that he voluntarily rejects all these and *chooses* that which is uplifting—this is the great goal of the teacher of reading. This is real character building.

To the boy or girl in training to be a missionary for God, reading is also a key to *soul winning*, for through reading he may open before others eternal truth. If the truth of God is presented in language that is distinct and clear, people will listen with pleasure. If it is given in tones that convey the depth of beautiful meaning, whether it be warning, sympathy, appeal, or love, the intelligence will be convinced, and the soul may be won to obedience.

This is the way Jesus read. When He stood up in the synagogue on the Sabbath day to read, He reached the very soul of His hearers. He read with such fullness of meaning in His voice that when He sat down "the eyes of all them that were in the synagogue were fastened on Him." They "wondered at the gracious words which proceeded out of His mouth." Such reading will prepare our boys and girls to be witnesses for Him.

In an endeavor to aid the teacher in placing these keys in the hands of our boys and girls, and also to give the children a balanced reading diet, the lessons in this book cover a wide range. A list of the reading projects is found under "Contents by Projects" in the Teachers' Edition. In this list are found the Bible, the great source book of all that makes reading worth while; nature, God's other book; experiences from the lives of men and women who have made God's word the guide of their actions; the noble deeds of missionaries who have followed their Lord in consecrating their best and their all to helping their needy brothers; the inspiration of those who through toil and perseverance have given up ease and personal pleasure in order to bequeath to the world their best in literature, in art, in music, in invention, in discovery—these are some of the sources that have been appealed to in the preparation of these lessons in reading for our growing boys and girls, the boys and girls who "if rightly trained" are to take an active part in finishing God's work in the earth in this generation.

In revising this series of school readers it has not been found necessary to draw from the unreal and purely imaginative. The books are therefore entirely free from myths, fairy tales, and all that tends to undermine faith in the Sacred Word, and to unfit the pupil for the highest service. Many conscientious educators and parents recognize the constantly increasing tendency in the world to-day toward a lack of faith in God and His word, which is but the natural result of much of the teaching of the present age. Many school readers abound with that which is false and fanciful, and this cannot but do much to unfit the mind to meet the realities of life and to appreciate sober truth. To help stem this tide toward the artificial and the skeptical, the subject matter in these readers is drawn entirely from the true and the beautiful in life, in nature, and in revelation. The author believes that "truth is stranger than fiction," fact more wonderful than fancy; and that the imagination of the child can therefore be best aroused, interested, and developed in the realm of truth and fact.

Such thoughts nourishing the minds of the young day after day and year after year will mold their lives and do much in winning them for "the joy of service in this world, and for the higher joy of wider service in the world to come."

CONTENTS

In this *Table of Contents*, S or O following a title indicates whether the lesson is best fitted for silent or oral reading. The *number* following the titles of certain poems is the number of words the poem contains.

FIRST PERIOD

	PAGE
READING TO LEARN	15
FIRST SILENT READING TEST	17
SERARPI [s]	19
HOW TO READ RAPIDLY [s]	24
A GRIEF-STRICKEN MONKEY [s]	25
A GRIEF-STRICKEN PIGEON [s]	26
HOW ESTHER'S PRAYER WAS ANSWERED [s]	28
MEMORY READING [s]	30
BABY CORN [245]	33
ORAL READING [s]	34
LITTLE CORNERS [o]	36
OUR WORDS [o] .... *Solomon*	39
THE LEAVES AND THE WIND [155] .... *George Cooper*	41
SILENT READING TEST	42
THE FOURTH GRADE DICTIONARY [s]	42
HOW THE LEAVES CAME DOWN [233] . *Susan Coolidge*	44
TELL THE WHOLE TRUTH [s] .... *Warren G. Harding*	46
HELPING FATHER [o]	48
EASY LESSONS [173] .... *Phœbe Cary*	49
DICTIONARY STUDY	51
CAPTAIN JOHN SMITH [s]	52
BE PLEASANT [o] .... *Eleanor A. Hunter, in Christian at Work*	56
STORY OF THIMBLES [s]	58
TRY AGAIN [116] .... *E. Hickson*	61
TREES IN OCTOBER [o] .... *Edith M. Thomas*	63
A TRIP TO MILK SPRINGS [o]	65
A TALKING CHIP [o]	68
READING TESTS AND SCORES FOR THE FIRST PERIOD	72

SECOND PERIOD

COLPORTEUR STORIES º	73
THE FOURTH MAN IN THE BOAT ˢ	77
THE FROST ¹⁹¹ .... *Hannah Flagg Gould*	79
DICTIONARY STUDY	81
A SQUIRREL FAMILY ˢ .... *Loretta Reisman*	81
A SUNBEAM ⁸²	87
A TALK ABOUT THE COW º	88
THE HANDIWORK OF GOD º .... *King David*	91
AMERICA'S GREATEST NATURALIST ˢ	93
WHEN GOD CONTROLLED A RAILROAD TRAIN º	96
"MUST" AND "MUS'N'T" º	98
A TALK ABOUT BONES º	99
THE TARDY MAIDEN ¹³²	104
SILENT READING TEST	104
A SCHOOL DESK'S EXPERIENCE ˢ	105
BE THE BEST OF WHATEVER YOU ARE ¹¹²	108
DOGS AND CATS ˢ .... *Harriet Beecher Stowe*	109
DICTIONARY STUDY	112
BABY HAS GONE TO SCHOOL ¹⁶⁰	113
THE DUKE OF WELLINGTON º	114
THE LITTLE FACTORY GIRL WHO BECAME A POET ˢ	116
IF I WERE A SUNBEAM ¹⁰⁸ .... *Lucy Larcom*	121
THE RIVULET ⁹⁰ .... *Lucy Larcom*	122
TARDY TWICE º .... *The Sunbeam*	123
CHILDREN AND DIAMONDS ˢ ...... *London Graphic*	125
OLD WINTER ˢ	128
READING TESTS AND SCORES FOR THE SECOND PERIOD	133

THIRD PERIOD

THE MISSIONARY SHIP "THE PITCAIRN" ˢ .... *Mrs. L. Flora Plummer*	134
MIRIAM'S SONG ¹³⁹ .... *Thomas Moore*	143
LITTLE "PRETTY SOON" º .... *The Sabbath Recorder*	144
A WONDERFUL WEAVER ¹²² ...... *George Cooper*	146
POLLY'S BIRTHDAY º .... *Ladies' Home Journal*	148
DICTIONARY STUDY	152
AN ANT FUNERAL ˢ	153

THE LITTLE ONES HE BLESSED [224]	*Margaret E. Sangster*	155
PRAY FOR YOUR ENEMIES [s]		157
THE LAND OF FUSS-AND-FRET [o]	*Our Youth*	159
CAN YOU? [o]		161
SILENT READING TEST		162
FRED'S VICTORY [s]	*Augusta C. Bainbridge*	162
BLACK BEAUTY [s]	*Annie Sewell, in "Black Beauty"*	166
WISHING [o]	*William Allingham*	172
DOG COMPANIONS [s]	*The Youth's Instructor*	173
DICTIONARY EXERCISE		179
THE LITTLE ORPHAN PRINCESS [s]		179
THE KINGDOMS [o]		184
THE LOST LAMB [212]	*Thomas Westwood*	186
ENGLAND'S MOST BELOVED ARTIST [s]		189
TRUE TO THE MASTER [s]		193
READING TESTS AND SCORES FOR THE THIRD PERIOD		196

FOURTH PERIOD

"HOW MUCH DOES A HORSE KNOW?" [o]	*Allan Forman, in Harper's Young People*	197
DICTIONARY STUDY		202
A MIRACULOUS DELIVERANCE [s]		203
HOW TO MAKE A WORD BOOK		206
THE CHILDREN'S POET [s]		208
THE VILLAGE BLACKSMITH [215]	*Henry Wadsworth Longfellow*	213
THE CHILDREN'S HOUR [252]	*Henry Wadsworth Longfellow*	215
FINDING MY CORNET [o]	*Eric B. Hare*	218
DICTIONARY EXERCISE		220
FOUR SUNBEAMS [298]	*St. Nicholas*	221
TABLE MANNERS [o]		224
THE BRAVE TIGER MOTHER [s]		225
RATU MELI AT HOME [s]		227
SILENT READING TEST		231
WHAT THE SNOWFLAKES DID [255]		232
A RICH POOR BOY [o]	*Sunday School Visitor*	234
THEY TWO [222]		235
STORIES OF GEORGE WASHINGTON [s]		237

STORIES OF ABRAHAM LINCOLN [s]	240
LINCOLN'S SAYINGS	244
WHAT WORDS DO [152]	245
THE NEW SKATES [o] .... *The Youth's Instructor*	246
RULES FOR GOOD BEHAVIOR .... *The Youth's Instructor*	248
GIVING TO MISSIONS [o]	250
IN THE TIME OF TROUBLE [243] ...... *Psalm 91*	253
THE BROKEN FLOWERPOT [o] .... *Edward Bulwer-Lytton*	254
THE THERMOMETER [s]	259
READING TESTS AND SCORES FOR THE FOURTH PERIOD	262

FIFTH PERIOD

A SCHOOL OF A CENTURY AGO [s]	263
"THE MOTHER OF A THOUSAND DAUGHTERS" [s]	268
BETWEEN TWO ANGELS [266]	270
DICTIONARY DRILLS	272
THE SUNSHINE BASKET [s]	272
DUTY AND INCLINATION [o]	275
LONGFELLOW'S ARMCHAIR [o]	276
FROM MY ARMCHAIR [258] .... *Henry Wadsworth Longfellow*	279
SAVED FROM A PANTHER [s] .... *Nina Case Baierle*	281
DICTIONARY TIME DRILL	287
HONESTY IS THE BEST POLICY [s]	287
SILENT READING TEST	292
A ROBIN'S HEALTH LECTURE [303]	293
THE HORSE THAT CARRIED DOUBLE [s] *Elizabeth Preston Allan*	295
THE LILAC'S DINNER [116] .... *Clara Doty Bates*	299
DICTIONARY EXERCISE	300
HOW FROGS GROW [s]	300
CRADLES [130]	304
ALWAYS TELL THE TRUTH [o]	306
NATURE'S TEACHER [144] .... *Florence Bass, in "Stories of Animal Life"*	309
ONLY A FEW DROPS [o]	310
THE HERO ARCHER OF THE SWISS MOUNTAINS [s]	316
GOD'S WONDERFUL PROMISES [171] ... *Psalm 34*	319
READING TESTS AND SCORES FOR THE FIFTH PERIOD	320

SIXTH PERIOD

"King Cotton" in Dixie's Land [s]	321
A Bird's Nest [129] .... *Florence Percy*	328
A Camping Trip [s]	329
Poor Robin [o]	336
The Mysterious Singer [o] ...... *Little Men and Women*	337
Taught by a Dream [s]	339
Who Stole the Bird's Nest? [334] . *Lydia Maria Child*	341
A Lesson Father Taught Me [s] .. *Edgar A. Guest*	344
When Shall I Be a Man? [282] .... *Edgar A. Guest*	346
Dictionary Exercise	348
A Bible in the Fiery Furnace [s]	348
The Way to Try [s] .... *Viola Woodville*	350
How Birds Learn to Sing [91] ..... *Mary Mapes Dodge*	353
A Modern Raven [s] .... *Maria White, M.D., in the United Presbyterian*	354
Silent Reading Test	356
The Missionary Pumpkin [o] ...... *Herald*	357
Temperance [134] .... *Bible*	363
Where to Drink [98]	364
What to Drink [135]	365
Horace Mann [s]	366
The Way for Billy and Me [103] ... *James Hogg*	369
The D. D. Class [o]	370
The Spider and the Fly [277] ..... *Mary Howitt*	373
Cornelia's Jewels [s]	375
Vacation [254] .... *Katherine Lee Bates*	379
Reading Tests and Scores for the Sixth Period	380
The Little Dictionary Teacher	381
Graphs of Pupil's Weekly Silent Reading Rate	393

xi

Contents by Projects—Fourth Grade, First Semester

Projects	FIRST PERIOD		SECOND PERIOD		THIRD PERIOD	
Bible	Our Words	39	The Handiwork of God	91	Miriam's Song	143
Answers to Prayer	Serarpi	19	When God Controlled a Railroad Train	96	Pray for Your Enemies	157
	How Esther's Prayer Was Answered	28				
Nature Stories	A Grief-Stricken Monkey	25	A Squirrel Family	81	An Ant Funeral	153
	A Grief-Stricken Pigeon	26	A Sunbeam	87	Can You?	161
	Baby Corn	33	A Talk About the Cow	88	Black Beauty	166
			Dogs and Cats	109	Dog Companions	173
			Old Winter	128		
Missions and Missionaries	A Talking Chip	68	Colporteur Stories	73	The Missionary Ship "Pitcairn"	134
			The Fourth Man in the Boat	77	True tp the Master	193
Health and Temperance	A Trip to Milk Springs	65	A Talk About Bones	99		
Stories of Famous People	Tell the Whole Truth	46	America's Greatest Naturalist	93	The Little Orphan Princess	179
			The Duke of Wellington	114	The Kingdoms	184
					England's Most Beloved Artist	189
Manners and Morals	Little Corners	36	The Tardy Maiden	104	The Land of Fuss-and-Fret	159
	Try Again	61	A School Desk's Experience	105	Fred's Victory	162
			Be the Best of Whatever You Are	108		
			Tardy Twice	123		
Home and Friends	Helping Father	48	"Must" and "Mus'n't"	98	Little "Pretty Soon"	144
	Be Pleasant	66	Baby Has Gone to School	43	Polly's Birthday	148
					Wishing	172
History Stories	Captain John Smith	52	Children and Diamonds	125		
Common Things	Story of Thimbles	58				
Poets and Literature	The Leaves and the Wind	41	The Frost	79	A Wonderful Weaver	146
	How the Leaves Came Down	44	The Little Factory Girl Who Became a Poet	116	The Little Ones He Blessed	155
	Easy Lessons	49	If I Were a Sunbeam	121	The Lost Lamb	186
	Trees in October	63	The Rivulet	122		
Reading Drills	Reading to Learn	15	Dictionary Study	81	Dictionary Study	152
	First Silent Reading Test	17	Silent Reading Test	104	Silent Reading Test	162
	How to Read Rapidly	24	Dictionary Study	112	Dictionary Exercise	179
	Memory Reading	30	Reading Tests and Scores for Second Period	133	Reading Tests and Scores for Third Period	196
	Oral Reading	34				
	Silent Reading Test	42				
	The Fourth Grade Dictionary	42				
	Dictionary Study	51				
	Reading Tests and Scores for First Period	72				

Contents by Projects—Fourth Grade, Second Semester

Projects	FOURTH PERIOD		FIFTH PERIOD		SIXTH PERIOD	
Bible	In the Time of Trouble	253	God's Wonderful Promises	319	Temperance	363
Answers to Prayer	Finding My Cornet	218	Saved From a Panther	281	Taught by a Dream	339
					A Modern Raven	354
Nature Stories	"How Much Does a Horse Know?"	197	How Frogs Grow	300	Poor Robin	336
	Four Sunbeams	221			The Mysterious Singer	337
	The Brave Tiger Mother	225			Who Stole the Bird's Nest?	341
	What the Snowflakes Did	232			The Spider and the Fly	373
Missions and Missionaries	A Miraculous Deliverance	203	"The Mother of a Thousand Daughters"	268	A Bible in the Fiery Furnace	348
	Ratu Meli at Home	227			The Missionary Pumpkin	357
	Giving to Missions	250				
Health and Temperance			A Robin's Health Lecture	293	Where to Drink	364
					What to Drink	365
Stories of Famous People	Stories of George Washington	237	The Hero Archer of the Swiss Mountains	316	A Lesson Father Taught Me	344
	Stories of Abraham Lincoln	240			Horace Mann	366
	Lincoln's Sayings	244				
Manners and Morals	Table Manners	224	Between Two Angels	270	The Way to Try	350
	What Words Do	245	The Sunshine Basket	272		
	Rules for Good Behavior	248	Duty and Inclination	275		
	The Broken Flowerpot	254	Honesty Is the Best Policy	287		
			Always Tell the Truth	306		
Home and Friends	A Rich Poor Boy	234	The Horse That Carried Double	295	The D. D. Class	370
	They Two	235	Only a Few Drops	310		
	The New Skates	246				
History Stories			A School of a Century Ago	263	Cornelia's Jewels	375
Common Things	The Thermometer	259			"King Cotton" in Dixie's Land	321
					A Camping Trip	329
Poets and Literature	The Children's Poet	208	Longfellow's Armchair	276	A Bird's Nest	328
	The Children's Hour	215	From My Armchair	279	When Shall I Be a Man?	346
	The Village Blacksmith	213	The Lilac's Dinner	299	How Birds Learn to Sing	353
			Cradles	304	The Way for Billy and Me	369
			Nature's Teacher	309		
Reading Drills	Dictionary Study	202	Dictionary Drills	272	Dictionary Exercise	348
	How to Make a Word Book	206	Dictionary Time Drill	287	Silent Reading Test	356
	Dictionary Exercise	220	Silent Reading Test	292	Reading Tests and Scores for the Sixth Period	380
	Silent Reading Test	231	Dictionary Exercise	300		
	Reading Tests and Scores for Fourth Period	262	Reading Tests and Scores for Fifth Period	320		
Closing					Vacation	379

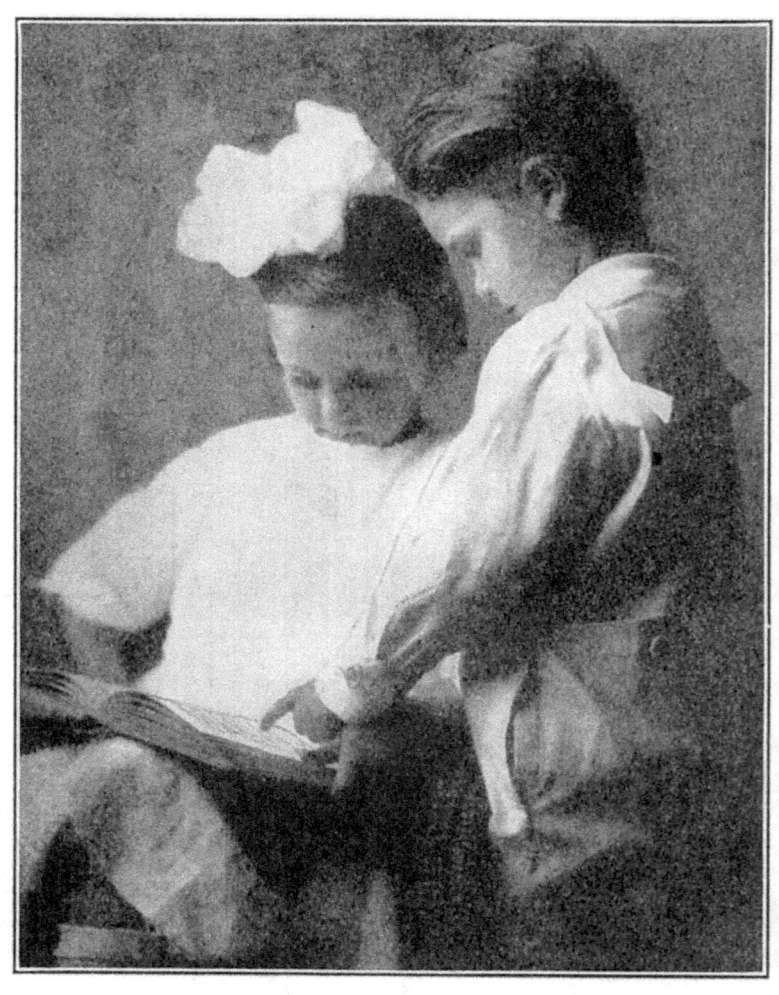

Reading to Learn

Reading to Learn[1]

To the Boys and Girls in the Fourth Grade:

Another year of school is here, and you are beginning your fourth grade. In your first and second and third grades you *learned to read*. This year you will *read to learn*. From now on through all the rest of your life you will get more and more pleasure and knowledge from reading. A great deal of all you learn will be through reading good books.

Your new reader is full of good things to read. There are nature stories from which you will learn some interesting things about animals and birds and flowers and trees and other things in God's great book of creation.

There are stories about children who have tried to do right. These will help *you* to do right. There are also stories about children in far-away lands.

Do you know how thimbles and buttons are made? Do you know what the cloth that is in the garments

---

[1] To the Teacher: Before teaching any of the lessons in this book, read carefully what is said in the Teachers' Edition for the third grade on pages v-xxix. "Reading to Learn" should be read and interpreted by the pupils, or it may be read to the class or given to them orally by the teacher. It is designed to suggest how the year's work in reading may be introduced. Read also in "Reading Tests and Scores for Fourth Grade" how to find and record the silent reading rate and comprehension grade of each pupil.

you wear is made of, and how it is made? It is very interesting to know something about the common things that we see or use every day. It helps us to appreciate the work that others are doing all the time for our benefit. It helps us to be grateful to them, and to respect and love those who toil day after day that we may have the comforts of life. In your fourth reader are stories from which you will learn about some of these common things.

There are other stories about great men and women who loved children. Some of them have written beautiful poems for children, and you will enjoy reading these poems and memorizing some of them.

Best of all, there are some wonderfully interesting stories about what God is doing for our missionaries, and how He has answered prayer. From every one of these stories you will learn something that will help you.

When you were in the third grade, you learned to read silently from 80 to 120 words a minute. In the fourth grade you will learn to read from 100 to 140 words a minute. Some of you will learn to read even more than that. I know you are all going to try hard to reach the fourth-grade goal of 140 words a minute by the end of the school year.

Of course, you must *think* about what you are reading, and *understand* what it *means*, or it won't count. If you read so rapidly that you do not understand what you read, it really is not reading at all; it is only a race with words.

First Silent Reading Test

Your first reading lesson this year will show how much you can read in a minute right at the beginning of the fourth grade. Then from time to time you will have other tests that will show how much you have improved. This first lesson test is in your "Reading Tests and Scores" pad for fourth grade.

Be sure that you understand what you read, so that after you finish reading you can answer all the questions in the "Comprehension Test." If you can answer *all* the questions after only *one* reading, you will be 100 in *comprehension*. For every question you fail to answer, 10 will be taken from this grade.

When you have read two minutes, the teacher will say, "Mark!" As soon as she speaks, make a light pencil dot after the word you are then reading, and go right on reading until you finish the story.

The number of words you read in two minutes divided by two will be the number you can read in one minute. This is called your *reading rate*. Your comprehension grade and reading rate will then be recorded on your "Reading Score Card."

What are you to do when your teacher says, "Mark"?

What are you to do after you make the mark?

Your teacher will now give you the first story from your "Reading Tests and Scores" pad.

Ready! Point with your pencil to the first word in the story. Then, all eyes on the teacher!

Read!

Serarpi was sold to an Arab chief.

FOURTH GRADE—FIRST PERIOD

Serarpi[1] (S)

This story is about a little girl who was driven from her home during the World War, which began in 1914. As you read silently, find out how God cared for her in her exile, and whether she ever found her way home again. Trace her wanderings on the map.

After you have read the story silently, practice parts 2, 6, and 7 for oral reading.

---

1. Se-rar'pi* was a little girl whose home was in Ar-me'ni-a.* When she was eight years old, her father's family, with many others, were driven from their home by soldiers. This was during the terrible World War. It would be impossible to tell what they suffered during their exile.*

While trying to find some way to get his family away from the cruel soldiers, the father lost his life. The mother knew that she, too, must soon die. Oh, how anxious she was for little Serarpi! What would become of her darling child?

2. An Ar'ab* chief offered the mother twenty-five cents for her daughter. The mother was deeply troubled. What *should* she do? If only he would be *kind* to her, it might be best to let her go. Otherwise, the

---

[1] To the Teacher: Frequently, stories marked for silent reading contain one or more paragraphs that are excellent for oral expression; and any story marked for oral reading may be used for silent reading, provided a proper balance in the pupil's reading development is preserved. An average of two lessons a week on silent, two on oral, and one on memory reading is a good proportion.

child would soon be left all alone in a strange land.

"I would not sell her for the world," the mother said. "But if you will promise to be a good father to her, I will let you have her as your daughter."

"I would rather die than go with strangers," Serarpi cried.

But the mother knew that she must soon die, so she took the child to the A-ra′bi-an family, and left her there.

Serarpi

"Do not forget your two brothers in the United States," were the mother's parting words to little Serarpi, "and your two brothers in the Turkish army. Remember who you are and where you came from, and some day may God bring you back to your brothers."

3. The Arabian family changed the child's name to Miriam. One day the woman tied her hands and feet, and tat-tooed′* her face. This was very cruel, but these people did not mean to be unkind to the child. They were Mo-ham′me-dans,* and this was one of their religious customs.

4. For four long years little Miriam waited and longed to get a message to her brothers. Her mother

had taught her to pray, to read the Bible, and to keep the Sabbath of the Lord. And now these lessons of her childhood led her in her loneliness and trouble to pray to God for help. Once, after the war, she met an Armenian who remembered her family name.

"Tell my brothers," she pleaded, "that I am here. Tell them to come and get me."

A little later this Armenian met a man who had the same family name as Miriam's parents. He also had lost a little girl during the war. What if this girl should be his daughter! He was too old to take the journey to Miriam, and he had no money to pay the expense of traveling.

He begged a young man, a distant relative of his, who had just been discharged from the Turkish navy,* to go in search of his daughter. This young man was Miriam's own brother.

5. The Ar'mis-tice* said that all who had been exiled from home might return. It also said that help was to be given to those searching for relatives among Mohammedans. Therefore two Turkish soldiers were sent with the young man to aid him in his efforts to find the lost child. Eagerly the young man started with the two soldiers. Oh, how he hoped that at the same time he might get some trace of his own little sister!

Village after village they searched. It seemed to him that every possible effort had been made. Every village had been searched. No; not *every* village. One more having a few scattered houses remained. He would search it, and then he would have to give up the search.

6. He went to the home of the Arabian chief. It was the very chief who had taken Serarpi five years before, but this young man did not know it. He asked if an Armenian girl was in his village. The chief did not dare to hide his captive. He sent a girl of his household to bring Miriam, who was herding sheep in a distant field.

"A young Armenian man has come and has asked to see you. Perhaps it is your brother," the girl said, when she found Miriam.

Serarpi and her brother

Miriam could not believe it; yet, with beating heart, she started for the house. While still a long way off, one of the soldiers went to meet her. He carried with him a photograph of the young man who was waiting for her, to see if she would know him. Without a word the soldier showed her the picture. Miriam looked at it a moment.

"That is *my brother!*" she exclaimed excitedly, as she eagerly reached for the picture.

7. On she hastened to the house.

"Do you know this girl?" the soldier asked the young man.

He saw, not a child of eight years, but a girl of twelve, her face carved with tattoo marks.

"I don't know *what to say*," he declared, still studying her face.

Miriam could wait no longer. She sprang to him. "Brother, I am your sister!" she cried.

She told the name of her mother and of her father. She told from what place they came. She told of her capture. She told of the Armenian by whom she had sent a message to her people. No longer could the brother doubt that she was his own sister.

8. The old chief was greatly disappointed. He did not want to give her up. But he was under orders from his government not to hold any Christian captives. Overjoyed, Serarpi and her brother left the home of the chief, left the Mohammedan village, left Arabia, and made their way back to Con-stan-ti-no′-ple.*

Serarpi afterwards went to another brother in America to study, so that some day she might go back as a missionary to the home of her birth.

Speed and Comprehension Test. See how quickly you can find, and write the number of, the part that tells about each of these topics:

Serarpi driven from home
Praying for help
Relatives searching for lost ones
Searching in the home of the Arabian chief
Tattooed
Leaving Arabia for her home in Constantinople
Sold to an Arab chief
Found by her brother

In America studying to be a missionary

This story is told in "Providences of the Great War," where many other wonderful stories of God's deliverance are told. You would enjoy reading more of them.

How to Read Rapidly[1] (S)

In the past, you have often tried to see several words at a time in your reading, for in this way you could read faster and easier than if you had to stop and look at only one word at a time. No one likes to hear a person read one word at a time, does he? How does this sound? "A-member-of-a-shooting-party-killed-a-mother-monkey-and-carried-it-to-his-tent." Such reading is not only slow, but it is so cut up that it is hard to get the sense from the reading. How much easier it is to get the thought by reading phrases, or *groups* of words, like this:

    A member of a shooting party
    killed a mother monkey
    and carried it to his tent.

And how much more pleasant it is to *listen* to such reading!

When you were in the third grade, you learned to read *short* phrases. In the fourth grade you should learn to read those that are a little *longer*.

---

[1] TO THE TEACHER: Phrase drills should help greatly in gaining speed and ease in reading, and in enabling pupils to hold the attention of their audience by frequently looking away from the book to the eye of the hearer. Give similar drills as often as needed, gradually increasing the length of the phrases.

Suggestive phrase, vocabulary, and dictionary drills are given on pages xvi, and xx, and xxi of the Teachers' Edition for the third grade. Grades three and four may unite in these drills.

The next two stories are divided into phrases. Each phrase tells something about the thought.

Boys, you may read silently the first story. It contains 165 words. See if you can read it in one and one-half minutes, and find out how the monkey showed its grief. Then tell the story to the girls.

The second story is for you to read, girls. It contains 164 words. See if you can read it in one and one-half minutes, and find out how the pigeon showed its grief. Then tell the story to the boys.

After you have told both the stories, practice reading the phrases orally as if each were a single word.

I. A Grief-Stricken Monkey [S]

A member of a shooting party
killed a mother monkey,
and carried it to his tent.
The tent was soon surrounded
by forty or fifty monkeys that made a great noise,

and seemed to want to attack* the hunter.
When he pointed his gun at them,
most of them seemed to understand, and ran away.
But the head of the group stood his ground,
chattering fu′ri-ous-ly.
The sportsman, who perhaps felt guilty
for having killed one of the family,
did not like to fire at the creature;
and nothing short of firing would drive him off.
At last, the monkey came to the door of the tent,
and began to moan pitifully.
By the most im-press′ive motions he seemed to beg
that the slain monkey be given back.
The dead body was therefore given to him.
He took it sorrowfully in his arms,
and bore it away to his waiting companions.
Those who saw these strange actions
re-solved′ never again to fire at another monkey.
—*Selected.*

II. A Grief-Stricken Pigeon [S]

Another story
that should arouse our sympathy for animals
happened in England.
A man was set to watch a field of peas,
which had been much preyed* upon by pigeons.
He shot an old male pigeon
that had long lived on the farm.
Its mate at once settled down by its side,
and showed her grief in the most impressive manner.

See how these pigeons appreciate the gentleness and kindness of the boy! How would you like to have them for pets?

The man took up the dead bird,
and tied it to a short stake,
thinking the sight would drive away other birds.
But the be-reaved'* bird did not forsake her mate.
She continued day after day
walking slowly around the stick.

At last, the kind-hearted wife of the farmer
went to comfort the poor bird.
When she reached the spot,
she found the hen bird much ex-haust'ed.
It had made a beaten track around the dead pigeon,
giving now and then a little spring toward him.
Not until the woman took the dead bird away
did the hen return to the dovecot.*

—*Selected.*

How Esther's Prayer Was Answered (S)

This story tells how a young girl was persecuted by her own parents because she wanted to be a Christian. The story has 497 words. See if you can read it silently in five minutes, and find out how they persecuted her and what God did for her because she was true to Him.

In a far-away heathen village of Africa, lived a young black girl named Esther. Esther at this time was about fourteen years old. She attended an Ad'vent-ist mission school which was taught by a native missionary. In the school she learned of the love of Jesus, and she gladly gave her young heart to Him.

When she became a Christian, she took her large ear'rings from her ears. She took the beads from her neck. She removed her brace'lets and her leg ornaments. All these she gave to her teacher to be sold for missions.

Esther's parents were heathen. When she was converted, she told them that she would still obey them in all that was right. But she re-fused' to attend the heathen dances. She refused to make beer for them. She refused to work on the Sabbath. She begged them to accept Christ and join her in living the new life.

Her parents were very, very angry because she would not do these wrong things. They decided that she must give up her religion and return to her heathen ways. At first, they tried to per-suade' her. But she could not be persuaded. Then they tried whipping her until she would almost faint from pain.

"Will you give up this religion now?" her parents then asked.

"I would rather die than give up my hope in Christ," she answered.

Then they shut her up in a dark hut for days without food or water until she was almost starved. Still she remained true to God. She did not feel angry with her parents. She only prayed that they might learn to love Jesus.

At last her father tied her to a small tree. He bound her so tightly that she could not move. Then taking a sharp, strong cord, he tied it around her forehead and the tree, twisting it with a stick until it cut into the flesh. Here they left her a whole day. Still she was firm in her faith in Jesus. Still she continued to pray for her parents.

About this time, a white missionary came to visit the native teacher at the village. He held some special meetings. Esther begged him to unite with her in prayer that God would lead her father and mother into the light.

One night, at the close of the sermon, the missionary invited those who had never known Jesus to come forward and give their hearts to Him. A number respond'ed. Then, to his great surprise, he saw Esther making her way down the aisle to the front, leading her old father with one hand and her mother with the other. The old man, trembling with e-mo'tion, laid his pipe at the feet of the preacher, and the mother placed her snuffbox beside it. Then they knelt down together, and asked Esther's God to accept them as His children. Later on, the three of them were together led into the water and baptized.

Comprehension Test. How many of these questions can you answer after reading the story only *once*?
1. Where did Esther live?
2. How old was she?
3. To what race did she belong?
4. Where did she learn to love Jesus?
5. What four changes did she make in her dress after she gave her heart to Jesus?
6. What three things did she tell her parents she could not do?
7. Was it right for her to disobey her parents? Read Ephesians 6:1 and Acts 5:29 before you answer.
8. When they tried to get her to disobey Jesus, what did she tell them?
9. What did she do for her parents?
10. How did God answer her prayers?

Memory Reading (S)

In the third grade you learned that there are three ways to read. Do you remember what they are? If you do, you can read the next few sentences and put in the missing word. Try it. I learn to read to myself quickly in my ———— reading. I can help others by reading to them if I do well in my ———— reading. I shall get beautiful word pictures to hang on the walls of my memory in my ———— reading.

How many pretty little poems did you learn to read from memory when you were in the third grade? About ten? In the fourth grade you will learn perhaps ten others. Maybe some of you will learn more than ten. You will enjoy these beautiful poems as long as you live, and they will help you to give others pleasure too, for every one likes to hear a beautiful poem well recited.

For memory reading you may choose from your fourth reader the poems you like best. After the name of each of those that are the finest ones to memorize is a number that tells how many words there are in the poem.

If your memory reading this period totals at least 300 words, and if you can recite the poems in an interesting way without any help, your grade will be 100. If it totals 250 words, your grade will be 95. If 200 words, it will be 90. If 160 words, it will be 85. If 140 words, it will be 80. And 120 words gives you a passing grade of 75. Of course, no one will go below 75, for *that* would be a failure.

The next lesson is a very pretty poem. How many words in it? If you memorize it, how much will it count on your grade in memory reading? Study it with your teacher, and see if it is one you would enjoy memorizing.

A Study on "Baby Corn"

I hope you have a stalk of corn in class to look at as you study this lesson.

What is the name of this poem? "Baby Corn" surely must have a mother; for all babies have mothers, don't they? Read until you find out what part of the corn the Baby is, and what Baby Corn's mother is.

1. Read the lines in stanza 1 that tell what the mother said to her baby. What are the "petticoats of green"? Do you see the "tucks" and "folds" in these petticoats?

2. The second stanza says that Baby Corn was a "funny little baby." Read until you find out what made it funny. This stanza also tells how the mother fed her baby. How did she feed it? Where did the "baby's milk" come from? Can you find the "thread of silk" on the ear of corn?

3. Stanza 3 tells when Baby Corn drank its milk.

4. What was it in stanza 4 that "grew strong and full and round"? What was the baby's "gown" made of? What word tells the color of its gown? Read what Baby Corn said. To what was it talking?

5. In stanza 5, read the words that Mother Stalk spoke to Baby Corn. Find the "soft brown plume" on an ear of corn. Read the words Baby Corn proudly said to its mother.

If you were to draw a picture for this poem, what would it be?

After you have studied the poem, listen as your teacher reads it to you. You may then read orally the first stanza. Read this stanza over and over silently, looking away from your book more and more, until you can read it without looking at your book at all. Then try reading it to the class *from memory*. See if you can do this in three minutes. If you can memorize one stanza in three minutes how long will it take you to memorize all five stanzas?

If you decide to make this one of your memory readings, have it all ready to recite to the class one week from to-day.

Baby Corn [245]

1. A happy Mother Stalk of corn
    Held close a Baby Ear,
   And whispered, "Cuddle up to me,
    I'll keep you warm, my dear.
   I'll give you petticoats* of green,
    With many a tuck and fold,
   To let out daily as you grow;
    For you will soon be old."

2. A funny little baby that,
    For, though it had no eye,
   It had a hundred mouths; 'twas well
    It did not want to cry.
   The mother put in each small mouth
    A hollow thread of silk,
   Through which the sun and rain and air
    Provided baby's milk.

3. The petticoats were gathered close
    Where all the thread'lets* hung,
   And still the summer day went on,
    To Mother Stalk it clung;
   And all the time it grew and grew,
    Each kernel drank the milk
   By day, by night, in shade, in sun,
    From its own thread of silk.

4. And each grew strong and full and round
    And each was shining white;
The gores* and seams were all let out,
    The green skirt fitted tight.
The Ear stood straight and large and tall,
    And when it saw the sun,
Held up its em′er-ald* satin gown,
    To say, "Your work is done."

5. "You're large enough," said Mother Stalk,
    "And now there's no more room
For you to grow." She tied the threads
    Into a soft brown plume.
It floated out upon the breeze
    To greet the dewy* morn,
And then the Baby said, "Now, I'm
    A full-grown ear of corn!"
                          —*Author Unknown.*

Oral Reading (S)

When you read silently, no one else can enjoy what you read because they cannot hear you. So you will sometimes want to read aloud. You have learned that this is called *oral* reading.

Almost any of your silent reading stories would be good to read orally to some one else. Your father or mother, I am sure, would be delighted to hear some of these stories, especially if you learn to read them well. Are there any old or sick or blind people living near your home? It would make them very happy to hear you read some of the good things from your reader. Try it sometime, and just see how much they enjoy it.

Do you remember the four things you should do when you are reading aloud to others? Let us review them:

When I read aloud to others,—

1. I must make my voice sound natural, as if I were talking.

2. I must pronounce my words cor-rect′ly and very distinct′ly.

3. I must read the words just as they are, without repeat′ing.

4. I must sometimes look away from my book to the one who is listening.

There is one more thing to remember about oral reading, and that is to read *slowly* enough so that others can easily understand what you are reading. It is very tiresome to listen to one who reads too rapidly. Besides, if you hurry over your words, you cannot pronounce them distinctly. You are likely to run them together, and that is very unpleasant. *Rapid* reading is for your *silent* work.

The next story is a good one for oral reading. At the beginning and near the end of each par′a-graph are always the best places to look away from your book. In some of the longer paragraphs it is well to look away more often, usually toward the end of some sentence. Be careful not to make your reading jerky. Keep it smooth and pleasant, and do not lose your place.

"Little Corners" is a story that tells how a little girl in the kitchen was a shining light for Jesus. I wonder what she did to be a light, and how many saw her light. Find out as you read. If you wish, you may read this story silently first, just to see how quickly you can read it, or how much you can read in three minutes.

Little Corners ^(O)

1. Georgia Willis, who helped in the kitchen, was rubbing the knives. Somebody had been careless and let one get rusty, but Georgia rubbed with all her might—rubbed, and sang softly a little song,—

> "In this world of darkness we must shine,
> You in your corner, I in mine."

2. "Why do you rub at those knives forever?" asked Mary. Mary was the cook.

"Because they are in my corner," Georgia said brightly. "'You in your corner,' you know, and 'I in mine.' I'll do the best I can; that is all I can do."

3. "I wouldn't waste my strength," said Mary. "No one will notice."

"Jesus will," said Georgia; and then she sang again,—

"You in your corner, I in mine."

4. "Cooking the dinner is in my corner, I suppose," said Mary to herself. "If that child must do what *she can*, I suppose *I* must. If Jesus knows about *knives*, it is likely He knows about *dinners*." And she took par-tic′u-lar pains.

5. "Mary, the dinner was nicely cooked to-day," Miss Emma said.

"That's all because of Georgia," said Mary, with a pleased face. And then she told about the knives.

6. "No," said Emma to her friend who urged, "I really cannot go this evening. I am going to prayer meeting. My 'corner' is there."

"Your 'corner'? What do you mean?" Then *Miss Emma* told about the knives.

"Well," the friend said, "if you will not go with me, I will go with you." And they went to the prayer meeting together.

7. "You helped us ever so much with the singing this evening." That was what their pastor said as they were going home. "I was afraid you wouldn't be there."

"It was owing to our Georgia," said Emma. "She seemed to think she must do what she could if it was only knives." Then she told *him* the story.

8. "I believe I will go in here again," said the minister, stopping before a poor little house. "I said yesterday there was no use; but I must do what I

can." In the house a sick man was lying. Again and again the minister had called, but the in′va-lid* would not listen to him. But to-night the minister said, "I have come to tell you a little story."

9. Then he told *him* about Georgia Willis, about her knives and her little "corner," and her "doing what she could." The sick man wiped the tears from his eyes.

"I will find my 'corner,' too. I will try to shine for Jesus," he said.

10. "I believe I won't go to walk," said Helen, hes-i-ta′ting-ly.* "I'll finish that dress of mother's. I suppose I can if I *try*."

"Why, child, are you here sewing?" her mother asked. "I thought you had gone to walk."

"No; this sewing seemed to be in my 'corner,' so I thought I would finish it."

"In your 'corner'?" her mother repeated in surprise.

Then *Helen* told about the knives.

11. The doorbell rang, and Helen's mother went thoughtfully to receive her pastor. "I suppose I *could* give *more*," she said to herself, as she slowly took out the money she had laid aside for missions. "If that poor child in the kitchen is trying to do what *she* can, I wonder if *I* am. I'll *double* it."

12. But Georgia knew nothing about all this. She had let her light shine; and others, seeing her good works, had, with her, glorified the Father in heaven. Jesus, looking down at her that day, said, "She hath done what she could." And He gave the blessing.

Comprehension Test

1. What did Mary, the cook, do because Georgia let her light shine?
2. What did Emma and her friend do?
3. What did Georgia's faithfulness lead the pastor to do?
4. How did Georgia's faithfulness help a sick man?
5. What did Helen do because of Georgia?
6. What did her mother do?
7. How many saw Georgia's light?
8. What did Jesus say about Georgia?
9. How can Georgia's light help *you?*

Our Words ^(O)

The verses in this lesson are called *proverbs.* A proverb is a short saying that tells some great truth. As you read these proverbs, pick out the one you like best and memorize it.

1. A word fitly spoken
   Is like apples of gold in pictures of silver.

2. Boast not thyself of to-morrow;
   For thou knowest not what a day may bring forth.

3. Let another man praise thee,
      and not thine own mouth;
   A stranger, and not thine own lips.

4. Seest thou a man that is hasty in his words?
   There is more hope of a fool than of him.

5. Lying lips are a-bom-i-na'tion* to the Lord:
   But they that deal truly are His delight.

6. The tongue of the just is as choice silver:
The heart of the wicked is little worth.

7. Pleasant words are as an honeycomb,
Sweet to the soul, and health to the bones.

8. Even a fool, when he holdeth his peace,
   is counted wise:
And he that shutteth his lips
   is es-teemed'* a man of understanding.

9. Bread of deceit is sweet to a man;
But afterwards
   his mouth shall be filled with gravel.

—*Selections From the Proverbs of Solomon.*

Appreciation Study

Verse 1. A word "fitly spoken" means a kind word spoken at the right time to help some one.

Verse 4. "Hasty" words are words spoken thoughtlessly, carelessly, or impatiently.

Verse 9. Words that deceive are words that give others a false idea. True words are like *bread*. What does this verse say deceitful words are like? How would you like to eat bread that was full of gravel?

Read the lines that tell what God thinks of "pleasant words."

Read the lines that tell what "a word fitly spoken" is like.

Read the lines that tell why we should not "boast" of what we are going to do.

Read the line that tells what God thinks of "lying lips."

How many proverbs did Solomon speak? 1 Kings 4:32 will tell you.

Who gave Solomon so great wisdom? 1 Kings 4:29, 30.

After studying these proverbs with your teacher, read them orally, verse around.

The Leaves and the Wind [155]

This little poem has some very pretty word pictures. See if you can find one in each stanza.

1. "Come, little leaves," said the wind one day,
   "Come o'er the meadows with me and play.
   Put on your dresses of red and gold;
   Summer is gone, and the days grow cold."

2. Soon as the leaves heard the wind's loud call,
   Down they came fluttering, one and all.
   O'er the brown meadows they danced and flew,
   Singing the soft little songs they knew.

3. "Cricket, good-by. We've been friends so long!
   Little brook, sing us your farewell song;
   Say you are sorry to see us go,
   Ah! you will miss us, right well we know.

4. "Dear little lambs, in your fleecy fold,
   Mother will keep you from harm and cold.
   Fondly we've watched you in vale and glade;
   Say, will you dream of our loving shade?"

5. Dancing and whirling the little leaves went;
   Winter had called them, and they were content.
   Soon, fast asleep in their earthy beds,
   The snow laid a coverlet over their heads.
   —*George Cooper.*

Find expressions in the poem that mean the same as those in the following sentences that are printed in italic, and tell which you prefer:

1. The green leaves *turned red and yellow*.
2. The leaves *rustled softly as the wind blew them off the tree*.
3. The little lambs *were in their warm pen*.
4. The leaves *lay quietly on the ground*.
5. The snow *covered them out of sight*.

Silent Reading Test

Your next lesson will be your second silent reading test. This test is in your "Reading Test and Scores" pad. It will show you how much you have improved in silent reading rate and comprehension since school began this year.

A
B
C
D

The Fourth Grade Dictionary[1] (S)

E
F
G
H

When you were in the third grade, you learned to use your "Little Dictionary Teacher." This year you have another dictionary, one for the *fourth* grade. It is in the back of your reader, beginning on page 381. Turn to it.

This dictionary will show you how to pronounce the new words in your fourth reader, so you will not

---

[1] TO THE TEACHER: Make this lesson a brisk time drill on quickly locating all the letters miscellaneously in the alphabet list. Drill from time to time until pupils can point to the entire list in thirty seconds. Complete familiarity with the order of letters in the alphabet is absolutely essential before the use of the dictionary can be practical.

Follow up this drill during the period with such drills as are given on page xx and page xxi of the Teachers' Edition for the third grade and other drills that will help the pupil locate quickly any word he wishes to find in the dictionary. Third and fourth grades may take all these drills together.

need to ask your teacher. It will also tell you what they mean.

The very first thing you will need to do is to find *quickly* the word you want to know about. Notice carefully the words in large, heavy, black letters on the first page of your dictionary. With what letter do they begin? *A* is the first letter of the al'pha-bet, isn't it? If in any reading lesson you should have a new word that begins with the letter *a*, you could find it right here, where all the new words are that begin with *a*. It wouldn't do any good to look anywhere else for it, because all the *a* words are *here*.

Look down the list of *a* words until you find the very last one. With what letter does the next black word begin? *B*, of course, because *b* comes next after *a* in the alphabet.

Look through all the *b* words, and next after them you will find all the words beginning with *c*. Then all the words beginning with *d*. Then the *e* words, the *f* words, the *g* words, and so on till you get to the very end of the alphabet. Like good children, every word is always in its own place. It is never out of place.

The better you know the alphabet, the quicker you can find any word you want your "Dictionary Teacher" to tell you about. See how quickly you can point to the letters on the side of these pages as your teacher calls them: T, N, J, D, W, O, L, C, Z, S, A, P, X, B, K, G, etc.

It may help you to remember them if you learn them in groups. Point quickly to the A-B-C-D group; the Q-R-S-T group; the I-J-K-L group.

I
J
K
L

M
N
O
P

Q
R
S
T

U
V
W
X
Y
Z

Point to the group in which G is found; O, T, etc.
What letter in the alphabet comes—
   Just before *s?*   Just after *s?*
   Just before *k?*   Just after *k?* etc.

You will need to learn the letters so well that you can point to any of them without stopping to think.

How the Leaves Came Down [233]

As you read this orally, see how real you can make the words of the Tree and his children sound, especially the sleepy answer of the leaves in stanza 7.

1. I'll tell you how the leaves came down.
    The great Tree to his children said,
"You're getting sleepy, Yellow and Brown.
    Yes, very sleepy, little Red,
    It is quite time to go to bed."

2. "Ah!" begged each silly, pouting leaf,
    "Let us a little longer stay,
Dear Father Tree. Behold our grief!
    'Tis such a *very* pleasant day
    We do not *want* to go away."

3. So, for just one more merry day
    To the great Tree the leaflets* clung,
Frolicked* and danced, and had their way,
    Upon the autumn breezes swung,
    Whispering all their sports among:

4. "Perhaps the great Tree will forget,
      And let us stay until the spring,
   If we all beg, and coax, and fret."
      But the great Tree did no such thing.
      He smiled to hear their whispering.

5. "Come, children, all to bed," he cried;
      And ere the leaves could urge their prayer,
   He shook his head, and far and wide,
      Fluttering and rustling everywhere,
      Down sped the leaflets through the air.

6. I saw them. On the ground they lay,
      Golden and Red, a huddled swarm,
   Waiting till one from far away,
      White bedclothes heaped upon her arm,
      Should come to wrap them safe and warm.

7. The great bare Tree looked down and smiled,
      "Good night, dear little leaves," he said.
   And from below each sleepy child
      Replied, "Good night," and murmured,*
      "It is so nice to go to bed!"

                                                  —*Susan Coolidge.*

Comprehension Test

    1. What did the Tree say to his children in stanza 1?

    2. Did you ever hear any children talk as the "silly, pouting" leaves talked in stanzas 2 and 4?

    3. What did the Tree do when the time really came for his children to go to bed? What season of the year was this?

    4. What are the "white bedclothes" spoken of in stanza 6?

    5. Who brought them?

6. Three words in this poem have a star after them. That means that you should find them in your dictionary, and learn their meaning or how to pronounce them.

Tell the Whole Truth ^(S)

This is a story that President Harding once told about his boyhood days. He says he told a lie. Read silently, and find out what the lie was, *how* he told it, and what lesson the experience taught him. The story has 311 words. See if you can read it in two minutes and forty seconds, and find out what you want to know.

When I was a boy about eight years old, it was my fortune to spend the summer at the home of my grandfather on the farm. One of my chores was to bring in the cows at milking time.

One evening, I got my orders to go for the cows. I obeyed rather unwillingly. As I slowly walked along, boylike I picked up a stone that we called a "sailer,"—a thin stone, you will remember, that you throw and it sails in the air,—and I let it go at a flock of geese, without any thought of the harm it might do. The sharp edge of this stone struck a fine gander* right in the side of the head. He whirled a half dozen times, and fell dead!

In my great sorrow that I had killed the gander, and my sense of injury to my grandfather, I rushed after the cows without making a word of explanation. When I came back, I found my grandmother plucking the gander to save the feathers. And grandfather was orating.*

He had examined the dead bird, and had concluded that it had been killed by a very ill-behaved turkey gobbler.* He reasoned that the gobbler had struck him in the side of the head and killed him. Thereupon he decreed* that the gobbler should die. And there I stood, a boyish culprit*—a liar through omission,* saying nothing in the gobbler's defense. Silently I saw him taken to the block; and a more innocent gobbler had never lived and died.

It may seem strange, but that event has returned to me a thousand times in my life; and the lesson it has taught me is that it always pays to make a fair statement of things, no matter if I myself am at fault, and even though there may be painful consequences.
—*Warren G. Harding.*

Dictionary Work: Find the following expressions in the story, and tell what you think they mean. After you guess, find the starred words in the dictionary in the back of your reader, and see if you guessed right.

1. plucking* the gander*
2. a boyish culprit*
3. a liar through omission*
4. painful consequences*
5. grandfather was orating*
6. ill-behaved turkey gobbler*

Helping Father [O]

This is a story of what a boy did that made him thankful to God all the rest of his life. Before reading orally, read silently, and find out what it was. How long does it take you to find in your dictionary the starred words?

"I wish you would take this package to the village for me, Jim," my father said in a hesitating* way.

I was a boy of twelve, not fond of work, and was just out of the hayfield, where I had been since early morning. I was tired, dusty, and hungry. It was two miles to town. I wanted to get my supper, and wash and dress for singing school. I was vexed that he should ask me after my long day's work, and my first impulse was to grumble. But if I refused, he would go himself. He was a gentle, patient father, and something stopped me—one of God's angels, I think.

"Of course, father, I'll take it," I said heartily.

"Thank you, Jim," he said, giving me the package. "I was going myself, but somehow I don't feel very strong to-day."

Father walked with me to the road that turned off to the town. As he was about to leave me, he put his hand on my arm.

"Thank you, my son," he said again. "You've always been a good boy to me, Jim."

I hurried to town and back. When I came back, I saw a crowd of farm hands at the door. One of them ran to meet me, tears rolling down his face.

"Your father," he said, "fell dead just as he reached the house. The last words he spoke were to you."

I am an old man now, but I have thanked God over and over, in all these years since that hour, that those last words to me were, "You've always been a good boy to me, Jim."

No human being was ever sorry for love or kindness shown to others. But there is bitter grief and regret* if we have the memory of neglect or coldness to loved ones who are gone. Do not give kind deeds and words unwillingly, especially to those about the same hearth.* It is such a little way we can go together. He is richest of all who is most generous in giving the love that blossoms continually in kind words and deeds.
—*Adapted.*

Easy Lessons (173)

Who wrote this poem? What other poems have you read that she has written? Which of her poems do you like best? Study with your teacher the questions following the poem. Then, before you try to read it, listen while she reads it to you.

1. Come, little children, come with me,
   Where the winds are singing merrily,
     As they toss the crimson clover;
   We'll walk on the hills and by the brooks,
   And I'll show you stories in prettier books
     Than the ones you are poring* over.

2. Do you think you could learn to sing a song,
    Though you drummed and hummed it all day long,
        Till hands and brains were aching,
    That would match the clear, untutored* notes
    That drop from the pretty, tender throats
        Of birds when the day is breaking?

3. So do not spoil your happy looks
    By poring always over your books,
        Written by scholars and sages;*
    For there's many a lesson in brooks and birds,
    Told in plainer and prettier words
        Than those in your printed pages.

4. And this is a very good reason why
    I would have you learn from earth and sky
        Their lessons of good, and heed* them;
    For there our Father, with loving hand,
    Writes truths that a child may understand,
        So plain that a child can read them.

        —*Phœbe Cary.*

Appreciation Study

1. What are the "prettier books" referred to in stanza 1? What great Teacher taught His pupils from these books? How can the winds "sing"?

2. What time of day is spoken of in stanza 2? In your own words ask the question of stanza 2. Why are the songs of the birds called "untutored notes"?

3. What is the "reason" spoken of in stanza 4 why we should learn lessons from earth and sky as well as from books?

4. Name one lesson that you have learned from a brook, a bird, a hill, or the wind. Who has written these lessons in earth and sky? Why?

DICTIONARY STUDY

Before your dictionary can tell you how to pronounce new words, you will need to know what the marks on the letters mean, and about the syllables in the words. You have had some of this work before, but this year you will need to review it. This period you will review the long and short sounds of a, e, i, o, u, and y. They are as follows:

ā, as in māy	ī, as in īce	ō, as in nō
ă, as in căt	ĭ, as in ĭn	ŏ, as in hŏt
ē, as in mē	ȳ, as in my	ū, as in ūse
ĕ, as in lĕt	y̆, as in lovely	ŭ, as in ŭs

Copy the following words in two columns, putting those that have long sounds in the first column, and those having short sounds in the second column:

wind	with	brains	that
toss	over	why	when
clover	think	drop	sky
hill	writes	though	day
show	song	hands	plain

Captain John Smith ^(S)

Did you ever stop to think that once upon a time there was not a single white man living in the whole of North America? It was the home of red men—the Indians. It was more than one hundred years after Columbus discovered this New World before white men came here to live. They had many interesting experiences with the Indians. This story tells about an experience of Captain John Smith, one of the first white settlers. He came from England. The village of Jamestown where he lived is in the state of Virginia. Find all these places on the map before you read.

The story has 779 words. Can you read it in seven minutes, and find out how Captain Smith helped the Jamestown settlers, and how he escaped from the Indians? Try it. Read so carefully that you can afterwards tell the story of how he saved his life when he was caught by the Indians.

Among the first people who came from England to live in the New World was a man named Captain John Smith. He and his people called the village which they built Jamestown, in honor of King James of England. This was in Virginia, in the year 1607. There were about one hundred men in the village. They had no families, or, if they had, they had left them in England. Most of the men had come to find gold and get rich, and then return to England. Some wanted to see this wonderful new world that everywhere in Europe people were talking about.

About half of the men in this company were so-called "gentlemen." They were not used to hard work. They did not want to chop wood. They did not know how to cultivate the soil. There were some who could refine* gold, and these might have been quite useful if there had been any gold to refine. There was even one man who could make perfume. But these gold seekers did not care for perfume. Fortunately, there were among them a few carpenters, a blacksmith, a mason, a barber, and a tailor.

The first summer at Jamestown was a hard one. Some of the people lived in tents. Some dug caves in the hillside to live in. A few built log cabins. The food they had brought with them from England was soon gone, and the corn they had planted was not ready to be gathered. The men did not know how to take care of themselves, and many of them became sick. By September, half their number had died.

Captain John Smith was then made president of the colony.* And he saved it from destruction. How did he do it? He set every man to work. He said, "Those who will not work, shall not eat." He trained the tender "gentlemen" till they learned how to swing the ax in the forest. He taught them that the surest way to make a fortune* is by hard, honest labor. He showed them how to build comfortable log huts for the winter. He made friends among the Indians, and from them he bought corn and other food.

A tribe of Indians, called the Powhatans,* were the nearest neighbors of the white men. Usually they were friendly, but not always. Once during the winter, when Captain Smith was among them, they caught him and prepared to kill him. They were going to tie him to a tree to be burned.

All at once, he thought of a little compass* that he

had in his pocket. He pulled it out, and began to explain it to the Indians. He showed them the trembling needle. He told them it kept him from being lost in the woods. He said it always told him just which way to go to find Jamestown. They wondered how that could be.

Then he told them about the shape of the earth. He talked to them about the motions of the moon and the stars. He explained how the sun and the moon and the stars chase one another. They were so interested and delighted that they forgot to kill him.

At last he promised to give his gun to the one who would take a piece of paper to his people in Jamestown. On this paper they saw him make a few marks, but they did not know what these marks meant. When the Indians who carried the paper to Jamestown found that it told his friends of his misfortune, they were astonished. They could not understand how the white man could make the paper talk. They thought he must be some kind of god, and they did not dare to kill him.

Before giving them his gun, he filled it with small pebbles. Then he pointed it toward the branches of some trees that hung thick with icicles. *Bang!* went the gun. *Crash! Crash!* went the branches and the icicles. This so frightened the Indians that they could not be persuaded to touch the gun.

Then Captain Smith gave them some powder. This they afterwards planted, expecting to reap a rich harvest for their next war. After that the Indians let the white man go free, and he returned to Jamestown in safety.

A few years later, Captain Smith was so badly burned by the explosion of some gunpowder that he had to go to England, where he could have a doctor's care. Here he stayed during the rest of his life. Captain John Smith will always be remembered as the man who saved from starvation and death the first English settlement in America.

Comprehension Test. Complete these sentences:

1. The first village built by the English in the United States was ———.
2. It was named ——— after ———.
3. This was in the year ———, ——— years after Columbus discovered America.
4. About ——— people lived in this village, and they were all ———.
5. They had come from ——— to ———.
6. Most of them were ———, who did not want to ———.
7. Fortunately, there were among them a ———, a ———, a ———, a ———, and a ———.
8. The first summer the people lived in ———, ———, and ———.
9. By the end of summer ——— of the people had died.
10. ——— kept the village from starvation by teaching the men to ———. He said, "———."

Be Pleasant [O]

This story contains 329 words. It is about a boy who made every one at his home feel pleasant one gloomy morning. Read silently for three minutes, and find out how he did it. Afterwards practice reading the story orally.

The other morning, we were in the midst of a three days' rain. The fire smoked, and the dining room was chilly when we came together for breakfast. Father looked rather grim.* Mother looked tired, for the baby had been restless all night. Polly was fretful, and Bridget was plainly cross.

Just then, Jack came in with the breakfast rolls from the baker's. He had taken off his rubber coat and boots in the entry,* and he came in rosy and smiling.

"Here's the paper, sir," said he to his father, with such a cheerful tone that the troubled look on his father's brow disappeared.

"Ah, thank you, Jack," he said quite pleasantly.

His mother looked up at him smiling, and he just touched her cheek gently as he passed.

"The top of the morning to you, Polliwog," he said to his little sister.

He gave the rolls to Bridget with a "Here you are, Bridget. Aren't you sorry you didn't go to get them yourself this beautiful morning?"

He gave the fire a poke, and opened the damper. The smoke stopped, and the coals began to glow. Five minutes after Jack came in, we were seated around the table and were eating our oatmeal as cheerily as if the sun shone brightly outside.

This seems very simple in the telling, and Jack never knew he had done anything at all. But he had, in fact, started a gloomy day pleasantly for five persons.

"He is always so," said his mother, when I spoke to her about it afterwards; "just so sunny and kind and willing all the time. I suppose there are boys in the world who are more brilliant than mine, but none with a more unselfish heart or a sweeter temper, I am sure of that."

And I thought, "Why isn't such a disposition worth cultivating? Isn't it one's duty to be pleasant, just as well as to be honest or truthful or industrious* or generous?

—*Eleanor A. Hunter, in Christian at Work.*

Comprehension Test

1. Name three things that made the morning unpleasant.
2. What shows that Jack was helpful? What shows that he was orderly?
3. How many persons did he help to feel pleasant?
4. What did he do for his father? for his mother? for Bridget?

5. What helpful act did he do without being told?
6. How was it that Jack didn't know he had done anything?
7. The next to the last paragraph tells the secret of Jack's power to do pleasant things for others. What is it?

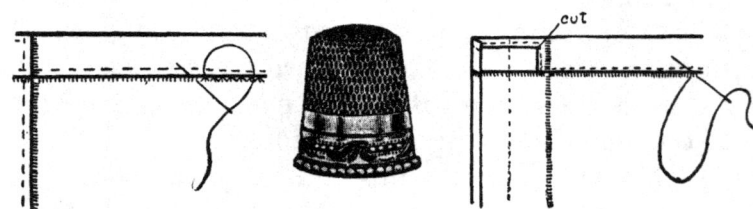

Story of Thimbles ^(S)

Read this story with your thimble in your hand. As you read, notice from your thimble all the steps in its making. The first thimble was made in 1684. How many years ago was that?

After you have read the story through, take your thimble and *show* the class the different steps used in making it.

There are eight starred words in this story. Write a list of these words, then find in the dictionary any that you cannot pronounce or tell the meaning of.

The making of thimbles is very simple and interesting. Some thimbles are made of celluloid.* Some are made of gold. But many thimbles are made of silver,—not silver from the mines, but bright new silver right from the smelter.*

First, the bright silver is melted. The melted silver is then made into round bars. These bars are cut into thin, round pieces just large enough for one thimble. A bar the shape and size of the thimble to be made comes down on one of the disks* of silver and bends it into the shape of a thimble. This bar goes up and down by machinery. These thimble shapes are made just as fast as the silver disks can be placed under the bar.

The thimble shapes are next put on a rod that turns round and round very rapidly. With a sharp chisel a thin shaving is cut from the open end of the thimble. This trims the open end, and makes it smooth. Another chisel cuts a thin shaving from the side of the thimble, a little way from the open end. A third chisel rounds off the rim so that it is not too sharp. Look at your own thimbles, and see if you can find these places.

The outside of the thimble is then polished with a rod dipped in oil.

Look again at your thimble. Do you see the little ornament* next to the rim? That is pressed into the thimble by a wheel that has the same pattern on it. Only the pattern on the wheel stands out, while the ornament on the thimble is pressed *into* the silver. A second wheel prints a different ornament around the thimble near its center. A third wheel with sharp points makes the little dents on the outside of the thimble to catch the needle.

The inside of the thimble is polished. Then the thimbles are washed in soapsuds to remove the oil. Last of all, they are dried and packed, ready for sale.

Thimbles were first worn on the thumb instead of on the finger. They were called "thumb balls." This word was afterwards changed to thimbles. The Germans used to call the thimble a "finger hat." Wasn't that a jolly little name?

>Little finger, slim and nimble,*
>Here am I, your friendly Thimble.
>Germans call me "Finger hat;"
>Jolly little name is that!
>
>Put me on, and you will see
>What a helper I can be.
>Brother Needle's very fine—
>Sharp and clever in his line,
>But he oft would puzzled be,
>If he had no help from me.
>
>When the cloth is stiff and hard,
>Oft his headlong dash is barred,
>And he balks, and frets, and pricks;
>Says, "I'm in a dreadful fix!
>This will never, never do—
>I shall really break in two."
>
>Then's my time! No fuss or rush,
>Just a steady, patient push—
>And the stiffened fiber* slacks,
>And the stubborn threads relax,*
>And Friend Needle darts along,
>Singing his triumphant* song.
>
>—*Author Unknown.*

Try Again [116]

In this poem there are four words that show the kind of character one has who keeps on trying until he succeeds. Two of these words are in stanza 1, one is in stanza 2, and one is in stanza 3. Read until you find them.

1. If at first you don't succeed,
    Try *again*.
 'Tis a lesson all should heed—
    Try, try *again*;
 Let your courage then appear;
 For if you will persevere,*
 You will conquer, never fear;
    Try, try, try again.

2. Twice or thrice though you should fail,
    Try *again*.
  If at last you would prevail,*
    Try, try *again*.
 When you strive, 'tis no disgrace
 Though you fail to win the race.
 Bravely, then, in such a case,
    Try, try, try again.

3. If you find your task is hard,
    Try *again*.
 Time will surely bring reward;
    Try, try *again*.
 That which other folks can do,
 Why, with patience, may not you?
 Only keep this rule in view—
    Try, try, try again!
        —*E. Hickson (adapted).*

I recommend this advice to all who are discouraged, and who think that the best thing they can do is to give up. Nobody knows *what* he can do till he *tries*.

The fox said, "Try," and he got away from the hounds,* when they had almost caught him. The bees said, "Try," and found honey in many flowers. The squirrel said, "Try," and up he went to the top of the beech tree.

The young bird said, "Try," and he found that his new wings took him over hedges and ditches, and up where his father was swinging. The ox said, "Try," and plowed the field from end to end.

No hill is too steep for Try to climb, no clay too stiff for Try to plow, no field too wet for Try to drain, no rent too big for Try to mend.

> "By many strokes
> Men fell great oaks."

What man *has* done, man *can* do; and what has never *been* done, *may* be done.

Do you wish to make something of yourself, young Hopeful? Begin now in earnest. "Where there's a will, there's a way." The sun shines for all the world. The road up the hill may be hard, but at any rate it is open, and they who set stout heart against steep hill shall climb it yet. What is hard to bear will be sweet to remember.

Believe in God and stick to hard work, and see if the mountains are not removed. *Cheer up*, boys! Cheer up!

Trees in October [O]

In reading this poem, find out the different trees named, and the colors of their autumn dress.

---

1. The maple owned that she was tired of always
     wearing green.
  She knew that she had grown, of late, too shabby*
     to be seen!
  The oak and beech and chestnut then deplored*
     their shabbiness.
  And all, except the hemlock sad, were wild to
     change their dress.

2. "For fashion plate *we'll* take the flowers," the
    rustling maple said,
   "And like the tulip I'll be clothed in splendid gold
    and red!"
   "The cheerful sunflower suits *me* best," the light-
    some* beech replied;
   "The marigold *my* choice shall be," the chestnut
    spoke with pride.
   The sturdy oak took time to think. "Give *me* no
    glaring hues;
   The gillyflower,* so dark and rich, *I* for *my* model
    choose."

3. So every tree in all the grove, except the hemlock
    sad,
   According to its wish erelong in brilliant dress
    was clad.
   And here they stand through all the soft and
    bright October days;
   They wished to look like flowers,—indeed they
    look like huge* bouquets!

   —*Edith M. Thomas.*

Comprehension Test

1. What five trees are spoken of in this poem?
2. How many of these trees have you seen?
3. What color does the maple have in autumn? the beech? the chestnut? the oak? What flowers have the same colors?
4. Which of these trees does not change color?
5. What is a tree called that remains green the year round?

A Trip to Milk Springs ^(o)

From this story find out how children should receive a visitor at school. Find how many food elements there are in milk, what they are, and what each one does for the body. Which friend living at Milk Springs do *you* need most?

A lady entered the schoolroom one morning. The teacher shook hands with her. She seemed glad to see her. Then she turned to the children.

"Boys and girls," she said. As she spoke to them, they all quietly rose and stood by their seats. "Miss Goodhealth, our school nurse, has come to visit us to-day."

"Good morning, Miss Goodhealth; we are glad to see you," said the children courteously and all together.

"Good morning, boys and girls," Miss Goodhealth answered, smiling.

The children remained standing until the teacher and the nurse sat down. Then all the children quietly took their seats and went on with their studies while the teacher and Miss Goodhealth talked together for a few moments.

"Boys and girls," the teacher said at last, "Miss Goodhealth has something interesting to say to you."

Every pupil closed his book, laid down his pencil, and took the position of attention. Then Miss Goodhealth began to talk to them.

"This morning," she said brightly, "I hope you are all on the fast express to Life and Health. We are going to the station called Milk Springs. Every train going through Milk Springs stops to let the passengers get a drink. Before we reach the station, I want to tell you what these wonderful springs can do for you.

"There are some people living at Milk Springs that I want you to know," she said as she drew a picture of a big bottle of milk on the blackboard, and colored it all white with chalk. Under it she wrote "Milk Springs."

"The last time I talked to you," she continued, as she went on drawing something else, "I found that some of you have a 'sweet tooth.' There is a sweet little girl in Milk Springs that I know you will all like." She had drawn a big tooth and put a face on it. Then she put a girl's hat on top of it. "Her name is Susie Sugar," she continued, as she wrote the name below the picture. "Susie Sugar will help to keep you warm.

"There are other people living at Milk Springs besides Susie Sugar," she went on, as she began to draw again. "I know you boys like to have strong muscles so you can do hard work. There is a strong little man in Milk Springs that can make fine muscles. His name is Peter Protein.*"

And there on the blackboard stood a strong-looking chap with an ax over his shoulder and the name "Peter Protein" written below.

"No one likes to look thin and skinny," she then said, as she began another drawing. "A round, plump body is the only kind to have on this train. How much better you feel when you are up to weight!

This smiling lad we will name Frank Fat. He is a twin to Susie Sugar, and helps her to keep you warm.

"It is just as important that we have good bones and teeth as strong muscles," she continued, as she began another drawing. "What a terrible thing it would be to have weak bones and not be able to walk, or poor teeth that would be sure to ache sometime. The name of this erect little girl with these pearly teeth is Minnie Mineral* Matter.

"There is one more very important person living at Milk Springs. He is a fine, tall lad, and he can make you grow, too. His name is Victor Vitamin.*

"But here we are just pulling into our station. How many can tell what living elements there are in milk, and what each element can do for you? How many of you are going to drink a glass of milk at every meal?" Every boy and girl raised the hand.

Miss Goodhealth then thanked the children for their courteous attention, and they were dismissed.

Comprehension and Speed Test. In the margin of your reader write lightly the number of each of these points next to the place where they are told. See if you can find them all in *three minutes. Ready! Go!*

1. The children remained standing until the visitor sat down.
2. When the visitor talked to the pupils, each one laid down his pencil.
3. The sugar in milk helps to keep you warm.
4. The protein in milk will make you strong.
5. The fat in milk keeps you warm.
6. The mineral matter builds bone and teeth.
7. The vitamin makes you grow.

A Talking Chip [O]

Do you know any missionary who has ever gone among cannibals? Who was it? Where did he go? This story tells about a famous missionary who went from England more than one hundred years ago to tell the cannibals of the South Sea Islands about Jesus.

Let us find these islands on the globe, and see how far away from home this missionary went. Find England, where John Williams lived when he was a boy. Find the great body of water that is called the Pacific Ocean. All these little black dots that you see in the Pacific Ocean are quite large bodies of land. They are called islands. The southern part of this ocean is sometimes called the South Sea. So the islands here are called the South Sea Islands. What a long, long way from home he went, didn't he? He never went back home to live, either. He spent the rest of his life teaching these cannibals about the Saviour.

John Williams

On page 135 you will find a map of the South Sea Islands. On this map find the group of islands where John Williams began his work.

Before you read this story guess what you think this "talking chip" was; then read and see if you guessed right. Read so carefully that you can afterwards tell the story to the folks at home.

John Williams was a famous missionary who went from England to carry the gospel to the cannibals* of the South Sea Islands. He began his work on a group of islands called the Society Islands. At this time he could not speak the language of the natives.

So the first thing he did was to learn how, so the people could understand what he said. Then he wrote parts of the Bible and other books in their language. These were the first books that had ever been written in that language. He also started schools, where hundreds of native children were taught. He trained some of these children to be teachers and preachers.

One time John Williams was building a church on one of the islands. He went to work one morning without his square. Picking up a chip, he wrote a line to Mrs. Williams, asking her to send it to him. Then he called a chief to take the chip to her.

"Friend," he said, "take this, go to our house, and give it to Mrs. Williams."

The chief was a queer-looking man, and very quick in his movements. He had been a great warrior, and in one of his battles he had lost one eye.

"Take *that?*" he asked, giving Mr. Williams a comical look with his one remaining eye. "She will think I am a fool, and scold me if I carry a chip to her."

"No," replied Mr. Williams, "she will not. Take it and go immediately. I am in haste."

"What must I say?" the chief asked, when he saw that Mr. Williams was really in earnest.

"You have nothing to say. The chip will say all that I wish."

With a look of astonishment and scorn, he held up the piece of wood.

"How can this speak? Has it a mouth?" he asked, as if it were a great joke.

Tahiti, one of the South Sea Islands

"Take it immediately," replied Mr. Williams, "and do not spend so much time talking about it."

When the chief reached the house, he gave the chip to Mrs. Williams. She read it, threw it away, and went to the tool chest. The chief followed her closely, for he was determined to see the result of this mystery.* She found the square, and gave it to the puzzled chief.

"How do you know that this is what Mr. Williams wants?" he asked.

"Why," she replied, "did you not bring me a chip just now?"

"Yes," said the warrior, "but I did not hear it say anything."

"If you did not, I did," she replied, "for it made known to me what he wanted, and all you have to do is to return with it as quickly as possible."

The chief leaped out of the house, and catching up the mysterious* piece of wood, he ran through the settlement* with the chip in one hand and the square in the other, holding them as high as he could reach.

"See the wisdom of these English people!" he shouted as he ran. "They can make chips talk! They can make chips talk!"

When he gave the square to Mr. Williams, he asked how it was possible thus to talk with persons at a distance. Mr. Williams tried to explain, but it was all such a mystery to the chief that he actually tied a string to the chip, hung it around his neck, and wore it for some time.

During several following days, he was often seen surrounded by a crowd, who were listening with great interest while he told of the wonders of this strange chip.

John Williams traveled from one island to another in boats. One of his boats he named "The Messenger of Peace." The natives called it "The Ship of God." Finally he was killed on one of the islands by cruel cannibals. Because he gave his life to help the cannibals of the South Seas, John Williams is often called "The Hero* of the South Seas." Of the islands where he labored it is said, "When he came, there were no Christians; when he left, there were no heathen."

Comprehension Test. Read the right words where the blanks are:

1. The name of the missionary in this story is ———.
2. He went as a missionary to the ——— Islands.

3. The people on these islands were ———.
4. First, he had to ———.
5. Next, he wrote ——— in the native language.
6. This was ——— that had ever been written in that language.
7. He started ——— to help the native children.
8. The natives called his boat ———.
9. This missionary is called ———.
10. At last, he was killed by ———.

Reading Tests and Scores for the First Period

To the Boys and Girls in the Fourth Grade:

You have now completed your reading lessons for the first period of school. You are ready for your first period tests. These tests will show you what your progress in reading has been during the past six weeks. Do your very best in these interesting tests.

In your *silent reading test,* remember that rate without comprehension is worthless. Read as quickly as you can, but be sure you understand what you read. Your rate for this period should be about 120 words a minute. Your silent reading memory test will show how much you remember of what you have read this period.

At this time, you will also have an *oral reading test.* For this test you may choose any story you have had this period. Study it beforehand as much as you please. Practice reading it at home if you like. When your test is given, your score should show your very best effort.

Your score, or grade, in *memory reading* will depend on the amount of memory reading you have prepared well enough to recite in public in an interesting way without any help from anyone. You can find out what your grade will be by reading about it again on pages 30 and 31.

SECOND PERIOD

Colporteur Stories ⁽ᴼ⁾

Here are two colporteur stories that tell how God answered prayer. The boys may read or tell the first one to the girls. The girls may read or tell the second one to the boys. See how interesting you can make your story. If you *read* it, look away from your book as much as you can. Where are the best places in reading to look away?

The first story took place in Czecho-Slovakia* in Europe.* The second story took place in Canada. Find these countries on the map or the globe.

Do you know who a colporteur* is? A colporteur is a person who carries and sells religious books and tracts from house to house. A real colporteur is a true Christian, a missionary for God.

This story is about a colporteur who lived in Czecho-Slovakia,* a small country in Europe.* One day, sixty miles from the nearest railway station, he went to a house and canvassed the lady for his book.

"I see you believe the Bible," the lady said, when he had finished telling her about his book.

"Of course I do," the colporteur answered.

"If you believe the Bible, you must keep the Sabbath," she continued.

"Yes, I do," he replied.

"Have you been baptized?"

"Certainly."

"Do you believe in the second coming of Christ?"

"Indeed I do!"

Then the lady became excited, and called to her husband.

"Come, come!" she cried. "The Lord has sent us the angel of Revelation 14, for whom we have prayed so long!"

There were ten persons in that place who had never seen a book, a tract, or a paper that told them about the second coming of Christ. They had never heard a preacher talk about the true Sabbath. But they had studied the Bible for themselves, and God had taught them about His holy Sabbath day. He had taught them the truth about baptism and about His near coming.

As they studied the messages of the angels in Revelation 14, they prayed that the Lord would send some one to them to explain this chapter in the Bible. And they believed God had answered their prayer by sending them this colporteur. As a result, every one of these ten persons were baptized and united with God's people.

Another Colporteur's Experience

It was in Canada in the winter, and the snow was deep. The colporteur was walking along the road, pulling a sled on which were books that told about the second coming of Christ. He was passing a small grass-covered shack almost buried in the snow. He wondered if anyone lived there. If so, he thought they would surely be too poor to buy a book. He decided not to stop at this little shack.

Suddenly the familiar song, "Pass me not, O gentle Saviour," flashed into his mind. If he should pass by this humble place, he feared the Saviour would pass *him* by. This thought caused him to stop at the humble door. He knocked.

"Come in," was the friendly call.

He entered. A man met him. As soon as he saw the colporteur, he called to his wife.

"Here is the man I have been telling you about this morning," he said to her.

Then he turned to the colporteur.

"You are the man I saw in my dream last night," he said. "I seemed to be riding past a field of grain. I noticed that it was wasting because it was overripe. I asked the driver why the owner of the field did not reap his grain.

"Just then I saw a man coming through the field with a scythe* on his shoulder. As he came out on the side next to us, I noticed heads of wheat clinging to his clothing. I asked about the field of grain, and why it was not being reaped.

"He took a book from under his coat, and began showing it to me. The book had red on it, and white letters on the cover. As he showed it to me, I noticed a picture of Jesus coming on the clouds with the angels. The book told about the coming of Christ.

"I wanted to buy the book, but he said he was only taking orders for it now. Then he pulled from his pocket a little book with a black cover and gold letters on it. He began to fill out the order, and I signed my name. You are the man I saw; but where is the book?"

Imagine the colporteur's surprise! He took "The World's Hope" from under his coat,—a book with a red back and white letters on the cover,— the very book the man had seen in his dream! The astonished man was filled with joy. He seized the book and pressed it to his heart, while tears of gratitude rolled down his face.

"This is the book," he exclaimed; "but where is the order book?"

The colporteur pulled the order book from his pocket, just as the man in his dream had seen him do. Immediately, the man signed his name in the order book. He wanted the book at once, but he had no money to pay for it.

What would you have done if you had been that colporteur? Could you have had the heart to take the book away with you? This colporteur could not. He left it with the happy man, who paid him for it two months later.

Truly this colporteur was passing through fields overripe for the harvest, gathering some of the golden grain in God's great harvest field.

The Fourth Man in the Boat [S]

This story was told by L. J. Borrowdale, at that time our missionary in Venezuela.* This and many other times when God has shown His wonder-working power in this "Neglected Continent"* make us feel that South America is no longer a neglected continent but rather a "Continent of Opportunity."* Find South America and Venezuela on the map or globe. This story has 362 words. See if you can read it silently in three minutes, and find out how it shows that God fulfilled His promise in Psalm 34:7.

It was in Venezuela,* a country in the northern part of South America. One of our missionaries, his assistant,* and a boy to help care for the boat were passing up a large river in the mission boat. When they came to a fork in the river, they did not know which way to go. They decided to try the right-hand branch of the river.

They had not gone far when they found that they could go no farther. They returned to the fork, and took the left branch. They passed up this branch until it began to grow dark. Then they cast anchor* and lay down in the boat to sleep.

The next morning they continued their journey

up the river until they reached a town where they were to hold meetings.

After the meetings were over, they returned to the fork of the river. Here they stopped at a house, and were given permission to stay all night. The missionary and his assistant went up to the house, leaving the boy to look after the boat.

"Where is your companion?" the owner of the house asked.

"He is at the boat, but he will soon be up," the missionary answered, thinking that the man was speaking of the boy.

"But where is the other one?"

"There are only three of us."

"I saw *four* men in the boat when you went up," he continued. "Your helper here was at the front, steering the boat; you were at the side, leaning over to watch; and the boy was on the other side, taking the depth of the river."

"Where was the *fourth* man?" I asked.

"He was standing right by your side, and was dressed in white."

Then he described how my two helpers and I were dressed. I knew by this that he had observed carefully and correctly. He told us that this part of the river was very dangerous.

With gratitude I thanked God that He had saved us from dangers that we knew not of. He had fulfilled to us His promise, "The angel of the Lord encampeth round about them that fear Him, and delivereth them."

The Frost [191]

Read the poem silently, and mark anything you do not understand. Then discuss these things in class. After that read orally, and see which lines you can read at one glance.

1. The Frost looked forth, one still, clear night,
   And whispered, "Now I shall be out of sight;
   So through the valley and over the height,
      In silence I'll take my way:
   I will not go on with that blustering* train,
   The wind and the snow, the hail and the rain,
   Who make so much bustle and noise in vain,
      But I'll be as busy as they."

2. Then he flew to the mountain and powdered its crest;*
   He lit on the trees, and their boughs he dressed
   In diamond beads—and over the breast
      Of the quivering lake he spread
   A coat of mail,* that it need not fear

The downward point of many a spear
  That hung on its margin far and near,
     Where a rock could rear its head.

3. He went to the windows of those who slept,
   And over each pane he daintily crept;
   Wherever he breathed, whenever he stepped,
      By the light of the moon were seen
   Most beautiful things—there were flowers and
         trees;
   There were bevies* of birds and swarms of bees;
   There were cities with temples and towers, and
         these
      All pictured in silvery sheen!*

                                —*Hannah Flagg Gould.*

Appreciation Study

Stanza 1. What is the "blustering train"? Why is it called "blustering"?

Stanza 2. Have you ever seen the crest of a mountain when it is "powdered" with frost?

What are the "diamond beads"?

What is the "coat of mail" that is spread over the lake?

What is the "spear" that hangs from the rocks?

Stanza 3. Did you ever see the frost pictures on a window? What did they look like? What word in this stanza tells the color of the pictures painted by the frost?

DICTIONARY STUDY[1]

Last period you had all the long and the short sounds of the letters. To-day you will study more of the sounds of *a*.

ā, as in nāme ä, as in ärm
ă, as in ăt a̤, as in a̤ll
â, as in câre

Write the following words in syllables, mark the accented syllable, and mark all the *a's:*

place	answered	caused	encampeth
prayer	wanted	grain	angel
can	prayed	gratitude	warning
small	chapter	farther	airplane
railway	father	called	hairs

Remember to find in the dictionary all the starred words in each lesson. But first see if you can tell what they mean by the thought of the sentence in which they are used.

Copy the five starred words from the last story. Then see how long it takes you to find these words in the dictionary. In this way test yourself often in lessons that follow.

A Squirrel Family (S)

Read this story silently, and see how many things you can learn about squirrels. Write these things in two lists. In one list put the things you knew before; in the other put the things you did not know before. See how far you can read in three minutes.

Paragraphs 1, 2, 3, and 4 are good for oral reading.

1. Such a chattering as there was in the branches of the old oak! Alice rubbed her sleepy eyes. Then

---

[1] TO THE TEACHER: Give sufficient drill on the sounds and markings of the letters, and on dividing words into syllables, to give the pupils a good working knowledge of them.

she slipped out of bed, and ran to the window to listen. There, in the branches of a tree close to the window were two squirrels with long, bushy tails of a reddish brown. They seemed much excited.

"Oh, how I wish I knew the squirrel language!" she said to herself.

The squirrels certainly had something worth talking about, and were losing no time over it, either.

2. "*Leo! Do* wake up and come here *quickly!*" Alice called to her brother. Then she added, in a warning tone, "*Come softly!*"

"What frisky little fellows!" said Leo, as he watched the pretty squirrels. "What can they want with old Dick's nest?"

Dick was an old crow that had lived in the tree for many years, but had finally died, as all crows must. The squirrels had decided to take his nest for *their* home. But it was too small, and they seemed to be discussing how to enlarge it.

3. After breakfast the children ran out under the tree to see if the squirrels were still there. Peeping through the leafy branches, they saw four bright, black eyes watching them.

"See! They are in Dick's nest," whispered Alice.

"I hope they'll stay," Leo said.

And they *did* stay. They made the nest larger. With long, tough grasses they fastened it more firmly to the branches. They lined it with soft, fresh leaves. Then they set up housekeeping in true squirrel fashion.

A SQUIRREL FAMILY
Match each picture with the paragraph in the story that tells about it.

4. After a time, they became so well acquainted with Alice and Leo that they would come down to the ground to get the corn that the children brought for them. One morning, the father squirrel came down, took a nibble, and then ran home as fast as he could go. In a moment he returned with the mother. But what were they carrying so carefully in their mouths? They laid their burdens down under the tree, and the father squirrel scampered up to the nest again.

"Oh! oh!" cried both children in a breath, "What dear little baby squirrels!"

When the father returned, he laid the third baby beside the other two. The baby squirrels began to run about a little. When they found how easy it was, they ran around quite briskly. After a while the father and mother took the babies back to their nest. This was their first lesson in learning to walk.

5. At the next lesson they had an exciting time. They took a long run on the branches of the tree and the high board fence. The father led the way, and called the baby squirrels to follow. They scampered along as they had seen *him* do. Then the mother called from the door of their house for them to come back. Back they ran, as fast as they could. What fun it was!

6. One day, the father took the young squirrels into the walnut tree to show them the nuts. The first young one leaped safely to the branch of a hickory tree. The next one tried and succeeded, but the effort made all the hairs on his bushy tail bristle.* Then

came the little sister. Her leap was too short, and she began to fall.

"Spread your feet and tail quickly!" called the mother squirrel. They were almost as good as wings, and the little squirrel came to the ground as safely and lightly as a bird.

7. When summer was over, the squirrels found a winter home in the hollow limb of an old oak tree in the woods. Through a hole in the limb, they carried leaves and straw for a soft, warm nest.

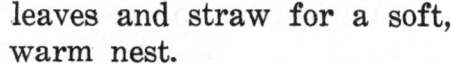

The squirrels stored some nuts in their winter home. But it would not hold all the nuts they gathered, so every hollow tree they found was turned into a storehouse.

8. One day, Leo and Alice went with their mother across the river to gather nuts. Here they saw their old friends, the squirrels. The squirrels were so busy hiding nuts that they did not stop to visit with the children.

9. When lunch time came, our nutting party sat down on the shady bank of the river to eat and rest. Soon they heard a rustle among the dry leaves. Looking up, they saw five yellowish-brown tails whisk through the air, and five little gray bodies skip down to the river's brink.* There they paused, running

first one way and then another. Finally, the father squirrel dashed into the water. The three children followed. They held their heads up to keep the nuts in their mouths from getting wet, and swam safely to the other side.

But the mother squirrel was a dainty creature. She did not like to get wet. Back and forth on the bank she ran till at last she saw a piece of bark floating on the water. She paused and looked at it. Then she jumped on to it, and spread her tail to catch the breeze. Thus she slowly drifted to the opposite shore.

10. The winter was bitterly cold and the snow was deep, but the little family in the hollow oak lay snug and warm in their thick fur coats. They slept soundly most of the time. When they woke up, they ate the nuts beside them. Before winter was over, the supply in the oak tree gave out. Then on bright, sunny days they would skip over the snow to their other storehouses. Here they would eat, and then go home again to sleep.

11. When spring came, the little squirrels had grown to be big ones. They left the home nest, and made homes of their own. The father and mother returned to their summer home in the old oak tree, and you may be sure Alice and Leo gave them a joyful welcome.

—*Loretta Reisman (adapted)*.

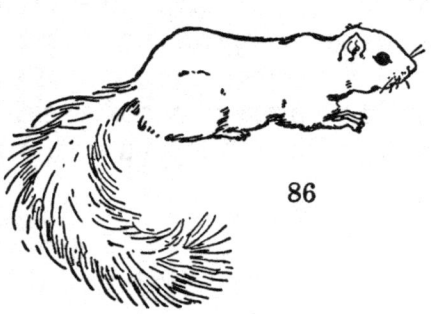

A Sunbeam [82]

Read this poem, and see if you like it. Then tell why.

1. A sunbeam touched my little bed;
   "Good morning, dear," he gently said.
   I opened wide my sleepy eyes,
   And said, "Good morning," with surprise.
   "I cannot think that night is gone;
   Are you quite *sure* that this is *morn?*"

2. The sunbeam laughed and shook his head;
   "Last night you would not go to bed,
   And that is why you sleep so late,
   And make me climb the window gate
   To say, 'Wake up, you sleepy dear!
   Wake up! Rise quickly! Morning's here!'"

   —*Selected.*

A Talk About the Cow ^(o)

This is a good story to read as a dialogue. How many persons would be needed to read it in this way? As you read this dialogue, read only the words that are spoken by the different persons. Try to read the phrases smoothly.

Once or twice a week try marking the reading phrases in one or two paragraphs of the lesson. Mark the longest phrases that you think you can read at a glance, and remember each phrase tells something about the story.

"Do cows run wild anywhere now?" asked Fred.
"Not entirely wild," said Uncle William.
"In Australia, however,
and in some parts of South America,
and in the western prairies* of the United States,
vast* herds of cattle roam as free as air.
They belong to different owners,
but they have the *habits* of *wild* cattle."
"I have read," said Cousin Kate,
"that many years ago some people clothed themselves with the skins of cattle,
and fed upon the flesh and milk of cattle.
They wandered with their herds from place to place,
stopping where pasture feed was most plentiful.
Their wealth was counted not in money,
but by the number of their cattle."
"Yes," added her father,
"the words *cattle, capital,** and *chattel,**
all come from the same parent word.
In those times property was always in motion."
"Cows have some of that old, roving* nature yet,"
said Uncle William.

The Runaway Cow

"Don't you remember
how grandpa's cow was always straying away?"
 "I do," said Fred;
"I have had to go and find her many a time."
 "And they have the old habit of keeping together,"
said Cousin Kate.
"I remember that when the neighbors
took their cows out of grandpa's field,
his cow was lonely, and grandpa said
she did not give nearly so much milk as before."
 "And, oh, Cousin Kate," said Nannie,
"don't you remember how she cried for her calf?"
 "Yes, indeed," replied Kate.
"She grieved and moaned, and showed her sorrow
almost as plainly as if she had spoken.

Grandpa says that cows have tones of joy
as well as of grief,
and that some cows
become strongly attached to places.
He told me
that they have been known to find their way back
twenty miles to their old homes."

"Well," said Uncle William,
"I don't think cows are so affectionate*
as some other domestic* animals,
but there is certainly no animal
that *does* more for us."

Comprehension Test

1. Find on the map three places where herds of cattle roam almost like wild cattle.

2. How was a man's wealth counted long ago?

3. Can you think of any man in the Bible whose wealth was counted in cattle?

4. Because one's wealth was first counted in cattle, what two words that mean wealth come from the same parent word as cattle?

5. What are some of the habits of a cow?

6. Name some things that a cow does for us.

7. If you have a cow, or know of one, tell the class something about her.

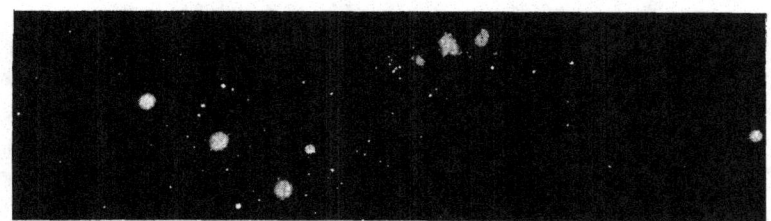

This group of stars is named Orion. It is the most wonderful group in the heavens. The three large stars in a slanting line toward the left are the belt of Orion. The three bright ones above are his sword. The center star in the sword is made up of many stars within which is "the open space" in Orion. Through this open space the New Jerusalem will descend to this earth when the earth is cleansed from all sin.

Some night, when the stars shine, try to find Orion and "the open space."

The Handiwork of God [O]

This lesson is taken from two of King David's most beautiful psalms. Can you find them in the Bible? After studying these psalms with your teacher, read them in concert.

Lesson Study

1. Did you ever stop to think that the earth and the sky can talk? Well, they can; the Bible says so. Read it in stanza 1. How do they talk? What do they say?

2. Which stanza says that the sun runs races? When does the sun begin his race, and how often does he run a race?

3. What is the "tabernacle" where the sun races?

4. Which stanza tells that man is very small compared with other things that God has made? What does Isaiah 40: 12, 15, 17 tell about man?

5. Read the two lines in stanza 3 that tell why God visits man.

6. Read the lines in stanza 4 that show what God has made man to rule over.

---

1. The heavens declare* the glory of God;
   And the firmament showeth His handiwork.*
   Day unto day uttereth speech,
   And night unto night showeth knowledge.

There is no *speech* nor *language* —
Their *voice* is not heard.
Their line is gone out through all the earth,
And their words to the end of the world.

2. In them hath He set a tabernacle* for the sun,
Which is as a bridegroom* coming out of his chamber,
And rejoiceth as a strong man to run a race.

3. When I consider* Thy heavens, the work of Thy fingers,
The moon and the stars, which Thou hast ordained;*
What is man, that Thou art mindful of *him?*
And the son of man, that Thou visitest him?
For Thou hast made him a little lower than the angels,
And hast crowned him with glory and honor.

4. Thou madest him to have dominion* over the works of Thy hands;
Thou hast put all things under his feet:
All sheep and oxen,
Yea, and the beasts of the field;
The fowl of the air,
And the fish of the sea,
And whatsoever passeth through the paths of the seas.

5. O Lord, our Lord,
How excellent is Thy name in all the earth!

—*From Psalms 19 and 8 (R. V. in part).*

This is John Burroughs in his study at "Slabsides."

America's Greatest Naturalist ^(S)

As you read this story, find out the name of America's greatest naturalist,* and what made him a great naturalist. Are you studying nature as this boy did?

John Burroughs* is called America's greatest naturalist.* A naturalist is one who knows a great deal about nature. John's parents lived on a farm in New York. Here he learned to love the birds and flowers and animals. Before he was fourteen years old, he knew every inch of ground about his home, and he had made a study of all the animals of the neighborhood.

When John was a boy, life was very different

from what it is to-day. In those days boys and men wore boots that were so heavy some one had to help pull them off at night. When John needed a new pair of boots, instead of going to a shoe store to buy them, he went to the village shoemaker and had a pair made.

When he needed a new shirt, his mother spun the thread, wove the cloth, and sewed it by hand. The thread was made from flax* that was raised on their farm. His socks and mittens were knit by hand from the wool that grew on their own sheep. Their mattresses and pillows were filled with feathers that grew on their own geese. Their lights were candles that they made from tallow which was melted from the fat of their own sheep and oxen. Even the children's pencils were made of soft slate that they found in the hills. And they made their fishing lines by braiding the hair they pulled out of the horses' tails.

John's father was a hard-working man, but he did not have very much money. And he did not need much, for he raised on the farm nearly everything his family needed. But there was one thing John wanted that they could not grow on the farm. John wanted books.

His father did not always think it was necessary to buy the books his son wanted. How was John to get them?

"I know what I'll do," he said to himself. "I'll get some sap from the maple trees about the farm, and make it into sugar, and sell the sugar. Then I'll take the money and buy books." And this he did.

The more he learned about animals and other

things in nature, the more he loved it. He often thought he would like to tell other boys and girls about nature because he thought they would love it too. So he began to study to learn how to write interesting stories about birds and animals. He studied every book he could find that would help him.

When he was about fifty years old, he gave up public life. Then he went back to his farm, where he built a log cabin. It was on the top of a high hill that sloped down to the Hudson River. He named the cabin "Slabsides." Here he spent much of his time studying nature and writing about it. Thousands of girls and boys have learned to love the woods and the fields because of what John Burroughs has written.

Comprehension Test. Complete these sentences:

1. ——— is called America's greatest naturalist.
2. He was born April 3, 1837. That was ——— years ago.
3. His mother spun her own ———, and wove her own cloth.
4. The thread was made from ——— that grew on their own farm.
5. John's mittens were knit from ——— that grew on their own ———.
6. His pillows were filled with ——— that grew on their own ———.
7. Their candles were made from ——— that came from their own ———.
8. They found the ——— for their pencils in the hills.
9. John made sugar from the ——— of ——— trees that grew about the farm.
10. John Burroughs named his cabin ———.

When God Controlled a Railroad Train ^(o)

This story tells how God answered the prayers of a poor woman and an engineer of a railroad train. First read silently and find out why they prayed, what they prayed for, and how God answered their prayer. After that, practice reading the story orally. See if you can call out, "All aboard!" in paragraph 4 as you have heard conductors call.

---

1. Not long ago an engineer brought his train to a stand at a little village in Massachusetts,* where the passengers had five minutes for lunch.

2. "The conductor tells me that the train at the junction leaves fifteen minutes before our arrival," said a sad-eyed lady on the platform to the engineer. "That is to be the last train to-night. I have a very sick child in the car, and no money for a hotel. I *must* get home to-night."

"It can't be done," said the engineer.

"Would it be possible for you to hurry a little?" asked the anxious, tearful mother.

"No, madam, I have the time-table, and the rules say I must run by it."

3. The woman turned sorrowfully away. In a moment she returned.

"Are you a Christian?" she asked.

"I trust I am," was the reply.

"Will you pray with me that the Lord may in some way delay the train at the junction?"

"Why, yes, I will pray with you; but I have not much faith."

4. Just then the conductor cried, "All aboard!" The poor woman hurried back to her sick child,

and away went the train, climbing the grade. The woman prayed in the rear. In front the engineer prayed, "Lord, keep them ten minutes, and I'll make the other five."

5. "Somehow," says the engineer, "everything worked like a charm. I prayed. I could not help letting my engine out just a *little*. We hardly stopped at the first station. People got on and off with wonderful speed. The conductor's lantern was in the air in half a minute, and then away again! I began to have more faith.

"Once over the summit,* it was easy to give the engine a little more steam, and then a little more, as I prayed, till she seemed to shoot through the air like an arrow. Somehow I couldn't hold her, knowing I had the road, and so we dashed up to the junction six minutes ahead of time. There stood the train and the conductor with his lantern on his arm."

6. These trains never connected with each other, nor were they intended to. There was no message sent ahead to stop. There was not the slightest business reason for waiting. Yet there stood the conductor with his train—waiting.

7. "Well," said he, "will you tell me what I am waiting here for? Somehow I felt that I must wait your coming to-night."

"I don't know why you are waiting," said the other conductor, "unless it is for this woman with her sick child, anxious to get home to-night."

But there were three who *did* know why he had waited—the engineer, the grateful mother, and God.

"Must" and "Mus'n't" (O)

Do you know any boys (or girls) like Tom in this story? What lesson did he learn from the trees?

---

1. "A fellow can't have *any fun*," growled Tom. "It's just *'must'* and *'mus'n't'* from morning until night. You *must* do this, you *must* learn that, you *mus'n't* go there, you *mus'n't* say that, and you *mus'n't* do the other thing. At school you're just tied right up to rules, and at home—well, a shake of mother's head means more than a dozen 'mus'n'ts.' Seems a pity a boy can't have his own way *half* of the time, and do *something* as he *likes*."

2. "Going to school this morning, Tom?" asked Uncle John, from the next room.

"Yes, sir, of course," answered Tom, promptly.

"Going across the common?"*

"Yes, sir; always do."

3. "I wish you would notice those young trees that have been set out the last year or two. There is something rather queer about them, it seems to me. Of course, the old trees will die sooner or later, and others will be needed, but—. Well, you just observe them rather carefully, so as to describe how they look."

4. "What about those trees, Tom?" asked Uncle John after lunch.

"Why, they're all right. Look a little cramped, to be sure; snipped off short on top, and tied up to poles, snug as you please, every twig of them. But that's as it should be to make them shipshape, don't you see? They can't grow crooked if they would. They'll make as handsome trees as ever you saw, one of these days. Haven't you noticed the trees in Mr. Benson's yard—tall and scraggy, and crooked, just because they were left to grow as they pleased?"

5. "But I wonder how the trees feel about *'must'* and *'mus'n't,'*" remarked Uncle John dryly.

Out goes Tom, wishing he had not said quite so much on the subject of trees—and boys.

—*Selected.*

A Talk About Bones [O]
(This may be read as a dialogue.)

MARGARET: Sit up, Carl. If you bend over your books in that way, you will grow crooked, just like poor Thomas Spear. Besides, your lungs cannot grow strong and healthy if you hold your body in such shape that they are always cramped.

CARL: Did Thomas grow crooked because he bent over his books when reading?

MARGARET: No, Thomas never had much chance for reading. You know his father died when he was quite young, and he and his brother William had to work to support the family.

CARL: That's so. They have been driving team ever since I can remember. It is a good thing their father left them those fine horses.

MARGARET: Perhaps you have noticed these boys, or rather young men, for they must be out of their teens by this time. William is so erect, and is so well and strong. But Thomas is stoop-shouldered, and looks pale. Shall I tell you how it came about?

CARL: Thank you, sister, I should like to know.

MARGARET: I remember when they were both quite small boys, not much larger than you. That was when they first began to drive team. Thomas was just as erect then as William. Day after day and week after week they rode behind those horses. William always sat erect, with his shoulders well back. Thomas sat with his shoulders thrown forward. I suppose he found it easier to sit in that careless position. His backbone was growing then, and of course it grew into just the position in which he sat. Now he cannot change, for the bone has become hard.

CARL: What do you mean, sister, by saying that the bone has become hard? Aren't bones always hard?

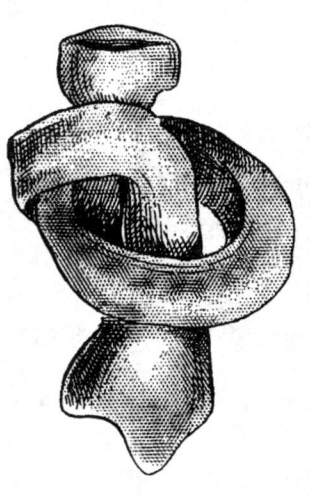

A bone with the mineral matter taken out can be tied in a knot.

MARGARET: Bones are made up of animal and mineral* matter. The bones in growing children contain more animal than mineral matter, and so are easily bent. But, as we grow older, our bones receive more and more mineral matter. In this way, they gradually become harder and less easy to change their form. I think you can now see why it is so necessary for children to sit in proper position, can you not?

CARL: You have made it very plain, sister. But how do people know what the bones are made of?

MARGARET: A very simple experiment will show that. If a bone is placed in weak muriatic* acid for a few days, the acid will eat up all the mineral matter that is in it. It will then be just like the gristle of meat, and can be bent into any shape. If a bone is burned in the fire, all the animal matter will be taken out of it, and only the ashes, or mineral matter, will be left.

CARL: I should like to try that and see it for myself.

MARGARET: You can easily do so, Carl. If you will get a long, slender bone from the meat market some day, I will help you. An old bone is not a good one to experiment on.

CARL: Thank you, sister. I wish all boys had such a kind sister as I have.

MARGARET: Here is a picture of a well-shaped backbone, Carl. See what a graceful curve it has! I think from this you can understand still better the importance of a correct position in sitting or standing. You see it is made up of a column of little bones very much alike. Can you tell me how many there are?

CARL: There seem to be twenty-four of those that are about the same shape.

MARGARET: That is right. This column of twenty-four bones is called the *spinal column*. Any injury done to the spinal column is very liable to injure the spinal cord that extends throughout its entire length.

CARL: Is it the spinal cord that has so many nerves fastened to it?

MARGARET: Yes, it is connected with the brain, too. If it is injured, the brain as well as all the nerves of the body suffer. But we were talking about the spinal column. Between all these twenty-four little bones that form the backbone, the wise Creator has placed a soft packing. If it were not for this, there would be great pain in walking. In fact, the suffering would be so great that we should hardly be able to walk at all. As one grows older, this packing hardens somewhat, and does not change easily. All our habits are formed while we are young, and when we become older it is almost impossible to change them.

CARL: Our habits are like the trees Uncle John was telling Tom about yesterday, aren't they? A young tree can be made to grow straight, but an old, crooked tree will always be crooked.

MARGARET: That is just it. And the child who slides down into his seat, the one who bends over his book, and the one who stoops over when he walks will not have a properly shaped backbone, or "grow straight," as you have said.

There is another thing about bones and habits that comes to my mind. Children who sit day after day with one shoulder high up on the desk and the other dropped down will finally grow that way, so that one shoulder will always be higher than the other. And not only this, but the backbone will be bent out of its proper shape.

CARL: My desk at school is too high for me, sister, and I cannot sit properly at it.

MARGARET: Your teacher will be glad to change it for you, if you will speak to her about it. It is just as important to stand well as to sit well. Some children have the bad habit of standing with the weight all on one foot. This throws the hip bones out of shape. It also changes the beautiful curve of the backbone.

CARL: But it seems so much easier to stand on one foot part of the time.

MARGARET: It may at times be easier to do wrong than to do right, but that is no excuse for wrong. If we persevere in doing right, it will soon become a habit, and then it will be easy. But we have talked long enough for this time. If mamma is willing, you might go and get the bone we spoke of, so that you may try your experiment.

Comprehension Test. Complete these sentences:
1. Bones are made up of —— and —— matter.
2. Children's bones contain more —— than —— matter.
3. Bones gradually become ——.
4. When all the —— matter is taken out of a bone, it can be easily bent.
5. The —— matter in a bone is like ashes.
6. The —— extends throughout the backbone.
7. The spinal cord is connected with the ——.
8. A —— is placed between the parts of the backbone.
9. The backbone has —— parts.
10. A wrong position in ——, ——, or —— will deform the bones.

The Tardy Maiden (132)

1. I know a little maiden who is always in a hurry.
    She races through her breakfast to be in time for school;
    She scribbles at her desk in a hasty sort of flurry,*
    And comes home in a breathless whirl that fills the vestibule.*

2. She hurries through her studying, she hurries through her sewing,
    Like an engine at high pressure, as if leisure* were a crime;
    She's always in a scramble, no matter where she's going;
    And yet—would you believe it?—she *never* is in *time!*

3. It *seems* a contradiction,* until you know the *reason;*
    But I'm sure you think it simple, as I do, when I state
    That she never has been known to *begin* a thing in season,
    And she's always in a hurry, because she *starts* too late.
    —Selected.

Silent Reading Test

This lesson will be a test to tell you how much you have improved in silent reading since your last test. The test is Number 4 in your "Reading Tests and Scores" pad. Remember, your real improvement is measured by the score you make in comprehension. If you fail in your comprehension test, you have not really read well, for true reading means understanding what you read.

A School Desk's Experience ^(S)

I was made in Philadelphia, in a cabinet* shop. When finished, my cherry wood was made dark, rich, and glossy by a handsome coat of varnish. Alas! little did I think how shamefully I should afterwards be treated.

I was placed with many other similar desks in a large and very pleasant room. A few days afterwards, a number of young ladies of different ages came in, and the school began.

A pleasant-looking girl was seated before me. I

never could find out her name, as it was not written upon the outside of any of her books. I soon found that she was quite pleased with me, for she took great pleasure in arranging all her books and papers in order, and often looked at me with much satisfaction. But she made one mistake; for not many hours after she took possession of me, while busy writing, she laid her pen, which was full of ink, down upon my face, and made an ugly ink spot.

However, she noticed it at once, and with a damp cloth she carefully and gently, but thoroughly, removed the spot. My coat of varnish was a great help, as it kept the ink from passing into the pores of the wood.

I found that my mistress was much beloved by her fellow pupils. I noticed, too, that when the teacher of this school came to speak to her, she always looked pleased and happy. She was not afraid to have her teacher look inside her desk.

This happy life, however, could not last long. I was one day surprised and grieved to find my mistress taking out her books and carrying them away. In her place there came another girl, who brought a most disorderly lot of books, maps, papers, rulers, boxes, pens, and paper.

She hastily crowded some of the largest books into the back part of the desk, pushed the other things this way and that, and then ran off to play. I thought that she would put me in order when she returned. But no, this was the usual treatment that I received from her.

When she wanted anything, she tumbled her books and papers over until she found it. Her luncheon was kept with everything else, and soon the crumbs were strewn all around. And what was worse than all the rest, again and again, without any care she inked my beautiful cherry wood. I made as much effort as I could, with the help of my varnish, to keep the ink from getting into my pores; but all in vain. It would get through.

I think the teacher of this school was very much to blame for not getting some old, inky, spoiled desks for those pupils who were so very slovenly,* instead of giving them such beautiful pieces of furniture as I was, merely to see them ruined. Once in a while the teacher would say something to his pupils about the importance of tidiness and of keeping the desks neat, and then my mistress would take it into her head to tidy up things.

She would put her books in a little better order, and would rub me with a wet cloth on the outside, in a vain effort to remove the spots. Ink spots, like bad habits, must be removed as soon as they are formed, otherwise they become fixed. The repeated rubbings that my mistress thus gave me had no effect but to wear away the varnish and to turn me from a glossy bright color to a dirty brown. I was soon spoiled. How I did wish my first mistress had never left me!

—*Adapted.*

Comprehension Test

1. What shows that the pleasant-faced girl was orderly? that she was neat and careful? that she was studious?

2. Why was she not afraid to have the teacher look into her desk?

3. How did the second girl differ from the first?

4. Which girl do you think will grow up into the better housekeeper? Why?

5. Which one would you rather have for a friend? Why?

6. Where was this desk made? Find the city on the map.

7. What is the difference between a cabinetmaker and a carpenter?

8. What is the cost of a single school desk?

9. What should you do to keep your desk looking bright and new?

10. What do you think *your* desk would say if it could talk?

Be the Best of Whatever You Are [112]

What lesson do you think these stanzas teach?

1. If you can't be a *pine* on the top of the hill,
    Be a *shrub* in the valley; but be
   The *best* little shrub by the side of a rill;
    Be a *bush* if you can't be a *tree*.

2. We can't *all* be captains, *some* have to be *crew*,—
    There's something for all of us here;
   There's *big* work to do, and there's *lesser* to do,
    And the task we must do is the *near*.

3. If you can't be a *highway*, then just be a *trail;*
    If you can't be the *sun*, be a *star*.
   It isn't by *size* that you win or you fail;
    Be the best of whatever you are."

—*Selected.*

Dogs and Cats [S]

After you have read this story silently, practice reading the third, fourth, sixth, and seventh paragraphs orally.

I want to say something to boys and girls who wish to adopt* as a pet either a dog or a cat. Don't do it without making up your mind to be really and thoroughly kind to your pet, and to feed it as carefully as you feed yourself, and to give it shelter from bad weather.

Some people seem to have an idea that throwing a scrap, or a bone, or a bit of waste food at odd times, to a dog is taking all the care of him that is needed.

"What is the matter with him? He *can't* be *hungry*. I gave him *that great bone* yesterday," they say.

Ah, my dear boy, how would *you* like to be fed in that way? When you show your hungry face at the dinner table, suppose papa should say, "What's that boy *here* for? He was fed *this morning.*" You would think this cruel.

In like manner dogs are often shut out of the house in cold, winter weather. A lady and I looked out once on a freezing, icy day, and saw a great Newfoundland* cowering in a corner of a fence, to keep from the driving sleet.*

"Do you have no kennel* for that poor creature?" I asked.

"No," said the lady; "I didn't know that *dogs needed* shelter."

She had taken into her family a living creature, without ever having thought about what that creature needed, or that it was her duty to provide for its wants. Most dogs can bear more cold than human beings, but they do not *like* cold any better than *we* do. When a dog has his choice, he will very gladly stretch himself on a rug before the fire for his afternoon nap, and show that he enjoys the blaze and warmth as much as anybody.

As to cats, some people seem to think that a miserable, half-starved beast, with no rights that anybody is bound to respect, is necessary to a family. This is a mistake. It is far kinder to have an animal killed in some quick and certain way than to treat it in this manner.

Cats are often said to have no hearts,—to be attached to *places*, but unable to give warm affection to *people*. A cat by the name of Juno has proved that this is not true. Her mistress was obliged to leave her

at home and go to a neighboring* city to live; so she gave Juno to the good lady who lived in the other part of the house. But no attention or care on the part of the new mistress could banish* from Juno's mind the friend she had lost.

The little parlor where she had spent so many pleasant hours was locked up; but Juno would go, day after day, and sit on the ledge of the window sill, looking in and mewing dolefully.* She refused food, and when too weak to mount the sill and look in, stretched herself on the ground beneath the window where she died for love of her mistress.

You see by this story the moral* I wish to teach. It is that watchfulness, kindness, and care will develop a nature in animals such as we little dream of. Love will beget* love. Regular care and attention will give regular habits, and thus domestic pets may be made agreeable and interesting.

—*Harriet Beecher Stowe (adapted).*

DICTIONARY STUDY

Learn these sounds of *e:*

ē, as in mē ẽ, as in hẽr ê, as in thêir
ĕ, as in lĕt ẹ, as in they ee (=ē), as in feed

Which sound of *e* is the same as ā?
Which sound of *e* is the same as â?
Copy the following words in syllables, mark the accent and all the *e's:*

either	fed	shelter	affection
really	here	better	neighboring
needed	fence	stretch	attention
yesterday	kennel	beast	pleasant
weather	creature	certain	herself

In the place of the starred word in each of the following sentences, put another word that means the same. Find the other word in the dictionary.

1. I have adopted* this dog as a pet.
2. Do you have a kennel* for your dog?
3. Nothing could banish* from Juno's mind the friend she had lost.
4. Juno sat on the window sill, mewing dolefully.*
5. What moral* does this story teach?

Practice until you can find the following words in the dictionary in two minutes.

| Newfoundland | neighboring | moral |
| beget | kennel | dolefully |

Baby Has Gone to School [160]

Check all the lines in this poem that you can read at a glance. ─────

1. The baby has gone to school. Ah, me!
    What will mother do,
  With never a call to button or pin,
    Or tie a little shoe?
  How can she keep herself busy all day,
  With the little "hindering thing" away?

2. Another basket to fill with lunch,
    Another good-by to say,
  And the mother stands at the door to see
    Her baby march away,
  And turns with a sigh that is half relief*
  And half a something akin* to grief.

3. She thinks of a possible future morn
   When the children, one by one,
Will go from their home out into the world,
   To battle with life alone,
And not even the baby be left to cheer
The desolate* home of that future year.

4. She picks up garments here and there,
   Thrown down in careless haste,
And tries to think how it would seem
   If nothing were displaced.
If the house were always as still as this,
How could she bear the loneliness?

—*Selected.*

Comprehension Test

1. What is there in stanza 1 which shows that the baby hinders the mother in her work?
2. Was the mother glad, or was she sorry, to send her baby to school?
3. Why was she glad? Why was she sorry?
4. What did it make her think of?
5. Were her thoughts happy ones? Why not?
6. Was the school near to the home, or far from it? How do you know?

The Duke of Wellington (O)

The boy in this story is called brave. Find out what he did which showed that he was brave.

One day in England, a farmer was at work in his fields. He saw a party of hunters riding over his farm. He had a field in which the wheat was just coming up, and he did not want the gentlemen to go into that, because the trampling of the horses and dogs would spoil the crop.

So he sent one of his farm hands, a bright young boy, to shut the gate of that field and to keep guard over it. He told him that he must not permit the gate to be opened.

The boy had only just reached the field and closed the gate when the hunters came galloping up. They ordered him to open the gate. The boy refused. "My master has ordered me to permit no one to pass through this gate," said he; "and I can neither open it myself nor allow anyone else to open it."

One of the men said he would thrash him if he did not open it. Another offered him a sovereign.* But the brave boy was firm. He was neither to be frightened nor bribed.*

Then a grand and stately-looking gentleman came forward.

"My boy," he said, "do you not know me? I am the Duke of Wellington. I am not accustomed to be disobeyed. I command you to open that gate, that I and my friends may pass in."

The boy politely took off his hat to the great man whom all England delighted to honor.

"I am sure the Duke of Wellington would not wish me to disobey orders," he answered. "I must keep this gate shut, and permit no one to pass without my master's permission."

The brave old warrior was greatly pleased at the boy's answer, and lifting his own hat, he said:

"I honor the man or the boy who can neither be

bribed nor frightened into doing wrong. With an army of such soldiers, I could conquer, not only the French, but the whole world."

As the party galloped away, the boy ran off to his work, shouting at the top of his voice, "Hurrah! hurrah for the Duke of Wellington!"

Comprehension Test
1. Find England on the map.
2. How did the hunters try to frighten the boy?
3. How did they try to bribe him?
4. What do you admire about this boy?
5. What do you admire about the Duke of Wellington?
6. What is a duke? Your dictionary tells.

The Little Factory Girl Who Became a Poet (S)

Lucy Larcom was one of a large family of children. She lived in an old-fashioned house in Massachusetts.* In those days, people knew nothing about electric light. They did not even have kerosene lamps, or stoves such as we have. The house where Lucy lived was lighted by a tallow* candle.

Lucy's mother had rosy cheeks and happy blue eyes. She pinned her dark curly hair back under a white lace cap. The father had a pale, noble face. Every evening before the children went to bed, they all gathered around the bright, warm fireplace. The father read from the big family Bible. Then he prayed. Lucy lived to be an old lady, but she never forgot her good father and her Christian home.

When Lucy was seven years old, her father died. Then it was necessary for the children to help earn a living. So the family moved to Lowell,* Massachusetts, where the older children might work in the cotton mill. Lucy's mother boarded a whole houseful of happy girls from the mill.

Lucy was too young to work in the mill, so she went to school. She loved books and school. When she was only three years old, she could read in the New Testament. Her Aunt Hannah was the teacher. Aunt Hannah was like all the other teachers in those days. She thought the best way to teach children was with a stick. She rapped them on their knuckles with a stick if they missed their lessons.

One day, when little Lucy came home, she said, "Aunt Hannah punished the scholars with the pudding stick." At this the whole family burst out laughing. The stick Aunt Hannah used in school looked to Lucy like the stick they stirred the pudding with at home, and she thought Aunt Hannah had taken it to school to use.

When Lucy was only three or four years old, she began to memorize hymns. She said she was going to learn all there were in the hymn book! But when she found out that there were a thousand, she thought that would be too many.

"I'll give you a nice book, Lucy," said her sister Emilie, "if you will learn fifty hymns. And if you will learn one hundred, I will teach you to write, besides."

Lucy wanted the book, and she wanted to learn to

"The Little Weaver," by Juan Planellay Rodriguez

write. So she began to memorize hymns. When she was five years old, she had learned between one and two hundred. Then Emilie gave her a book of poems, and taught her to write.

Before Lucy was seven years old, she had read "Pilgrim's Progress," and at least a dozen other books that people nowadays think interest only grown-ups.

"Let's write some poetry, Lucy, just for fun," said her brother John one day.

"What fun that would be!" said Lucy.

They both began to write. John soon got tired of that kind of fun, but Lucy wrote two stanzas. Here are the stanzas she wrote:

> "One summer day," said little Jane,
> "We were walking down a shady lane,
> When suddenly the wind blew high,
> And the red lightning flashed in the sky.
>
> "The peals of thunder, how they rolled!
> And I felt myself a little cooled;
> For I before had been quite warm;
> But now around me was a storm."

John was delighted. He thought his sister Lucy was a wonderful little girl. He was so proud of her that he read her verses to the family and to all the neighbors.

When Lucy was thirteen, she had to stop going to school, and begin to work in the cotton mill with the other girls. These girls were bright and interesting. They decided to publish a magazine.* They named it *The Lowell Offering*. They tried hard to write interesting stories for their magazine, so every one would like to read it.

Lucy wondered if she could write some poetry that would be good enough to print in the magazine. She decided to try. She thought hard. She wrote. She corrected. Then she tried again. She had never been so happy in all her life as she was when she saw one of her own poems in the magazine.

After that, Lucy often wrote poems that were printed in *The Lowell Offering*. They were the best things in the magazine. Every one liked to read them. The great poet, John G. Whittier, was delighted with them. He asked who wrote them. He said she would one day be a great poet. And she was. She wrote so many beautiful poems that some one said her whole life was a poem. People enjoyed her poems so much that they soon forgot she was once only a poor factory* girl.

Comprehension Test

1. What was the name of the little factory girl who became a poet?

2. She was born in 1826. How long ago was that?

3. What did people have instead of electric lights when she was a child?

4. With what did they heat their houses?

5. How many hymns had she learned when she was five years old? How many can *you* sing from memory?

6. What book had she read when she was only seven years old? Have you ever read it?

7. How did she learn to write poetry for *The Lowell Offering?*

8. Who said she would one day be a great poet?

9. What do you think is the most interesting part of this story?

10. Lucy Larcom was sixty-seven years old when she died. In what year did she die?

If I Were a Sunbeam [108]

Who wrote this poem? What pretty picture do you see in stanza 1? in stanza 2? What does stanza 3 mean?

---

1. If I were a sunbeam,
    I know what I'd do;
   I would seek white lilies
    Rainy woodlands through:
   I would steal among them,
    Softest light I'd shed,
   Until every lily
    Raised its drooping head.

2. If I were a sunbeam,
    I know where I'd go:
   Into lowliest hovels,*
    Dark with want and woe:
   Till sad hearts looked upward,
    I would shine and shine;
   Then they'd think of heaven,
    Their sweet home and mine.

3. Art thou *not* a sunbeam,
    Child whose life is glad
   With an inner radiance*
    Sunshine never had?
   Oh, as God has blessed *thee*,
    Scatter rays divine!
   For there is no sunbeam
    But must *die*, or *shine*.

—*Lucy Larcom.*

The Rivulet [90]

1. Run, little rivulet,* *run!*
   Summer is fairly begun.
   Bear to the meadow the hymn
   of the pines,
   And the echo that rings where
   the waterfall shines;
   Run, little rivulet, *run!*

2. Run, little rivulet, *run!*
   Sing of the flowers,
   every one:
   Of the delicate harebell* and
   violet blue;
   Of the red mountain rosebud,
   all dripping with dew;
   Run, little rivulet, *run!*

3. Run, little rivulet, *run!*
   Stay not till summer is done!
   Carry the city the mountain bird's glee;*
   Carry the joy of the hills to the sea;
   Run, little rivulet, *run!*

—Lucy Larcom.

Comprehension Test

1. Read the lines that tell where this little river comes from; where it goes; what kind of country it flows through.
2. Find the names of four things that are in the hills where the stream begins.
3. Did you ever hear "the hymn of the pines"?
4. What flowers grew near this stream? Have you ever seen any of them?

Tardy Twice ^(o)

This story is about two boys who attended the same school. Something happened one day that made the teacher proud of both these boys. Read, and find out what it was.

In your second reading of the story, pretend that you are Bert (or Eli), changing words to make the story read right.

1. "Any pupil who is tardy twice this month will miss the usual half holiday," the teacher said.

2. Bert Green looked over at Eli Wells, and Eli looked over at Bert. Both had been tardy once. It was very easy to be tardy again,—much easier than to be on time.

As soon as school was out, they talked it all over.

"We *must* be here on the *dot*," Bert said, "or we can't play ball next Friday."

"That's what *I* was thinking," agreed Eli.

3. The next two days, both boys were ahead of time. They got up early, and were off in good time. But Friday was different. Something went wrong with both Eli and Bert. When Eli called Bert, Bert was about to call him; and it was then fifteen minutes of nine.

"We'll have to *run*," said Bert.

"We can't run *all* the way. Let's *walk* fast, and run toward the *end*."

They walked fast, and did not stop for a minute.

"I think we'll be in time," said Eli. "Let's run now."

4. But just as they started to run, a voice called to them. Bert paused.

"Come on," said Eli, "we'll be late if we wait to see what that old man wants."

"But he's blind," urged Bert. "See him feeling his way with a stick."

"Well, *we* can't help it. Come on, or you'll miss the fun this afternoon."

"I can't," said Bert, shaking his head.

5. Eli ran on to school, but Bert stopped and helped the blind man. The pupils had taken their seats when he arrived, red and breathless. The teacher looked greatly displeased. "Bert Green, tardy twice," she said. Then she marked something in her book.

Bert knew it was his lost holiday she had marked. "But I'm not sorry," he thought. Yet when he saw all the others filing out, he found it hard to sit still in the schoolroom.

6. Eli went out slowly. Bert waved his hand to him as if to say, "Have a good time." But Eli shook his head.

Soon Eli came hurrying back.

"Did you forget something, Eli?" the teacher asked.

"Yes, Miss Laven. I forgot to tell you that you ought to have kept *me* instead of *Bert*. *He* stopped to help a blind man, and *I* went on. Please keep me in, and let Bert have his holiday."

"Bert," said Miss Laven, "it is a fine thing to be punctual;* but there is something finer. You have earned your half holiday by something better than punctuality.* I'm proud of both you and Eli."

—*The Sunbeam.*

Children and Diamonds (S)

As you read, find out *how*, and by *whom* diamonds were first discovered in South Africa.

The discovery of diamonds in South Africa was brought about one day in 1867, by two Dutch children who tossed a diamond in the air and caught it, thinking it was a common pebble. While they were playing, John O'Reilly,* a trader, stopped at their father's farm near the Vaal* River, to trade for skins.

He noticed the peculiar clearness of the pebble, and asked one of the children to show it to him. After he had examined it, he was satisfied that it was a stone of some value. The father laughed when O'Reilly of-

Open mine near Kimberley. This is said to be the largest hole in the earth.

fered to buy the stone, and said that plenty of them could be found in the river.

O'Reilly accepted the stone as a gift, and promised that if he succeeded in selling it, he would give half of the money toward educating the girl, which was the Dutch farmer's greatest desire.

The stone was examined by many traders, but nobody thought it was a stone of any special value, its size being too great. O'Reilly kept it carefully until he had time to send it to a man in Grahamstown, who knew all about diamonds. This man said it was a diamond of very great value.

Some time afterwards, the governor of the Cape bought the diamond for two thousand five hundred dollars. When O'Reilly returned to the Vaal, he gave one thousand two hundred fifty dollars to the little girl, and asked her if she had any more pebbles.

If the stone came from the river, as the Dutch farmer had said, more must be there, O'Reilly thought. So he hired natives to collect all the stones like it that they could find on the river banks. Sackful after sackful was examined, but O'Reilly found only one more diamond. It was a stone of much less value than the first one.

This is the story of the discovery of diamonds in Africa. It agrees with other stories that say children were the first to find diamonds, and the whole story is probably true.

The news of O'Reilly's find spread among the traders and settlers, and for three years after this the banks of the Vaal River were washed for diamonds. But not many were found. The finding of some diamonds in the mud walls of a hut led to what is called the dry diggings. Soon after this the most profitable search for diamonds was in the ground of the now famous DeBeers and Kimberley Mines. Here thousands of diamonds are found every year.

—*London Graphic (adapted)*.

Comprehension Test. Complete these sentences:
1. One day in Africa two ——— children were playing with a pretty stone.
2. A trader, named ———, thought the stone was ———.
3. It was found near the ——— River.
4. This was in the year 1867, ——— years ago.

5. Other traders said the stone was too ——— to be a diamond.

6. A man who knew all about diamonds said it was worth ———.

7. The governor paid O'Reilly ——— dollars for this stone.

8. O'Reilly gave ——— of this money to the child who had given him the stone.

9. Most of the diamonds of Africa have been found in the ——— Mines.

10. These mines are near the city of ———.

Old Winter (S)

1. All the things that God has made are His servants. They obey His voice. He speaks to the rain, and the gentle showers refresh the earth. He calls the sleeping flowers from their lowly beds, and they bud and blossom. He speaks to the twinkling stars, and they give light in the darkness. He sends the sunshine to warm the air. "By the breath of God frost is given." "He saith to the snow, Be thou on the earth."

You never thought that these things are God's servants? But they are, and I hope we shall sometime be better acquainted with them all. But in this lesson let us study one whose name every child knows very well. I mean Old Winter.

2. You all know that this servant pays us his yearly visit after the autumn is over, and the fruit has all been gathered; when the leaves have put on their dresses of red and gold, and fallen in showers from the trees.

3. But he does not come to the children of all countries in the same months of the year. In the Southern Hemisphere* his visits are made in June, July, and August. But in the Northern Hemisphere he comes in December, January, and February. Can you tell why this is?

4. In different countries he does not act the same at all. In fact, I doubt if you would know him if you should meet him far from your own home. But the One who sends him knows that the fruits and flowers and soil in different parts of the earth need to be treated differently. So, while in warm countries he comes in heavy showers of rain, in cold countries he comes on the wings of the wild north wind, and brings with him frost and snow and ice.

5. In these cold countries, he is first seen on the mountain tops, and from here he looks down to see if all is ready for him. Before he leaves the mountains, he gives them each a present of a white cap and mantle,* which they wear the whole winter. If in warm countries the mountains are very high, he dresses them just the same. Can you guess what this cap and mantle are made of?

6. When he has enjoyed his view from the hills,

"He saith to the snow, Be thou on the earth."

he rushes down into the valleys,* with a sharp, cold wind that warns all the children to put on their winter garments in honor of his arrival.* His first visits are generally paid at night, and in the morning he disappears again. But by and by he gets bolder and stays all day, often filling the air with the most beautiful white snowflakes.

Sometimes the snowflakes come gently down, and form a warm blanket over the fields. Sometimes they come on the wings of a stormy wind, which tosses them about, and beats them against the windows, and whirls them up in deep masses in the dens and hollows.

7. Sometimes Old Winter hides the sun with his mantle of dark, gray clouds. At other times he comes with a strong wind, driving the clouds through the sky, and shaking the tops and twisting the limbs of the tallest trees. Many a sly piece of mischief he does at night. He steals into the pantry, and breaks the pitchers and the glasses if water or some other liquid has been left in them. He touches with his icy fingers any tender plant that is left in his way, and it withers at his touch.

8. He pinches the fingers and toes of the poor children so badly that he often leaves large red swellings where his icy touch has been. In some countries he has been known to bite men's noses and take off their fingers.

9. No doubt you think this servant is rough and rude. And he certainly is not always very gentle. But we must remember that the enemy of God and man has marred everything that the Creator has made. Through his evil influence many strange things are done.

10. But this will not always be. Our Saviour has given His life, that all things may at last be beautiful and perfect as they were when this earth was created. When sin and Satan are destroyed, and the earth is made new, there will be no sharp, cold winds that make people shiver. Neither will there be any icy

winter that freezes the children's fingers and toes and destroys the pretty plants.

11. But are the plants all dead? Oh no! The Lord takes care of everything that He has made. Many of the plants are only sleeping until the cold winter is gone. And after their long rest, He who never slumbers or sleeps, but who keeps watch over all His creatures, will call them forth to a beautiful new life.

12. However, Old Winter is not always mischievous* and cruel. Sometimes he prepares for the children pretty pictures on the windows of their rooms. He draws trees, ferns, and flowers, all white, on the glass. He draws these pictures, not with a pencil but with your breath.

13. At other times he touches the ponds and little lakes, and hardens them into a smooth playground for the children to run and slide and skate upon; and he ornaments the houses with a fringe around the roof, of long, clear, bright icicles.*

14. He is a good friend to the gardener and the farmer. He destroys many of the troublesome insects that hurt their crops. He keeps the tender plants covered with his fleecy* blanket of snow, that they may not be hurt by his cold footsteps and icy touch, as he passes over the fields. He breaks up and crumbles the stiff, hard clods of soil and makes them fit to receive the seed.

So, for the good he does, many persons welcome Old Winter. They rejoice when he comes, and find him a merry companion in a rough game.

Comprehension and Speed Test. Write a list of the paragraph numbers that tell about the things given in the list following: See how quickly you can find all these paragraph numbers. There is more than one paragraph number for some of the topics.

 When Winter comes in different parts of the earth
 What he does to the mountain tops
 The mischief that he does
 The pleasure he gives children
 The good he does the farmer
 When he will never do any more harm
 How he acts in different countries
 What he does in the valleys
 Who made him rough and rude
 The Lord watching the plants that Winter put to sleep

Reading Tests and Scores for the Second Period

Boys and girls, you are now ready for your last reading tests for the second period. This is test No. 5.

Your score in *silent reading* will depend on how much you can read in a minute, and at the same time understand and remember the important things you read about.

Your score in *oral reading* will depend on your ability to do four things. What are these four things? Remember that for this test you may *choose* from the lessons in this period any story you wish to read, and you may practice on it as much as you like beforehand.

Your score in *memory reading* will depend on how much poetry you have memorized this period. By reading again about memory reading on pages 30 and 31 you can find out your own score.

THIRD PERIOD

The Missionary Ship "The Pitcairn" (S)

Read this story silently, and find out what good "The Pitcairn" did, and what finally became of it.

Part I of this story has 614 words. Practice reading it silently until you can read it in five minutes and answer the first eight questions in the Comprehension Test.

Part II has 523 words. Practice reading it until you can read it in four minutes and answer correctly questions 9-12.

Part III has 381 words. Practice reading it until you can read it in three minutes and answer the last five questions of the Comprehension Test.

I. Building "The Pitcairn"

"A missionary ship! We must have a missionary ship! The time has come for the light of the third angel's message to shine to the islands of the sea." This is what our people said when our parents and grandparents were children.

Look at a map of the world, and try to count the islands of the sea. Here and there are little groups of irregular shapes, some large, others mere specks. They seem close together; but if you were to sail among them, you would find that they are separated from one another by miles and miles of water. Each little island seems a tiny world in itself, with its peo-

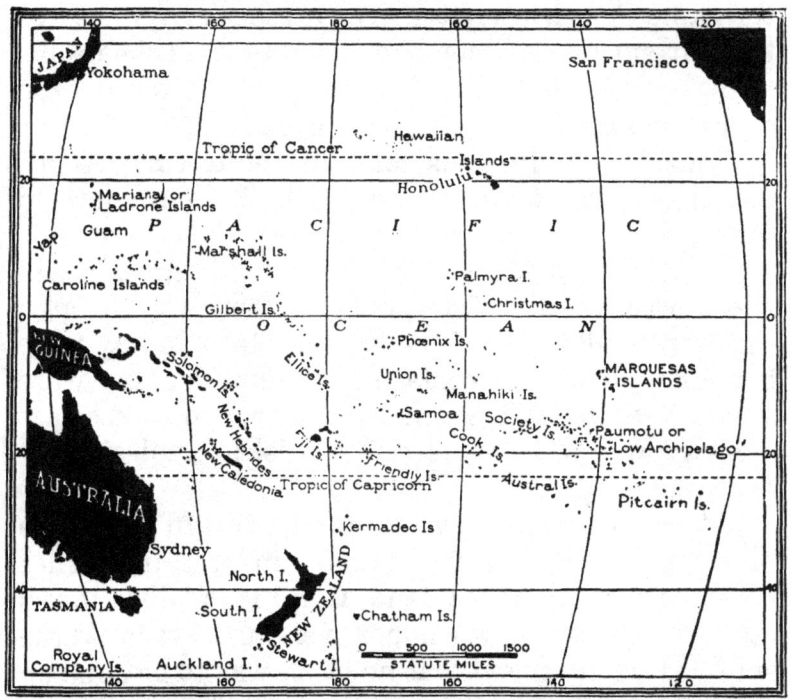

This a map of the South Sea Islands. Can you find Pitcairn Island?

ples of strange tongues and strange customs, and its storm-beaten, wave-washed shores.

As our parents looked at this part of the world, they remembered that God has said that the gospel of the kingdom should be preached to every nation, and kindred, and tongue, and people. Across the map with the eye of faith they seemed to see in burning letters the words of the Bible, "The isles shall wait for His law."

One tiny dot in the great South Pacific Ocean with

the name *Pitcairn* written near it especially attracted their attention, for they had heard that all the people living on this island had already accepted the true gospel message for these last days.

"Surely the time has come for us to carry God's message to the islands," was echoed from shore to shore.

In those days there were not so many great ocean steamers as there are now, plowing their way through the deep to all parts of the world. Many, many little islands that dot the surface of the great ocean were seldom* visited. It seemed plain that if God's last message was to be carried to the isles, a missionary boat was needed.

At last, the matter was settled. A ship was to be built in San Francisco Harbor* about thirty miles north of the city of Oakland, California. It is interesting to know that when men were hired to build the ship, it was arranged that no work was to be done on the boat on the Sabbath. As the workmen did not work on Sunday, they called it "the five-day boat."

In about three months after the building began, the boat was ready to be launched.* At one minute past ten o'clock, on the beautiful moonlight night of July 28, 1890, the last prop was removed and the missionary boat glided into the waters of San Francisco Harbor. That night hour was chosen in order to take advantage of the high tide.*

Two or three hundred people had gathered on the shore to witness* the event. The workmen asked, "Is this to be a 'wet' or a 'dry' launch? Since we are temperance people, of course we could not follow the custom of treating workmen to wine or beer; but a good, wholesome lunch was served, which all seemed to enjoy.

J. N. Loughborough,* a veteran* laborer in the Advent Movement, made a few remarks in which he told why the ship had been built. He then prayed that God's eye would watch over the little craft, and make it a real messenger of truth to the island world. Those who saw the launching of this missionary ship said it was one of the most interesting and successful launches they had ever witnessed.

After the boat was launched, there was still considerable work to do before it would be ready for service. The sails had to be put on, the rigging* adjusted,* and the whole boat furnished. This required about two months longer.

II. Naming and Dedicating the Boat

To the Sabbath schools had been given the privilege of paying for the boat. Many of our parents and grandparents well remember how, when they were children in Sabbath school, they gave their pennies and dollars to this interesting and noble work. And they proved themselves worthy of the responsibility placed upon them. A steady stream of pennies, nickels, dimes, and dollars flowed into the treasury.* Every payment was made on time, until the entire amount for building the ship, buying the furniture, and supplying provisions for a two years' trip was provided. This amounted to nearly $19,000.

The next step was to give the ship a name. Since the Sabbath schools had paid for the boat, they were given the privilege of selecting a name for it. How

This is "The Pitcairn" sailing away to the islands.

interesting! Did your family ever try to find a name for the new baby that was your very own? How difficult it was to think of a name that would really be good enough for the little treasure! Mother and father and each brother and sister suggested some name, and there was a great deal of discussion before a name was finally decided upon.

It was something like this in trying to name the new boat, which was so dear to the heart of every Sabbath school. Some thought "Glad Tidings" was a good name. Others suggested "Carrier Dove," "Angel of Mercy," "Joyful News," "Island Visitor," "Present Truth," "The Pitcairn." The "father and mother" of the new boat—the General Conference Committee—were asked to decide the question. They discussed all the names. They were all such beautiful names, it was difficult to choose. But finally they chose the name "The Pitcairn."

Next came the dedication,* for this boat must be dedicated* just the same as a new church is dedicated. The dedication took place at Oakland, September 25, 1890. The little vessel was attractively decorated with flags and streamers. It was fastened to the wharf,* so that the many people who attended the service could get within hearing distance.

The opening song, "Father, We Come to Thee," brought tears to many eyes. Psalm 107:21-31 was the Scripture reading. J. N. Loughborough prayed that God's richest blessing would follow the little boat in all its life on the wide, wide sea. O. A. Olsen, at that time the President of the General Conference, gave the address.* R. A. Underwood offered the dedicatory* prayer, in which the little craft was consecrated* to carrying God's last message to the isles of the great ocean.

III. The Work of "The Pitcairn"

About a month later, October 20, 1890, the sturdy little ship passed out through the Golden Gate* into the broad Pacific, to meet the dangers of sea life. She was on her way to the little island from which she had received her name. Fourteen missionaries were on board, and from many hearts earnest prayers went up to God that He would safely keep them on their sea voyage.

In a little more than one month, on November 25, 1890, the missionaries caught their first sight of Pitcairn Island. This was one hundred years after the ship "The Bounty" brought the first people who ever lived on this island. Imagine the joy of those on board! Imagine the joy of those on the island! With open arms the missionaries were received and taken to the quaint* little island village. Before they left the island, eighty-two persons were baptized.

On January 23, 1890, the people had celebrated the century of years since "The Bounty" arrived at the island. The same year is still held in sacred memory as the time when God sent them a knowledge of His last message to the world.

When "The Pitcairn" sailed away to other islands, Mr. and Mrs. E. H. Gates remained on Pitcairn Island to teach the people the word of God more fully.

For two years "The Pitcairn" carried its message of love and salvation to different islands. It then returned to San Francisco.

In 1892 the second trip began. At this time, missionaries, teachers, and Bible workers were taken to

The first church school on Pitcairn Island. Miss Andre, teacher, standing in center.

various islands. One of these missionaries was Miss Hattie Andre, who was going as a teacher to the children of Pitcairn Island. After this, the Pitcairn made a third, a fourth, and a fifth trip. Each time the noble little boat carried workers and supplies to the isles that were waiting for God's law.

As the years passed, many steamers were added to the ocean travel. This made it so easy and safe to reach the islands that it seemed unnecessary to continue the expensive travel with "The Pitcairn." Therefore, in 1900, the faithful little craft* was sold. At that time its name was changed to "The Florence," and for many years it steamed over the sea, carrying supplies to many islands.

—*Mrs. L. Flora Plummer (adapted).*

Comprehension Test

1. Point on the map to Pitcairn Island. How far is it from the islands where John Williams went as a missionary?
2. What does the Bible say about the islands? Isa. 42:4.
3. Why was a missionary boat needed?
4. Find on the map the place where the boat was built.
5. Why was it called "the five-day boat"?
6. How long ago was it built? How long did it take to build it?
7. Why was it launched at night?
8. Was it a "dry" or a "wet" launch? What does that mean?
9. How much did the boat cost? Who paid for it?
10. What were some of the names suggested for the new boat? Which one do you like best? Why?
11. What scripture was read when the boat was dedicated? Read it, and then tell whether you think this was an appropriate scripture and why.
12. Name some of the men who took part in the dedication.
13. On the map trace the journey of "The Pitcairn" from Oakland through the Golden Gate to Pitcairn Island.
14. How long did it take to make the trip?
15. How long ago was this?
16. What was the name of the boat that brought the people who first lived on this island?
17. How many trips did "The Pitcairn" make? Why was it sold?

Miriam's Song (139)

Find the place in the Bible where Miriam's song is given. As you read this poem, mark all the places that you do not understand, and discuss these things in class.

---

1. Sound the loud timbrel* o'er Egypt's dark sea!
   Jehovah has triumphed—His people are free!
   Sing!—for the pride of the tyrant* is broken:
     His chariots, his horsemen, all splendid and brave—
   How vain was their boasting!—the *Lord* hath but *spoken*
     And chariots and horsemen are sunk in the wave!
   Sound the loud timbrel o'er Egypt's dark sea!
   Jehovah has triumphed—His people are free!

2. Praise to the Conqueror! Praise to the Lord!
   His *word* was our *arrow*, His *breath* was our *sword!*
   Who shall return to tell Egypt the story
     Of those she sent forth in the hour of her pride?
   For the Lord hath looked out from His pillar of glory,
     And all her brave thousands are dashed in the tide.*
   Sound the loud timbrel o'er Egypt's dark sea!
   Jehovah has triumphed—His people are free!

   —*Thomas Moore.*

Little "Pretty Soon" ^(o)

This story tells how a little girl learned to do her duties at once, without waiting to be told a second time. Read silently, and find out how she learned this lesson.

1. The little girl's real name was a very pretty one, Evelyn, but her friends were in the habit of calling her "Pretty Soon," because those were the words she almost always spoke when she was asked to do anything.

2. "Please set the table for me, dear," or, "I want a little girl to go to the store for me," were some of the things her mother would say to her.

"Pretty soon," Evelyn would answer, and then often forget all about it. This was, of course, a great trial to her kind mother, and the cause of many tears to the little girl.

3. Then sometimes mother would call, "Come here, Evelyn!"

"Pretty soon," Evelyn would say. But when she finally came, she would find that she had lost a delightful ride or some long-desired treat.

4. Evelyn did not like to be called "Pretty Soon," and would often say, "I am going to stop saying that." But over and over again she would forget, and bring sorrow to herself and those who loved her by saying many times a day, "Pretty soon. Oh, pretty soon!"

5. One cold winter day, when the steps and walks were coated with ice, Evelyn's mother started to the market. The little girl was busy making a fine dress for her doll, Be-lin'da, which she wanted to finish before her cousin Grace came to spend the afternoon with her.

"Oh, Evelyn, come here quickly!" she heard her mother call faintly. She was wondering whether she should put two, or three, ruffles on Belinda's dress.

"Yes, mother dear, pretty soon," she answered. But she soon forgot that her mother had called her.

6. After some minutes the door opened suddenly and her father came in with her mother, very white and still, in his arms. She had fallen on the icy steps and broken her hip, had called Evelyn, and then fainted from the pain. If father had not come home a half hour early, she might have frozen to death.

How sorry and frightened the little girl was as she hurried to get the doctor!

"Oh, if I had only gone at once when mother called! I will never, *never* say 'pretty soon' again!" she said over and over through her sobs.

7. It was many weary weeks before the dear mother was able to walk, and Evelyn found many chances to do things for her, but never once did she say, "Pretty soon."

It was a hard lesson, and one that Evelyn remembered all her life. Whenever she was tempted to put off a duty, she would think of that terrible time when mother lay so white and still.

—*The Sabbath Recorder.*

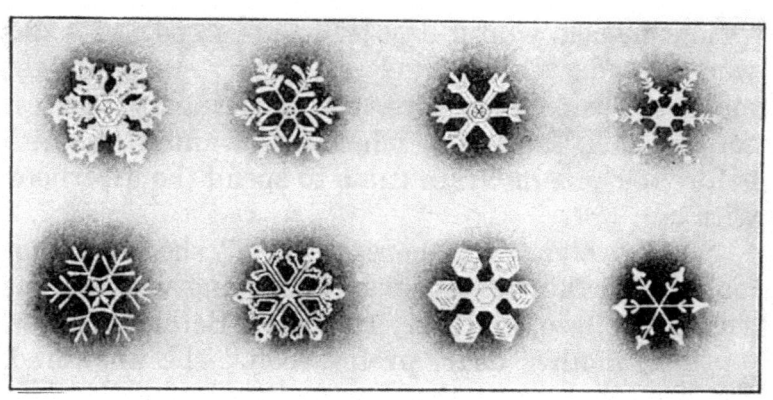

A Wonderful Weaver [122]

Listen as your teacher reads this poem to you, and see if you can find two pictures in it.

---

1. There's a wonderful weaver
    High up in the air,
   And he weaves a white mantle*
    For cold earth to wear.
   With the wind for his shuttle,*
    And the cloud for his loom,*
   How he weaves, how he weaves,
    In the light, in the gloom.*

2. Oh, with finest of laces
    He decks bush and tree;
   On the bare, flinty* meadows
    A cover lays he;
   Then a quaint cap he places
    On pillar and post;

146

And he changes the pump
To a grim,* silent ghost.

3. But this wonderful weaver
Grows weary at last;
And the shuttle lies idle
That once flew so fast.
Then the sun peeps abroad
On the work that is done,
And he smiles, "I'll unravel
It all, just for fun."

—*George Cooper.*

Appreciation Study. The first picture is in stanzas 1 and 2. Read the lines that tell,—
1. Where this wonderful weaver is
2. Three things that he weaves (Have you seen these things?)
3. Seven things that wear what he weaves (Have you ever seen them wear them?)
4. What his shuttle is
5. What his loom is
6. When he weaves

Who *is* this "wonderful weaver"? What makes the meadows "flinty"? What picture do you see in "a grim, silent ghost"? Tell what you see in the picture that stanzas 1 and 2 have painted for you.

The second picture is in stanza 3. Read the lines that tell that the snowstorm is over. How can the sun "smile"? How does he "unravel" the work of the weaver? What season of the year is described in stanzas 1 and 2. In stanza 3? Why do you think so?

Try to read this poem as well as your teacher did. You can if you try.

How many of you can memorize the first stanza in three minutes? Try it.

Polly's Birthday ^(O)

Before you read this story, read Luke 6:38. Then see if you can tell how the story illustrates this verse.

Polly lived on a large farm with plenty of chickens, cows, and horses. But Polly never thought much about how nice all these were, for her father and mother were always hard at work. The two brothers worked with their father. Her sister helped her mother in the house. Polly washed the dishes, scoured the knives, fed the chickens, and ran errands for the family and for all the summer boarders besides.

One of the boarders, Miss Cary, was watching Polly shell peas one morning, and thinking that she did a great deal of work for such a little girl.

"How old are you, Polly?" she asked finally.

"Eight," Polly answered.

"You're almost nine," said her mother.

"When is her birthday?" Miss Cary asked.

"Why, let me see. It is this month sometime—the seventeenth of July. I declare! I would have forgotten all about it if you had not spoken." And Mrs. Jones went on with her work again.

"What *is* a birthday?" Polly asked shyly.*

"Why, Polly!" exclaimed Miss Cary, "don't *you* know? It is the day of the year you were *born*. Did you never have a birthday present, Polly?"

"No," said Polly, looking puzzled.

"We never have much time for those things," Polly's mother said.

Miss Cary resolved then and there that Polly should "have a birthday."

When she came down to breakfast the next morning, Miss Cary met Polly in the hall, and putting a little purse into her hand, said kindly, "Here, Polly, is something for you to buy birthday presents with."

Polly opened the little bag, and found in it nine bright silver quarters. She ran as fast as she could to tell her mother.

"Why, child!" her mother said, "that is too much money for you to spend. Better save it. It will help buy you a pair of shoes and a warm dress for school next winter."

Polly's eyes filled with tears. But, as her mother wanted her to help put the breakfast on, she took the plate of muffins into the dining room. Miss Cary noticed the wet lashes.

"Mrs. Jones," she said, "please let Polly go down to the stores to-day and spend her birthday money."

Mrs. Jones could not refuse this request. So after Polly had put the baby to sleep, she was allowed to go down to the village, a good two miles away, all by herself.

It was late in the afternoon when she came back, and the boarders were waiting for the supper bell to ring. They all smiled at the little figure toiling up the road, with her arms full of bundles. Polly smiled back through the dust that covered her round little face, as she called to Miss Cary, "Oh, I've bought such lots of things! Please come into the kitchen and see."

"No, it is too warm there," Miss Cary said. "Come

into the living room, where it is cool, and we can all see."

So they went into the house, and Polly began to unwrap her packages.

"There," she said, as she tore the paper from a queer-shaped bundle, "this is for mother," holding up an egg beater. "It takes so long to beat eggs with a fork."

The boarders looked at one another in surprise, but Polly was too busy to notice. She fairly beamed as she held up a green glass necktie pin.

"Isn't it lovely?" she said. "It is for father."

"This isn't much," she continued, opening a small bundle; "only a rattle for baby. It cost five cents."

The boarders looked on in silence, as the busy little fingers untied strings. No one knew whether to laugh or to feel sorry.

It was wonderful what nine quarters would buy, and not strange that the little girl had spent a whole half day shopping. There was a blue tie for brother Dan and a pink one for Tim, a yellow hair ribbon for sister Linda, some hairpins for grandma, a small bottle of perfume for Jake, the "hired man," and then there was but one package left. Polly patted this lovingly as she opened it.

"This is the nicest of all, and it is for *you*," she said, as she handed Miss Cary a box of pink writing paper. "It seemed too bad that you had only plain white paper to write on, when you write so beautifully. So I got you this. Isn't it pretty?"

"Why, it is *beautiful*, Polly dear," Miss Cary

said; "but what have you bought for *your* birthday present?"

"Why, *these*," said Polly. "These are *all* my presents. Presents are something we give away, aren't they?" And Polly looked around, wondering why all were so still.

"It is more blessed to give than to receive," said one of the boarders softly, and Miss Cary put her arms around Polly, and kissed the hot, dusty little face again and again.

"It has been a lovely day!" Polly exclaimed. "I never had any presents to give away before; and I think birthdays are just *lovely!*"

The next month, after Miss Cary returned to the city, *she* had a birthday, and there came to Polly a most wonderful doll, with beautiful clothes, and a card saying, "For Polly, on my birthday, from Lena Cary."

Miss Cary was not the *only* one who caught Polly's idea of a birthday, for the rest of the boarders remembered; and through the year, as each one's birthday came, Polly received a gift to delight her generous little heart.

When the seventeenth of July came again, Miss Cary was not on the farm, but she sent Polly a little silk bag with ten silver quarters in it; and Polly still thinks "birthdays are just lovely!"

—*Ladies' Home Journal.*

Speed Test. See how quickly you can find the paragraphs that begin with the following phrases, and write the number of each *lightly* in your reader next to its paragraph:

1. It was late in the afternoon ———.
2. "This is the nicest of all, ———."
3. It was wonderful ———.
4. "You're almost nine," ———.
5. "It is more blessed to give ———."
6. When the seventeenth of July came again, ———.
7. Polly lived on a large farm ———.
8. The boarders looked at one another ———.
9. Mrs. Jones could not refuse ———.
10. Polly opened the little bag, ———.

DICTIONARY STUDY

Learn the sounds and markings of *i* and *y* as follows:

ī, as in īce
ĭ, as in ĭt
î, as in bîrd
ï, as in machïne

ȳ, as in mȳ
y̆, as in lovely̆
ŷ, as in mŷrrh

Which sounds of *i* and *y* are alike?
Which sound of *i* is like ē?
Which sound of *i* is like ĕ?

Copy the following words, divide them into their syllables, mark the accent and all the *i*'s and *y*'s:

story	filled	finally
first	quite	birthday
body	quickly	shyly
		kindly

Mark *a, e, i,* and *y* in:

every	behind	plenty
recall	jaws	sister
remember	share	family
where	grave	errands
ready	form	besides

Divide the following words into syllables. Then find them in the dictionary and see if your work is right:

entered   arrival   occasionally   icicles

An ants' nest

An Ant Funeral [S]

Read this story through once, then try to recall each step. If you cannot remember every step, read it again. Be able to tell it well in class. The next time you have a chance, watch some ants at work, and tell your classmates what you saw.

One time in Australia, a lady killed a number of soldier ants. In half an hour she returned to the spot where she had left their dead bodies. What do you suppose she saw?

A large number of ants were surrounding the dead ones. Soon four or five started off from the rest toward an ant hill a short distance away, in which was an ants' nest. This they entered. In about five minutes they came out, followed by others. All fell into line, walking regularly and slowly, two by two, until they arrived at the spot where lay the dead bodies of the soldier ants.

In a few minutes two of the ants advanced and took up the dead body of one of their comrades; then two others, and so on, until all were ready to march. First walked two ants bearing a body, then two with-

PLOCKHORST

out a burden; then two with another dead ant, followed by two without a burden, and so on until the line extended to about forty pairs. This procession moved slowly onward, followed by an irregular body of about two hundred ants.

Occasionally, the two laden ants stopped, and laid down the dead ant; it was taken up by the two walking behind them. Thus by occasionally relieving each other, they arrived at a sandy spot near the sea. The body of ants now began digging with their jaws a number of holes in the sand. Into each hole a dead ant was laid. They labored on until they had filled up all the ants' graves.

This did not quite complete the funeral of the ants. Six or seven of the ants had attempted to run off without doing their share of the task of digging. These were caught and brought back, and at once attacked by the other ants and killed upon the spot. A single grave was quickly dug, and they were all dropped into it.

—*Selected.*

The Little Ones He Blessed [224]

1. I wonder if ever the children
    Who were blessed by the Master of old,
  Forgot He had made them His treasures,
    The dear little lambs of His fold!
  I wonder if, angry and willful,
    They wandered far astray,*—
  The children whose feet had been guided
    So safe and so soon in the way.

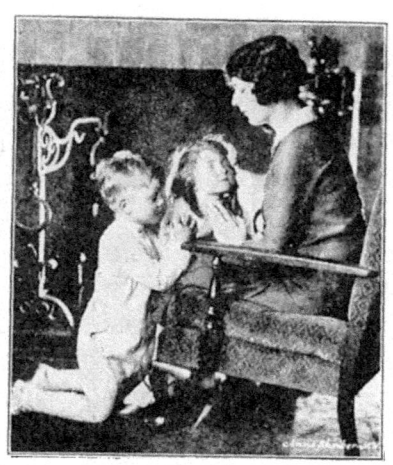

2. One would think that the mothers, at evening,
    Soft smoothing the silk-tangled hair,
  And low leaning down to the murmur
    Of sweet, childish voices in prayer,
  Oft* bade the small pleaders to listen,
    If haply* again they might hear
  The words of the gentle Redeemer
    Borne swift to the reverent* ear.

3. And my heart cannot cherish* the fancy*
    That ever those children went wrong,
  And were lost from the peace and the shelter,
    Shut out from the feast and the song.
  To the day of gray hairs they remembered,
    I think, how the hands that were riven*
  Were laid on their heads when Christ uttered,
    "Of such is the kingdom of heaven."

4. He has said it to you, little darling,
    Who spell it in God's word to-day;

You, too, may be sorry for sinning,
　You, also, believe and obey;
And 'twill grieve the dear Saviour in heaven
　If one little child shall go wrong—
Be lost from the fold and the shelter,
　Shut out from the feast and the song.
　　　　　　　　　　—*Margaret E. Sangster.*

Appreciation Study. Find the stanza that has these pictures:
 1. Little children getting ready for bed at evening
 2. Jesus watching for the children to come home to Him
 3. Jesus blessing the children when He was on earth
 4. The children grown old

What is the meaning of: the "lambs of His fold," "wandered far astray," "the children whose feet had been guided so safe and so soon in the way," "the silk-tangled hair," "the reverent ear," "the peace and the shelter," "the feast and the song," "the hands that were riven"?

Can you find the place in the Bible where Jesus said of the children, "Of such is the kingdom of heaven"?

Pray for Your Enemies [S]

This story took place in Southern Europe. Find Europe on the map. As you read the story, see how these children obeyed the words of Christ in Matthew 5:44.

A few years ago, just after a baptism in Southern Europe, a mob* attacked* the eleven people who had been baptized. The people ran over a bridge to escape, but they were caught and thrown into the river. One of them, a widow with two little children, was cruelly killed. It seemed as if the gospel work must stop at this place. But in a few weeks others, some even of her relatives, were ready for baptism.

And this is not all. Her little boy and girl, about ten years of age, were taken and put into the home of unbelievers, who declared they would train the children to be unbelievers.

But this little boy and girl did not forget their mother's instruction, and *God* did not forget *them*. The first Sabbath, they hid away in the haymow,* and studied their Sabbath school lesson and the New Testament. In the afternoon the man in whose home they were, found them and whipped them very cruelly. The next Sabbath, the children hid away in the woods, and studied their lesson as before. They were found again and beaten. The man said he would kill them if they continued to keep the Sabbath. But just as he began to strike them, some neighbors came upon him, and he was arrested.

When the story was told in court, the judge became very angry. He sentenced the man to be flogged just as he had beaten the children. Then the little boy arose with tears in his eyes.

"Judge," he said, "it is true that this man has beaten both me and my little sister very hard, just because we love Jesus and keep His Sabbath as mother taught us. But I do not want him beaten. In our Sabbath school lesson this week we learned that we must pray for those who hurt us. And so I pray you please to forgive him."

The court was much moved by the kind words of the child. The man was freed. He soon accepted the truth, and later became the elder of our little Adventist church there, and did his best to train those very children for the kingdom of heaven. Indeed, we have found again and again that those who have persecuted our brethren the most severely often turn to the truth later, and become some of our very best members. Paul was not the last persecutor* to become a faithful believer and an earnest servant of the Lord.

The Land of Fuss-and-Fret^(o)

1. Have you heard of the land called Fuss-and-Fret,
   Where the people live upon woes and regret*?
   Its climate is bad, I have heard folks say;
   There's seldom, if ever, a pleasant day.
   'Tis either too gloomy from clouded skies,
   Or so bright the sunshine dazzles one's eyes.

2. 'Tis either so cold one is all of a chill,
   Or else 'tis so warm it makes one ill;
   The season is either too damp or too dry,
   And mildew* or drought* is always nigh;
   For nothing that ever happened yet,
   Was just as it should be in Fuss-and-Fret.

3. And the *children*—it really makes me sad
   To think they never look *happy* and *glad*.
   It is "Oh dear me!" until school is done;
   And 'tis then, "There never is time for fun!"
   Their teachers are cross, they all declare,
   And examinations are never fair.

4. Each little duty they're apt to shirk,
   Because they're tired or 'tis too hard work.
   Every one is as grave* as an owl,
   And has pouting lips or a gloomy scowl;
   The voices whine, and the eyes are wet,
   In this doleful* country of Fuss-and-Fret.

5. Now, if ever you find your feet are set
   On the downhill road into Fuss-and-Fret,
   Turn and travel the other way,
   Or you never will know a happy day.
   Follow some cheerful face—'twill guide
   To the land of Look-at-the-Pleasant-Side.

6. There, something bright you will always see,
   No matter how dark the day may be;
   You'll smile at your tasks, and laugh in your dreams,
   And learn that no ill is as bad as it seems.
   So lose no time, but haste to get
   As far as you can from Fuss-and-Fret.

   —*Our Youth.*

Comprehension Test

1. Find all the expressions in these stanzas that tell about what kind of land "Fuss-and-Fret" is.

2. In the first four stanzas change all the words that mean unpleasant things to words that give the opposite meaning. This will be the land of "Look-at-the-Pleasant-Side."

3. In which land would you rather live?

4. In which one *do* you live?

5. Read Proverbs 17:22. How does it apply to these lands?

6. When things seem to us unpleasant, where is the trouble generally?

Can You? (O)

Read these stanzas, and count the things that we cannot do. How many do you find? What is the lesson these stanzas teach us?

1. Can you put the spider's web back in place
    That once has been swept away?
   Can you put the apple again on the bough
    Which fell at our feet to-day?

2. Can you put the lily cup back on the stem,
    And cause it again to grow?
   Can you mend the butterfly's broken wing
    That you crushed with a hasty blow?

3. Can you put the bloom again on the grape
    And the grape again on the vine?
   Can you put the dewdrops back on the flowers
    And make them sparkle and shine?

4. Can you put the petals back on the rose?
    If you could, would it smell as sweet?
   Can you put the flour back in the husk
    And show me the ripened wheat?

5. Can you put the kernel back in the nut,
    Or the broken egg in the shell?
   Can you put the honey back in the comb
    And cover with wax each cell?

6. Can you put the perfume back in the vase
    Once it has sped away?
   Can you put the silk back on the corn,
    Or the down on the catkins* gay?

7. You think that my questions are trifling, friend,
   Let me ask you another one:
   Can a hasty word ever be unsaid
   Or an unkind deed undone?

   —*Author Unknown.*

Silent Reading Test

You are now ready for another silent reading test which your teacher will give you.

This test is number six in your "Reading Tests and Scores" pad.

Fred's Victory (S)

This story shows some of the dangers of using tobacco. It has 636 words. See if you can read it through in exactly five minutes, or less, and find out what the dangers of using tobacco are, and how Fred won the victory over it. If you read it in five minutes, what is your reading rate a minute?

Little Fred Smith led his class in the first and second grades. When I became his teacher, he carried the banner all through the *third* grade. He was good in every study, an all-round bright boy. Though I knew his father was a smoker, I saw no sign of it in Fred.

During the next vacation, Fred's Uncle Ned came to be a member of the family. Ned was a smoker. He was a tall, slender boy, very backward in his studies. He was a leader in the sports on the playground, and Fred looked up to him with genuine pride.

Fred held his excellent standing in the fourth grade for some time. But there came a change. He began to miss a word or two in spelling. His arithmetic suffered. He forgot whether three times six are sixteen or eighteen. His papers were untidy and carelessly written. In penmanship and drawing the downward trend was most clearly marked.

I knew something was wrong. It could not be the fault of the weather, though we had an unusually warm spring. Every month he slipped lower down in his grades. One day, after the lunch hour, I smelled his breath. Then I knew! I took him aside, and had a very serious talk with him. He made a clean con-

fession, and, with tears, promised to drop the habit. He found it harder than he thought. Oh, how the dear boy suffered! When he found his grades the lowest in the class, he broke down completely. Knowing looks and nods went around the room. The children knew!

I visited his parents, and after a serious talk, they agreed to help Fred win the battle. Mr. Smith agreed to smoke no more in the house, and as little as possible around the yard and barn. It was agreed that Uncle Ned could stay if he, too, would quit smoking. If not, he must go home to his parents. I told them about the frequent warm baths to cause perspiration,* and, most of all, the benefits of an abundant fruit and tomato diet. This fruit was to be eaten freely, with very little, if any, seasoning. Water should be drunk morning and night, as well as during the daytime, between meals.

During the short summer vacation, the reform progressed steadily day after day. When school reopened, Fred was in his usual seat. All smoking was forbidden on the school grounds. The coöperation of the school board made this possible, even before the measure became a part of the State school law.

Ned's seat was empty, and perfect harmony* reigned.* Fred noticed that it was harder for him to study, and harder still to remember. He took his place bravely at the foot of the spelling class. But there was something that shone out of his determined eyes that told us that he would not *stay* there.

You should have heard the hand clapping when he

regained his place at the head of the class, and held it for a week against all efforts to dislodge him.

Month by month, his percentages crept out of the sixties and seventies into the eighties and nineties. Fred was himself again. At the end of the fall term, Fred had his old place at the head of the grade. All the pupils rejoiced together. No one was jealous, not even when he led the physical culture class on the day of the closing entertainment.*

Tomatoes and other fruits were often in his lunch pail. It was an object lesson not only to the school but to the entire community.* It took no urging to have the pledge cards signed. Years afterwards, I learned of many who had kept that pledge faithfully, and had helped others to see the advantages of a clean life.

—*Augusta C. Bainbridge (adapted).*

Here is the pledge card that Fred and others signed. Perhaps your teacher will get some of these cards, so that each pupil in the fourth grade may sign one.

PLEDGE

For strength and purity, I promise, with the help of God, never to use tobacco in any form, and to help others to abstain from its use.

Name ....

Address ....

Date ....

Black Beauty [S]

This is a good story to practice on timed silent reading.

Part I contains 219 words. If you cannot read this in two minutes, practice until you can.

Part II has 194 words. You should be able to read this in one minute and 40 seconds.

Part III has 1,261 words. How long does it take you to read this?

I. _____

The first place I can well remember was a large, pleasant meadow with a pond of clear water in it. Some shady trees leaned over it, and rushes and water lilies grew at the deep end. Over the hedge at one side we looked into a plowed field, and on the other we looked over a gate at our master's house, which stood by the roadside. At the top of the meadow was a grove of fir trees, and at the bottom a running brook overhung by a steep bank.

In the daytime I ran by my mother's side, and at night I lay down close by her. When it was hot, we used to stand by the pond in the shade of the trees, and when it was cold, we had a nice warm shed near the grove.

As soon as I was old enough to eat grass, my mother used to go out to work in the daytime, and come back in the evening.

There were six young colts in the meadow besides me. They were older than I was. Some were nearly as large as grown-up horses. I used to run about with them, and have great fun. We used to gallop all together round and round the field as hard as we could go.

II. ──────────

Our master was a good, kind man. He gave us good food, good lodging, and kind words. He spoke as gently to us as he did to his little children. We were all fond of him, and my mother loved him very much. When she saw him at the gate, she would neigh* with joy and trot up to him. He would pet and stroke her, and say, "Well, old Pet, how is your little Darkie?" I was a dull black, so they called me Darkie. Then he would give me a piece of bread, which was very good, and sometimes he brought a carrot for my mother. All the horses would come to him, but I think we were his favorites.

I was now beginning to grow handsome. My coat had become fine and soft, and was a bright black. I had one white foot, and a pretty white star on my forehead. I was thought very handsome. My master would not sell me until I was four years old. He said lads ought not to work like men, and colts ought not to work like horses till they were quite grown up.

III. ──────────

When I was four years old, Squire* Gordon came to look at me. He examined my eyes, my mouth, and my legs, and then I had to walk and trot and gallop before him. He seemed to like me, and said, "When he has been well broken in, he will do very well." My master said he would break me in himself, as he would not like me to be frightened or hurt. And he lost no time about it, for the next day he began.

Every one may not know what breaking in is; therefore, I will describe it. It means to teach a horse to wear a saddle and bridle, and to carry on his back a man, woman, or child; to go just the way they wish, and to go quietly. Besides this, he has to learn to wear a collar, a crupper,* and a breeching,* and to stand still while they are put on. Then he must have a cart or a carriage fixed behind, so that he cannot walk or trot without dragging it after him. And he must go fast or slow, just as his driver wishes. He must never start at what he sees, nor speak to other horses, nor bite, nor kick, nor have any will of his own, but always do his master's will even though he may be very tired or hungry. But the worst of all is that when his harness is once on, he may neither jump for joy nor lie down for weariness. So you see this breaking in is a great thing.

I had, of course, long been used to a halter and a headstall,* and to being led about in the fields and lanes, but now I was to have a bit and bridle. My master gave me some oats as usual, and after a good deal of coaxing he got the bit into my mouth and the bridle fixed. One who has never had a bit in his mouth cannot think how bad it feels; a great piece of cold, hard steel as thick as a man's finger to be pushed into the mouth between the teeth and over the tongue, with the ends coming out of the corner of the mouth and held fast there by straps over the head, under the throat, round the nose, and under the chin. In no way in the world can you get rid of it. It is very bad! yes, very bad! At least, I thought so. But I knew my mother always wore one when she went out, and all horses did when they were grown up. And so, what with the nice oats and what with my master's pats, kind words, and gentle ways, I got to wear my bit and bridle.

Next came the saddle, but that was not half bad. My master put it on my back very gently, while old Daniel held my head. He then made the girths* fast under my body, patting and talking to me all the time. Then I had a few oats, then a little leading about, and this he did every day until I began to look for the oats and the saddle. At length one morning my master got on my back and rode me about the meadow on the soft grass. It certainly did feel queer. But I must say I felt rather proud to carry my master, and as he continued to ride me a little every day, I soon became used to it.

The next unpleasant business was putting on the iron shoes. That, too, was very hard at first. My master went with me to the smith's forge* to see that I was not hurt or frightened. The blacksmith took my feet in his hand one after the other and cut away some of the hoof. It did not pain me, so I stood still on three legs until he had done them all. Then he took a piece of iron the shape of my foot and clapped it on, and drove some nails through the shoe quite into my hoof so that the shoe was firmly on. My feet felt very stiff and heavy, but in time I got used to the shoes.

And now, having got so far, my master went on to break me to harness; and there were more new things to wear. In time, however, I got used to everything, and could do my work as well as my mother.

I must not forget to mention one part of my training, which I have always considered a great advantage. My master sent me for a fortnight* to a neighboring farmer's where there was a meadow which was skirted on one side by the railway. Here were some sheep and cows, and I was turned in among them.

I shall never forget the first train that ran by. I was feeding quietly beside the pales* which separated the meadow from the railway, when I heard a very strange sound at a distance. Before I knew whence it came,—with a *rush* and a *clatter* and a *puffing* out of smoke,—a long black train of something flew by and was gone, almost before I could draw my breath. I turned and galloped to the farther side of the meadow as fast as I could go, and there I stood snorting with astonishment and fear. In the course of the day many other trains went by, some more slowly. These drew up at the station close by, and sometimes made an awful shriek and groan before they stopped. I thought it very dreadful; but the cows went on eating very quietly, and hardly raised their heads as the black, frightful thing came puffing and grinding past.

For the first few days I could not feed in peace. But as I found that this terrible creature never came into the field or did me any harm, I began to pay no attention to it, and very soon, I cared as little about the passing of the train as the cows and sheep did.

Since then I have seen many horses much alarmed at the sight or sound of a steam engine. But thanks to my good master's care, I am as fearless at a railway station as in my own stable.

Now if anyone wants to break in a young horse well, that is the way.

My master often drove me in double harness with my mother, because she was steady and could teach me how to go better than a strange horse could. She told me the better I behaved, the better I should be treated, and that it was wisest always to do my best to please my master. "But," said she, "there are a great many kinds of men. There are good, thoughtful men like our master, that any horse may be proud to serve. And there are bad, cruel men who never ought to have a horse or a dog to call their own. Besides, there are a great many foolish men,—vain, ignorant, and careless,—who never trouble themselves to think. These spoil more horses than all the others, just for want of sense. They don't mean it, but they do it for all that. I hope you will fall into good hands. But a horse never knows who may buy him. It is all a chance for us. Still, I say, do your best whatever it is, and keep up your good name."

—*Annie Sewell, in "Black Beauty."*

Comprehension Test

Draw a plan of the home of "Black Beauty" as told in Part I. On your plan write words, or make small drawings, of the things named. Put each in its right place.

When should a colt be "broken in," and *how?* Tell the steps in their order.

Decide on a good name for Parts I, II, and III.

This story is taken from "Black Beauty," a book that tells many interesting and useful things about horses. You will enjoy reading more from this book.

Wishing (O)

As you read this poem, find out *who* is doing all this wishing.

1. I wish I were a *primrose,*
    A *bright yellow primrose* blooming in the spring.
    The drooping boughs above me,
    The wandering bee to love me,
    The ferns and moss to creep across,
    And the elm tree for a king!

2. I wish I were an *elm tree,*
    A *great, lofty elm tree* with green leaves gay!
    The winds would set them dancing,
    The sun and moonshine glance in,
    The birds would house among the boughs,
    And ever sweetly sing!

3. I wish I were a *robin,*
    A *robin* or a little *wren,* everywhere to go,—
    Through forest, field, or garden,
    And ask no leave or pardon,

Till winter comes with icy thumbs
To ruffle up our wings!

4. Where should I fly to?
Where go to sleep in the dark wood or dell?
Before a day was over,
Home comes the rover,
For mother's kiss,—sweeter *this*
Than any other thing!

—*William Allingham.*

Appreciation Study
1. What picture do you see in stanza 1?
2. Tell what you see in the picture in stanza 2.
3. Describe the picture in stanza 3.
4. What picture in stanza 4?
5. Which of these pictures do you like best?

Dog Companions (S)

After you have read these dog stories silently, choose one to tell to the class. Tell the dog's name, the kind of dog he is, what he did, and the trait of character he showed. Or if you prefer, you may tell a story about some dog you have known.

I. Fido, the Spitz

I believe there is no other animal with so much affection as the dog.

You start away from home in the morning, and Fido, your cunning little spitz, wants to go too. You say, "Go back, Fido!" He stops. His tail droops down, and his eyes fill with disappointment. You start on, but have gone only a little way, when here comes Fido, determined to go with you to protect you from danger! You drive him back again, and at last think he has gone home.

All at once you see something in the road away ahead of you. You ask yourself, "What is that in the road?" Just Fido! He simply took a circle, and came in ahead. You say, "Well, Fido, you have defeated me *this* time, but you will not do it *again*."

The next time you leave home, here comes Fido! You drive him back, but it is the same old story. He follows you. You scold him, and at last cuff his ears. He makes up his mind at last that it is not exactly safe to follow this time. He goes back home. He stands where he can see as far as possible down the road. He watches you until you are out of sight. What then? Does he go off and forget you? Not at all. He stays right there all day, unless disturbed, watching for your return.

The first glimpse he catches of you, off he starts like a fuzzy hurricane,* down the road to meet you. He is so glad to see you that you have to scold him again and again, and finally cuff his ears, to prevent him from soiling your clothes in his wild efforts to lick your hands and face. Was ever such affection shown in any other animal except the dog? No other member of the family acts more glad to see you.

Where is there another animal so unselfishly devoted to the service of man? In the South, cattle and hogs run at large, sometimes in large numbers. In the fall, when these are in good order, some of them are quite fierce. How often I have seen the noble dog, standing with anxious eyes watching every move of the animals, ready to brave any danger or even to lay down his own life to care for his master.

There are many animals that will serve you when compelled to do so. But the noble dog will follow you at all times, patiently awaiting an opportunity to do you a favor. The night is never too dark or too stormy to cause him to slacken his watchfulness over you or your property, or to prevent his waking you at the first sign of danger. Oh that we might be as devoted to the service of *our* Master!

II. Bruno, the Shepherd

I believe there is no other animal that shows such a sense of right and wrong as does the dog.

A noble shepherd dog belonged to a neighbor of mine. This neighbor and his wife were suddenly called away from home, and in their haste they left poor old Bruno shut up in the kitchen, with the breakfast dishes containing food still upon the table.

They were gone three days and nights, but faithful and honorable Bruno stood guard all that time, and never touched a mouthful of that which he seemed to think was not his. Where is there another animal, man not excepted, so true to right? I believe that dog would have starved to death with food within his reach before he would have taken anything that was not given to him.

III. Rover, the Newfoundland

Many animals may be taught some tricks, but I believe there is no animal that shows more general intelligence than the dog.

About fifteen years ago a gentleman came from Boston, Massachusetts, to Minnesota, a distance of some fifteen hundred miles. He brought with him on the train a Newfoundland* dog, named Rover. Rover seemed perfectly at home and contented.

One day, however, the gentleman gave the dog a sharp scolding. That night Rover was missing. A search was made for him, but he could not be found, and he was given up as lost.

About three months later a letter came from Boston saying the dog was there. It is not known whether he took the train or not, but from the time taken to make the journey, it is safe to suppose that he made the trip on foot and alone. This is a true story, and it is the most remarkable dog journey I ever heard of.

IV. Old Ben, the Mastiff

I used to know two brothers who owned a large mastiff.* One of the brothers finally moved to a town twelve miles west. Old Ben, as they called the dog, used to board the train, and visit back and forth. Everybody in the neighborhood, and all the trainmen, knew Old Ben.

V. Jip, the Fox Terrier

Some dogs are quite sensitive, and often understand more words than we think.

An old gentleman once told me a story about a fox terrier named Jip. He used to send Jip on errands to his daughter's home fifteen miles away. The dog at last grew old and cross, and one day snapped at the cat, and chased her off. The dog was not scolded, but the man simply said to his wife that he would have to kill the old dog some day. The dog drooped his head and tail, and sneaked away.

No more was seen of him till three weeks later, when the man and his wife went to visit their daughter. There they found the missing dog. He must have understood what was said, and thought his only safety was in flight.

VI. Dick, the Airedale

Dogs are also very jealous of other dogs. How often do we see two dogs quarreling, even fighting, for a place closest to their master! Just pet one dog, and see how quickly the other will come for a share of your caresses.*

I know two little boys who own a very affectionate Airedale* dog. One of the boys took sick, and as he lay on the lounge, Dick would stand by him, and once in a while would raise his paws and tenderly place them upon the boy, as if to say, "Master, I am very sorry you are sick, and would gladly do for you anything in my power." Finally, Dick became so jealous of a little pup that took up a good deal of the family's attention that he almost left the place.

VII. Pan and Paris, the Collies

It has often been questioned why great men are so fond of dogs. The reason is not far to seek. The world is full of hypocrites,* and the loyalty and honor of the dog are like water in a barren place to the thirsty traveler. The sympathy of your dog never fails. If you are sad, so is he. If you are merry, no one is so willing to leap and laugh with you as he is. To your dog you are never poor. To your dog you are never old. Whether you are in a palace or a cottage he does not care. Fall as low as you may, you are his idol* still.

The affection of the dog for man is greater than his affection for another dog. He will follow his master to the grave, and sometimes die on it; but the loss of his own kind leaves him unmoved. I never knew of more than one dog where this was not true.

I once had two puppies. They were fine, white collies. In size they were between a Newfoundland and a fox terrier. These puppies, named Pan and Paris, lived, fed, played, and slept together, and for seven months were never separated. In the seventh month, Paris fell ill and died.

Pan nursed his brother as faithfully as any boy could nurse another. He licked him, brought him tempting bits to eat, and did all that he could think of. When, at last, his brother lay there cold and still, it was painful to see his grief and astonishment. From that time he ceased to play. From being a very lively dog, he grew grave* and sad. He had a longing, wondering look in his eyes, which made one's heart ache. Though he lived for many years after, and was as happy as a dog can be, he never was the same as before. He had buried his mirth in the grave of Paris. Something was lost for him with his brother, which he never found. This is the only dog I have known that had such love for another dog.

—*The Youth's Instructor (adapted).*

DICTIONARY EXERCISE

Learn these sounds and markings of *u:*
ū, as in ūse
ŭ, as in ŭs
u̜, as in pu̜t
ṳ, as in rṳle
û, as in fûr

Copy these words in syllables and mark each *u:*

true	under	hurricane
fuzzy	sudden	Massachusetts
used	upon	return
just	such	number
Bruno	disturbed	journey

Divide the following into syllables, then find them in the dictionary and see if you did your work right:

princess	mastiff	forge
caresses	affection	breeching
hypocrites	rover	crupper
		reigned

The Little Orphan Princess [S]

1. This is a picture of good Queen Victoria. She was born May 24, 1819. When a child, she was often called "the little Mayflower." She was not the daughter of a king, and she did not know that she might some day be the queen of England. She was very much like other little girls. She liked to play with toys, and to run and play at the seashore.

2. She had no brothers or sisters, but she had many dolls. The little princess* herself made the bodies of some of these dolls, to which she fastened china heads. Others of them, however, were quaint,* jointed, wooden dolls, such as few children of the present day have seen, but their grandmothers remember.

3. The little princess had few playmates, but her dolls were to her as real people. She dressed them like famous men and women she had heard about. Several of her English dolls represented Henry VIII, one of the kings of England, and others represented Queen Elizabeth. One group of dolls were dressed to represent the well-known English poet Shakespeare, and many other famous literary* people. The dolls were all properly dressed in such costumes* as were then worn.

4. But not all the dolls of this little maiden were English. Her French dolls represented Napoleon Bonaparte,* who was a great French general, Empress* Josephine, and some others. Her Russian dolls showed the czar's* uniform of white broadcloth, gold-laced and corded. There were also many dolls in Swiss* and Italian* costumes. Little Victoria was taught to sew, and her dolls' costumes were made with the greatest care.

5. Her father died when she was a baby. Victoria was brought up very carefully by her mother. One day, she saw a beautiful doll in a shop window. How she did want the doll! But she had spent all the money her mother had given her for that month, and

she knew it would do no good to tease for more. So into the shop went little Princess Victoria and begged the shopkeeper to keep the doll for her until she could save the money to pay for it. Then for a month she saved her pennies until she had enough for the beautiful doll. She went to get it at seven o'clock in the morning, before the shopman had opened his doors for the day.

The Princess Victoria

6. The king of England was Victoria's uncle. He had no children, and Victoria's mother knew that when he died her little girl would be queen. But Victoria knew nothing about this.

Her mother was a sensible woman, and the little princess was brought up in a wise and simple manner. She was taught to be regular in eating, exercising, studying, and sleeping. It is said that as a child her breakfasts consisted of bread and milk and fruit, and that for the evening meal she had bread and milk. Her dinner was also very simple.

7. Princess Victoria received her education under her mother's loving care. From ten to twelve every morning and from two to four in the afternoon were her regular hours for study. She was taught to speak and to write French and German. Still more carefully was she taught to use her own language well. She was taught history and arithmetic. She was taught to sing and to draw. Nor did her wise mother neglect to teach her to cook, and to sew, and to be useful at home. Victoria learned to spend money wisely, to think before speaking, to be careful of the feelings of others, and to try to make others happy.

8. When she was eighteen years old, all the people of England had a holiday. One of her birthday presents was a piano from her "uncle-king." Four weeks later, King William IV died. When Victoria received the sad news, tears came to her blue eyes. She was no longer a happy princess; she was a queen.

9. Queen Victoria tried to govern her people justly. In every way she sought to make them happy.

She was always kind to the poor and needy. When an Eastern ruler asked her the secret of England's success, that noble woman placed her hand reverently* on the Bible and said, *"That Book* is the secret of England's success."

10. Victoria reigned a little more than sixty-three years. When she lay on her deathbed, Dean Farrar,* a very dear friend, came to see her.

"Do you think my Lord will come soon?" she asked. "I wish He would come before I go. I would lay the diadem* of England at His feet. I would place my country's crown on His brow. He alone is worthy to wear a royal crown."

When she died, thousands of people all over the world felt that they had lost a friend.

Comprehension Test

1. Why do you think Victoria was called "the little Mayflower"? Find England on the map.

2. Whom did she dress her dolls to represent? See if you can find pictures of these people dressed in the costumes of their day.

3. How was Victoria related to William IV, king of England?

4. Who was Victoria's teacher? What was she taught?

5. Victoria's mother is called a sensible woman. Why do you think she was sensible?

6. See if you can figure out when Queen Victoria died.

7. Who is the present ruler of England?

8. What do you like best about Queen Victoria?

9. Tell the story of the first doll this little princess bought.

10. Think of a good name for each of these paragraphs: 3, 4, 7, 8, 10.

The Kingdoms [O]

This story happened in Prussia, a country in Europe. Find it on the map before you begin to read.

1. It was a fine day in June, many years ago. Frederick William, king of Prussia,* wanted to get away from the noise of the city. So he went for a walk along a quiet road through the country.

As he walked along, he listened to the songs of the birds. He picked some wild flowers that grew by the way. After a while he came to a little schoolhouse. The children were at play. It made him glad to see the children happy.

2. Soon they were called to their lessons. The king followed them into the schoolroom. At first the children were almost afraid to be in the presence of the king. But his kind face and pleasant ways soon won them. He was pleased to see how well they recited their lessons. After a time the teacher asked him to talk to the children.

3. "I will now ask you some questions," said the king, "and the child who gives the best answer shall have a prize."

Then the king held up an orange.

"You know that we all live in the kingdom of Prussia. But to what kingdom does this belong?" he asked.

The children were timid. They did not know just what to say. Every one sat quite still. At last a bright little boy spoke.

"It belongs to the vegetable kingdom," he said.

"How do you know?" asked the king.

"It is the fruit of a plant, and all plants belong to the vegetable kingdom," said the boy.

"That is a good answer," said the king. "You shall have the orange for your prize."

4. Then the king took a gold coin from his pocket. He held it up so that all the children could see it.

"To what kingdom does this coin belong?" he asked.

"It belongs to the mineral kingdom, sir," said another boy.

"Why so, my lad?" asked the king.

"Because it is a metal, and all metals belong to that kingdom," the boy answered.

The king was pleased.

"You are quite right," he answered. "You shall have the coin for your prize."

The children were delighted. With bright eyes and smiling faces they wondered what he would say next.

5. "I will ask you only one more question," said the king, with a twinkle of fun in his eye. "Tell me, children, to what kingdom do *I* belong?"

The king thought some one would say, "To the animal kingdom." And then he meant to act as if he were greatly offended.

The children looked at him, but no one spoke. They were a little afraid, because he was the king.

At last, Christel, a little blue-eyed girl, looked up into his kind eyes.

"I think you belong to the kingdom* of heaven," she said softly.

6. For a moment there was a breathless silence in the room. You might have heard a leaf fall as all eyes turned to little Christel. Even the surprised king hardly knew what to say.

Then he caught the timid child in his arms and kissed her again and again. With tears in his eyes, he said, "May God help me to prove the truth of what you have said!"

From that day, so the story goes, the Lord had a better servant, the people a wiser king.

Comprehension Test

1. What are the three kingdoms to which all things belong?
2. How many prizes did the king give that day?
3. Which prize was the best one?
4. What does the last sentence in this story mean?

The Lost Lamb (212)

As you read or recite this poem orally, take special pains with the line, "Left *alone, alone!*" in stanzas 1, 2, 3, and 4. Try to make your voice express the terrible loneliness of the poor lost little lamb.

1. Storm upon the mountain,
     Night upon its throne!
   And the little snow-white lamb,
     Left *alone, alone!*
   Storm upon the mountain,
     Rainy torrents* beating,
   And the little snow-white lamb,
     Bleating, ever bleating!

2. Down the glen* the shepherd
      Drives his flock afar;
   Through the murky* mist and cloud,
      Shines no beacon* star.
   Fast he hurries onward,
      Never hears the moan
   Of the pretty snow-white lamb,
      Left *alone, alone!*

3. At the shepherd's doorway
      Stands his little son;
   Sees the sheep come trooping home,
      Counts them one by one;
   Counts them full and fairly,—
      Trace he findeth none
   Of the little snow-white lamb,
      Left *alone, alone!*

4. Up the glen he races,
      Breasts the bitter wind,

  Scours across the plain and leaves
   Wood and wold* behind;
  Storm upon the mountain,
   Night upon its throne,—
  There he finds the little lamb,
   Left *alone, alone!*

5. Struggling, panting, sobbing,
   Kneeling on the ground,
  Round the pretty creature's neck
   Both his arms are wound;
  Soon within his bosom,
   All its bleatings done,
  Home he bears the little lamb,
   Left alone, alone.

6. Oh, the happy faces,
   By the shepherd's fire!
  High without the tempest* roars,
   But the laugh rings higher.
  Young and old together
   Make that joy their own,—
  In their midst the little lamb,
   Left alone, alone.

       —*Thomas Westwood.*

Appreciation Study
1. When is "night upon its throne"?
2. What kind of night was it when the lamb was lost?
3. What was the country like?
4. How do you think the little lamb felt when found?
5. Read the line in stanza 5 which shows that the lamb was contented?

Tell the story that this poem tells you, and help other children to see the place where the lamb was lost.

England's Most Beloved Artist (S)

1. A group of people were talking together in London. One of them was an artist.*

"Have you ever tried to draw two pictures at the same time, one with each hand?" asked one.

"That cannot be done," said another.

"It *can* be done," said the artist as he took a pencil in each hand and began to draw.

The others all crowded around to watch him. In just a few minutes he had the head of a horse on one paper and a stag's* head with its long antlers* on the other. This artist's name was Edwin Landseer.

2. Edwin was a bright, gentle little boy with blue eyes and curly hair. Like so many other boys and girls who became famous men and women he lived in the country. The father often went with the children for walks through the fields. They learned to love the beautiful things God has made.

One day little Edwin saw some cows grazing

This is a picture of Edwin Landseer and two of his dogs. See how closely the dogs are studying the picture Landseer is drawing. The artist has made them look as if they were deciding whether the picture is well done. That is why he named his picture "The Connoisseurs." Ask your dictionary what *connoisseurs* means.

in the field. He asked his father to show him how to draw them. His father gave Edwin his first lesson in drawing. After this, Edwin came to this field nearly every day to study the cows. His father said the field was Edwin's studio.*

Edwin's father taught him to draw from real animals instead of copying pictures.

"Study things as God has made them," he would often say.

3. When Edwin was only five years old, he could draw remarkably well. When he started off with his sister for his first day at school, how proud she was of her little artist brother! When he was thirteen years old, two of his pictures were put on exhibit with the pictures of other great artists. One of these was a picture of a mule, the other was a dog with her puppies.

When Edwin was sixteen years old, he drew a wonderful picture of dogs. A rich man bought this picture, and after that, Edwin Landseer was known as the great artist, Landseer.

4. For many years this artist lived and worked in a poor little room with only three chairs and an easel.* Later he bought a small house with a garden and a barn. He changed the barn into a studio.* Here he painted pictures to his heart's content. He seemed to like best to paint dogs, and many of his finest pictures are of dogs.

5. One of his dog pictures is named "Highland Shepherd's Chief Mourner." This is a picture of a dog leaning close against his dear master's coffin.

The dog belonged to Sir Walter Scott, who lived in Scotland. When Landseer died in London, this picture was carved on a tablet, and placed in Westminster Abbey. Above the dog's picture on the same tablet, a picture of Landseer was carved.

6. One day, Landseer was visiting a friend of his, who had a great Newfoundland dog named Paul Pry. While Landseer and his friend were visiting, Paul Pry came in with a basket of flowers in his mouth.

"Give the flowers to Mr. Landseer," said the dog's master.

Paul Pry proudly obeyed. This so pleased the artist that he asked his friend to send the dog to his studio to have his picture painted. When the gentleman came with the dog, Paul Pry remembered Landseer at once. The dog went up to him, wagging his tail, and offered him his paw. Newfoundland dogs can be taught many wonderful things. They are very strong swimmers, and often save people from drowning. So one picture which Landseer painted of Paul Pry shows a child that the dog had just saved from drowning. He named the picture "Saved."

7. But dogs were not the only animals that Edwin Landseer drew. In a shop window in London there was a lion. When it was a baby, it had been given to a Newfoundland dog to be cared for. Edwin and his brothers never tired of watching this lion with its strange mother. Sometimes the dog would strike the lion on its head with her paw when it did not behave well. Edwin made many pictures of this lion. Pic-

Saved

tures of monkeys, horses, cats, squirrels, and deer hung in Landseer's studio.

Edwin Landseer loved animals. He said that animals understand and feel as people do. So when he painted their pictures, they looked sad or happy, dignified or foolish, rich or poor. This is one reason why people were so fond of his pictures.

Queen Victoria was a friend of Landseer's. One time, when he went to the queen's castle, he told her about a new hippopotamus* that had been put into the zoo. The queen had not seen it. She asked him to draw it for her. In fifteen minutes he had made four sketches of the animal in different positions.

Queen Victoria loved Landseer's pictures so much that she made him a knight.* After that, instead of being just plain *Mr.* Landseer, he was called *Sir* Edwin Landseer. No English painter has ever been more loved in his own country than Sir Edwin Landseer.

Comprehension Test

1. What three things in this story show that Landseer was a great artist?
2. How old was he when he became known as a great artist?
3. Where was his native country?
4. Name some of his pictures that you have seen. Which do you like best?
5. Who made him a knight? Why?
6. Edwin Landseer was born in 1802, and died in 1873. How long ago did he die? How old was he then?
7. Which paragraphs do these topics fit?
    Drawing for Queen Victoria
    Drawing a picture with each hand at the same time
    Edwin's first studio
    Edwin becomes a great artist
    Paul Pry

True to the Master ^(S)

What do you think you would do if some day your father would become very angry and drive your mother away from home because she kept the Sabbath? How terribly lonely and unhappy you would be without her, wouldn't you? This story tells what two little girls in Tokyo, Japan, did under these circumstances.

Find these places on the map.

As you read, decide whether you think these children did right or wrong.

Two little girls, whose home is in Japan, faithfully attended Sabbath school every Sabbath. Their mother became a Christian, and joined the Seventh-day Adventist Church, but the girls seemed too young

to join the church. Their father, like many of the Japanese, is a Buddhist.* After a while he became very much opposed to the Christian religion.

"I will not have this religion in my house any longer," he said. And he drove his wife from home.

She went to a town about forty miles away, and began to sell books for her living.

The girls were very lonely without their mother, so they finally decided to go where their mother was.

About two days after they arrived the father came and found them. He began to scold and beat them for running away. He tried to take them back to his home by force, but they said they would not go without their mother. After spending all that day trying to persuade them, he went away.

Two days later he returned with police officers, and demanded that the girls go to court. As they went to court, the younger one comforted her sister with the text, "God is faithful, who will not suffer you to be tempted above that ye are able; but will with the temptation also make a way to escape, that ye may be able to bear it."

They reached the police court, and the judge looked at them from his high seat.

"Why did you run away from home?" he asked sternly.

"Our mother is a Christian," the girls explained, "and our father will not let her live at home. And we cannot get along without our mother."

"In Japan, women and children must do as the men say," the judge declared. "You must go with your father."

So the girls were forced to return home with their father. Soon they wrote a letter to their mother. They promised her that they would not give up the Christian religion, but would always be faithful, and some day they would be with her again.

Their father grew more and more bitter. He took away their Bibles and song books, and what little money they had. At last they decided to leave home again. This time they had no money, so they started to *walk* the forty miles to their mother.

They had walked about a mile along the railroad track when they came to a station. Here a man stepped up to them and, without saying a word, handed them some money. They had never seen him before, and they have never seen him since.

The girls went into the station and counted the money. Then they asked the fare to the place where they wished to go. They found that they had just enough money to pay their fare. They bought their tickets, and were soon with their mother again.

Their father finally gave up trying to get the girls, and they later went to our training school at Tokyo to prepare for a part in God's closing work.

Reading Tests and Scores for the Third Period

You have now reached the middle of the school year. Are you halfway toward your goal in silent reading? The test for which you are now ready will show. You will take this test in just the same way as you took your tests at the end of the first and second periods. It is test Number 7 in your "Reading Tests and Scores" pad.

Remember that it is better to get 100 in comprehension even if your rate is not quite so high as it should be than to score a high speed and fail in comprehension. So when you read your silent test, *read thoughtfully*. Your silent reading test includes also a memory test for the period. Your memory test will show how well you have remembered the important things in the stories you have read during this period. Review for this test if you wish.

For your *oral test*, choose any story you like from the third period. Study and practice it as much as you please. Then remember to make your voice sound right, to speak all your words correctly and distinctly, to read only the words that are in the story, and to look often away from your book without losing your place. *Read slowly*. Remember, *rapid oral* reading is *not good*.

You can give *yourself* a grade in *memory reading* by finding out how many words there are in the poems you have learned. I wonder how many of you have a grade of 100. This will be your grade if your memorized poems for the period total at least 300 words.

FOURTH PERIOD

"How Much Does a Horse Know?" (O)

Did you ever know that horses sometimes go to school? The horses in this story did. And they learned some of the very things you learn, too. As you read, count the things that the horses in this school had learned.

1. "How much does a horse know?" I asked Mr. Bartholomew,* the successful horse trainer.

"About as much as the average man—more than a great many," he answered promptly. "You can't believe it? Will you give me just half an hour to prove it?"

"But," I said, "you can teach a horse certain tricks, which become a mere matter of habit. But that proves nothing of the horse's intelligence."*

"I won't argue with you. Wait," he said, smiling pleasantly.

2. "*Nellie!*" he called.

A slight shuffling followed in the stalls.* Then a beautiful little bay* mare came trotting up to where we stood. She stopped beside the teacher and rubbed her head lovingly against his arm, gazing curiously at me the while.

"Bow to the gentleman," the teacher said.

Nellie nodded her pretty head toward me.

3. "Now shake hands."

She lifted her left forefoot.

"HOW MUCH DOES A HORSE KNOW?"
Match each picture with the paragraph in the story that tells about it.

"Is *that* the right foot?" he asked.

One could actually see a look of confusion* on her intelligent face as she quickly corrected her mistake.

"Nellie is like some children. She can't seem to tell the difference between her right hand and her left," said he, patting her affectionately.

4. "Now count one, two, three," he added.

Tap, tap, tap, went the iron-shod hoof on the floor.

"Good!" said the teacher.

5. "Now get the gentleman a chair."

I must confess I thought this was going a little too far. The tricks she had shown were ordinary enough. They were the result of careful training. But this quiet request to bring a chair rather surprised me. I watched to see what she would do. She trotted over to the opposite side of the room, and in a few minutes returned, bringing a chair in her teeth.

"Here," said Mr. Bartholomew, pointing to the place where he wanted me to sit. "Now," he said, "wait until I bring on the rest of my scholars."

6. He crossed the room, and put his hand on the swinging door that led to the stalls. Nellie started to follow him.

"Why don't you stay with the gentleman?" he said quietly, without turning his head, just as one would speak to a child.

7. Nellie turned obediently, and came back to my side. I confess I felt rather embarrassed, and hardly knew how to treat this little lady horse. Suddenly, I thought of some candy that I had in my pocket, and

soon we were getting on rather finely, eating candy together.

8. In the meantime, Mr. Bartholomew had returned. He was followed by a dozen horses. They marched soberly in and arranged themselves along one side of the room.

It would be impossible to describe all they went through; marching back and forth, dancing in perfect time to Mr. Bartholomew's whistle, lying down, kneeling, bowing, jumping,—all at the quiet command of the teacher. In fact, his voice was so low and gentle that it could hardly be called a command. It was more like a request, which they very promptly obeyed.

9. One handsome Arabian attracted my attention, and the teacher at once called this horse to him.

"How do you do, Se'lim?" he said.

The horse bowed.

"Is *that* the way you bow in Arabia?"

Selim at once dropped on his knees, and touched his forehead to the floor.

The teacher gave him the signal to get up.

"That is an extremely difficult thing to do," he said, turning to me.

10. "Does he understand what you say?" I asked.

"Does he not *act* as if he did?" was the teacher's answer. "There is no doubt that the horses understand every word I say to them. I could see no reason why, if a horse can understand the meaning of 'Go 'long,' 'Whoa,' he could not learn more, so I began to teach two or three, and soon I had this school around me."

11. "I notice you speak in a low, quiet tone, while so many who have anything to do with horses seem to think it necessary to yell at the top of their lungs."

"A horse is not deaf. His hearing is more quick than a man's, and yelling only tends to make him harder to manage. You can lay it down as a rule that the louder a man shouts at a horse the less he knows about horses. But then, half the men who have charge of horses now should be made to practice ten years on a sawhorse* before they are allowed to touch a live one."

12. "How do you manage to teach them so much?" I asked.

"Anyone with patience can train horses, and almost any horse can be trained. The trouble is that most people have very little patience, and a great many horses are spoiled by half-witted* owners who are not fit to have charge of a sawhorse."

13. By this time the pupils were becoming restless.

"School is dismissed," the teacher said to them.

Each horse left his place, came up to the teacher, and walked away to his stall.

"How much does a horse know?" asked Mr. Bartholomew, turning to me and repeating my own question.

"A good deal *more* than some *men;* for he knows enough to do his duty carefully and to the best of his ability," I answered promptly, as I took my leave.

—*Allan Forman, in Harper's Young People (adapted).*

Comprehension Test

1. What did these horses do that you think shows most of all that they really understood what their teacher said to them?
2. How much did the visitor finally decide that a horse knew?
3. Find on the map the home of the famous Arabian horses.
4. What do you think is the key to the professor's success in training horses?
5. Do you know anything a horse has done that shows intelligence?
6. How will the horses in the new earth differ from the horses here?

DICTIONARY STUDY

Learn all the sounds and marks of o, as follows:

ō, as in nō
ŏ, as in nŏt
ô, as in ôr
ǫ, as in dǫ
ȯ, as in dȯne

o͞o, as in to͞ol
o͝o, as in fo͝ot
oi, oy, as in **oil, boy**
ou, ow, as in **out, now**

What sound of u is like ȯ? What sound of u is like ǫ? What sound of o is o͞o like? What sound of u is o͞o like?

Divide the following words into syllables, mark the accented syllable in each word, and mark all the o's:

horse	followed	two	over	around
about	stood	won't	room	almost
more	lovingly	hoof	dozen	south
nothing	forefoot	floor	voice	school
proves	some	good	bowed	looked

A Miraculous Deliverance ⁽ˢ⁾

This story happened near Lake Titicaca* in South America. Find this place on the map. It tells how Satan tried to trap two of our missionaries, and how God worked a miracle to save them. After you have read the story, make a drawing of the place where these missionaries were trapped.

Practice reading paragraphs 6 and 8 orally.

1. It was in South America, in the region of Lake Titicaca.* In this section there are millions of Inca* Indians, and for this reason this part of the country has been called the Inca Union Conference.

Our missionaries first came to this field in the year 1912. They started schools where the Indians might learn to read the Bible and know about the soon coming of Christ. In this work there has been much bitter persecution. But this has only given God a chance to do wonderful things for His workers.

2. One time two of our missionaries in this field, Mr. J. M. Howell and Mr. E. P. Howard, were called to one of the towns to talk about starting a school. They mounted their horses and, taking a friendly guide, rode away. As they entered the town, hardly a person was to be seen on the streets, and everything was unnaturally quiet. It looked strange, for when these people are unfriendly, they often hide just before they plan to do harm.

3. Our missionaries were about to turn their horses and leave the town when two young men came to meet them.

"You will surely come up to our house and rest a

little before going on," these two young men said pleasantly.

"We would be glad to visit you in your home," the missionaries answered, going with them.

4. The young men led them about two blocks, then turned to the right and up a hill on a street shut in on both sides by a solid stone wall ten feet high. At the end of the street was a house which completely closed the street, the walls turning in to each end of the house.

Twice, as they were passing along this road, Mr. Howard said to his companion, "What a fine trap this would be if the men had anything against us!" But not for a moment did they have the least idea that any evil was intended.

5. They tied their horses just outside the house and went in. Brother Howard talked with one of the young men while Brother Howell talked with the other. Some fifteen minutes passed in interesting conversation. The young men seemed delighted with the hope of having a school in their midst.

6. Suddenly there rang from the street below a loud cry.

"Long live the evangelists!"*

"They *talk* all right, although they are drunk, don't they?" one of the young men said.

"Yes, they do," answered the missionary.

Hardly had the words been spoken when up went the angry cry: "*Down* with the evangelists! *Kill* the heretics!"* These words were followed by loud and wicked cursing.

7. The young man with whom our missionary had been talking became very nervous, but did not try to explain.

"I think we would better be going now," one missionary said to the other just as calmly as he could.

When they were outside the house, they saw that they were trapped. There were about thirty men in the street below, with large stones in their hands. They were cursing and calling loudly for help. There seemed but one of two things for the missionaries to do, either to mount their horses and go down and try to turn the evildoers from their wicked purpose or to go through their midst and away.

8. As Mr. Howell mounted his horse, the young man with whom he had been talking stepped up, his lips quivering.

"God grant that it go well with you to-day, sir," he said.

He really seemed sorry for the part he was playing in the wicked deed.

"Thank you, it always goes well with God's children. It shall go well with us to-day," Mr. Howell answered.

9. He then turned his horse to meet the mob. Brother Howard and their Indian guide came close behind. When they were about halfway to the ruffians,* they saw a hole in the wall on the side next to the mission compound.* It must have been a new hole, for the mob did not know it was there, else they would have been there instead of down below. Also, Brother Howard's remarks about the wall as they

were going up proved that it had just been made. The stones that had fallen were still lying by the side of the street.

10. The missionaries with their guide turned their horses and went through the hole in the wall. The ruffians looked at one another, said something, then ran around the wall to get at them on the other side. They succeeded in part, for the first stone hit one of the stirrups,* and the second struck Brother Howard a terrible blow in the back. However, the missionaries escaped without serious injury, thankful to God for His love and care in their hour of need. Truly "the angel of the Lord encampeth round about them that fear Him, and delivereth them."

In these experiences of our missionaries, how wonderfully Christ fulfilled His promise, "Lo, I am with you"! And in these experiences Jesus is calling us to stand by the mission work, to pray, and to give, and to go.

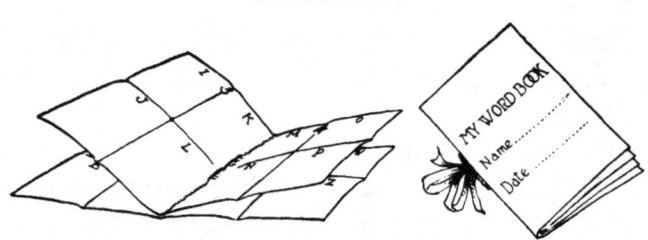

How to Make a Word Book

To-day, you are going to make a "word book," a sort of dictionary. See if you can make it without any help from anyone—just by following these directions:

1. Take two sheets of paper about eleven inches long and eight inches wide.
2. Fold both sheets through the middle across the narrow way.
3. Put them together like a book.
4. Sew them together through the fold with a cord or piece of ribbon, tying it on the outside.
5. Number the six inside pages.
6. With pencil and ruler draw the vertical and horizontal diameters on each page.
7. At the *top* of the *upper left* part of page 1 write the capital letter *A*.
8. At the *top* of the *lower left* part of page 1 write the capital letter *B*.
9. At the *top* of the *upper right* part of page 1 write the capital letter *C*.
10. At the *top* of the *lower right* part of page 1 write the capital letter *D*.
11. In the same way write the other letters of the alphabet in their order on pages 2, 3, 4, 5, and 6. Write four letters on each page. In the last space on page 6 write the three letters *X Y Z* at the top.
12. On the outside front cover, near the middle, write "*My Word Book.*"
13. Below this write your name and the date.
14. Your "word book" is now ready to use. Under the proper letter write all the new words you find in your reader from day to day, or any words your teacher may give you.

The Children's Poet [S]

If you were to visit the city of Portland, in the state of Maine, you could see an old wooden house where Henry Wadsworth Longfellow was born. You could walk down some of the same streets where he walked when he was a boy, and see some of the places where he played.

When Longfellow was just a little boy, his mother wrote to a friend: "I think you would like my little Henry W. He is such an active little rogue."* This "little rogue," as his mother lovingly called him, had rosy cheeks and brown hair. He was a healthy little boy, with well-bred manners, and with bright blue eyes that sparkled with fun.

Henry W. Longfellow

When Henry W. was about nine years old, his teacher told the class to write a story about a turnip. Henry W. remembered the turnips that grew behind Mr. Finney's barn. He thought a while, and finally wrote these lines:

> Mr. Finney had a turnip,
>   And it grew behind the barn,
> And it grew and grew,
>   But the turnip did no harm.

And it grew and it grew
    Till it could grow no taller,
Then Mr. Finney pulled it up
    And put it in the cellar.

There it lay and it lay
    Till it began to rot,
Then his daughter Susan took it
    And put it in the pot.

There it boiled and it boiled
    As long as it was able,
Then his daughter Peggy took it
    And put it on the table.

There it steamed and it steamed
    Till they all sat down to sup,
And they ate and they ate
    Till they ate the turnip up.

"Mr. Finney's Turnip" was the first poem that Henry W. ever wrote. Now I will tell you about the first one that was published. One summer vacation, Henry W. stayed on a farm with his grandfather. His grandfather dressed as old people did in those days. He wore knee breeches, and ruffles down the front of his shirt. His hair was long and was tied with a ribbon. Henry W. would sit by the hour and listen to stories about Indians that his grandfather told. One of these stories was about a fight with the Indians, at a place called Lovell's Pond. He thought about this story so much that he wrote a poem named "The Battle of Lovell's Pond."

Henry W. was now thirteen years old. He wondered if the newspaper editor would print his poem. He decided to send it to him, but he was afraid to sign his name to it. No one but his sister knew that he had sent it, and she promised not to tell. Every day after that he watched the paper to see if his poem was printed. Finally, there it was! Right in "The Poets' Corner," just as he had written it! At that moment there was no happier boy in all Portland than Henry Wadsworth Longfellow. After that, he tried harder than ever to write poetry that people would enjoy reading.

On his way home from school, Henry W. had to pass a blacksmith shop. He loved to see the fire burn in the forge.* He loved to watch the blacksmith fit the shoes to the horses' feet. When he became a man, he wrote a poem about this, which he called "The Village Blacksmith."

After Mr. Longfellow finished college, he spent some years studying in Europe. He learned to speak French, German, Italian, and Spanish. He made friends wherever he went, for he could talk to the people in their own language. He said he was their American uncle.

When he returned to America, he taught languages in a great university. He was a very kind and sympathetic teacher. But at last he decided to stop teaching and give all his time to writing poetry. He had six children, whom he loved dearly. Often when they would wake in the morning, they would find little letters under their pillows that their father had written to them.

Henry Wadsworth Longfellow wrote so many beautiful poems for children that he is called "the children's poet." He is also called "the home poet." One of his poems is named "The Children." Another, which was written for his three daughters, he named "The Children's Hour."

The poet's oldest son was named Charles. The next one was Ernest. When they were still little boys, their baby sister Fannie came to live in the nursery.* This nursery was a room in a house in Cambridge, Massachusetts, where George Washington once stayed. This became the Longfellow home. Do you suppose the poet ever told the children stories about the first President of their country? Poor little Fannie died when she was just old enough to run about.

The first schoolhouse where the two boys went to school was near the same elm tree under which General Washington took command of the American army.

After Fannie died, Longfellow had three other children—"Grave Alice, and laughing Allegra,* and Edith with golden hair." Allegra means "merry."

Besides the stories that Longfellow had heard about Indians, he knew a great many Indians himself. So he wrote a long poem about an Indian boy, which he named "Hiawatha."* Another long poem he wrote was "Miles Standish." Mr. Longfellow had heard this story many, many times, for Priscilla, the beautiful girl that the story tells about, was his great-great-great-grandmother. This was a story of the early days in New England.

The Village Blacksmith

Henry Wadsworth Longfellow was one of the best loved of all American poets. When he died, thousands of people who had never seen him mourned the loss of "the children's poet."

Comprehension Test. Fill the blanks with the right word or words.

1. Henry Wadsworth Longfellow was born Feb. 27, 1807. That was ——— years ago.
2. He died in 1882. He was ——— years old when he died.
3. His first poem was ———.
4. His first published poem, ———, was written when he was ——— years old.
5. His children's names were ———.
6. His great-great-great-grandmother's name was ———. His poem, ———, tells about her.
7. Some other poems that he wrote are ———.
8. I have read Longfellow's poems named ———. I like ——— the best.

The Village Blacksmith (215)

Is there a blacksmith shop near where you live? Did you ever visit it? Why are they not so common now as they used to be?

After your teacher has read this poem to you, see if you can tell the lesson Mr. Longfellow wanted to teach.

1. Under a spreading chestnut tree,
    The village smithy* stands;
The smith, a mighty man is he,
    With large and sinewy* hands;
And the muscles of his brawny* arms
    Are strong as iron bands.

2. His hair is crisp, and black, and long;
   His face is like the tan;
   His brow is wet with honest sweat,
   He earns whate'er he can,
   And looks the whole world in the face,
   For he owes not any man.

3. Week in, week out, from morn till night,
   You can hear his bellows* blow;
   You can hear him swing his heavy sledge,
   With measured beat and slow,
   Like a sexton* ringing the village bell
   When the evening sun is low.

4. And children coming home from school
   Look in at the open door;
   They love to see the flaming forge,*
   And hear the bellows roar,
   And catch the burning sparks that fly
   Like chaff* from a threshing floor.

   * * * * *

5. Toiling, rejoicing, sorrowing,
   Onward through life he goes;
   Each morning sees some task begin,
   Each evening sees it close;
   Something attempted, something done,
   Has earned a night's repose.*

6. Thanks, thanks to thee, my worthy friend,
   For the lesson thou hast taught!
   Thus at the flaming forge of life,

Our fortunes must be wrought;
Thus on its sounding anvil* shaped
Each burning deed and thought.
—*Henry Wadsworth Longfellow.*

Appreciation Study

1. What picture do you see in the first stanza? in the second stanza? in the fourth stanza?
2. In stanza one what are the blacksmith's strong muscles said to be like?
3. In stanza three what is like a sexton ringing a bell?
4. In stanza four what is like chaff flying away?
5. What does a blacksmith use the bellows for? the forge? the anvil?
6. Which stanza tells the lesson we may learn from the blacksmith? What is this lesson?

The Children's Hour (252)

This is a poem that every child should be able to recite. As you read it, find the meaning of the words that are starred, so that you can better understand and enjoy the poem.

In this poem Longfellow pretends that he is the keeper of a great prison house, or castle, with a tower that turns round and round. The children are bandits, or robbers, plotting to kidnap him. The battle is on, and the bandits—they are called *banditti* in the poem—rush in from every side. They are trying to capture the fortress of the enemy. They succeed in climbing over the wall around the castle or fortress, or getting through it, but then they themselves are taken captive and put down into a dungeon, or prison, where they are kept forever—till the dungeon "shall crumble to ruin, and molder in dust away." As your teacher reads the poem to you, try to keep in mind what Longfellow is pretending. Then see if you can read it as well as she does.

1. Between the dark and the daylight,
	When the night is beginning to lower,
   Comes a pause in the day's occupation,*
	That is known as The Children's Hour.

2. I hear in the chamber above me
	The patter of little feet,
   The sound of a door that is opened,
	And voices soft and sweet.

3. From my study I see in the lamplight,
	Descending* the broad hall stair,
   Grave Alice, and laughing Allegra,
	And Edith with golden hair.

4. A whisper, and then a silence!
	Yet I know by their merry eyes
   They are plotting and planning together
	To take me by surprise.

5. A sudden rush from the stairway,
	A sudden raid* from the hall!
   By three doors left unguarded
	They enter my castle wall!

6. They climb up into my turret*
	O'er the arms and back of my chair;
   If I try to escape, they surround me;
	They seem to be everywhere.

7. They almost devour me with kisses,
	Their arms about me entwine,
   Till I think of the Bishop of Bingen*
	In his Mouse Tower* on the Rhine!

8. Do you think, O blue-eyed banditti,*
  Because you have scaled* the wall,
  Such an old mustache* as I am
  Is not a match for you all?

9. I have you fast in my fortress,*
  And will not let you depart,
  But put you down into the dungeon*
  In the round tower of my heart.

10. And there will I keep you forever,
  Yes, forever and a day,
  Till the walls shall crumble to ruin,
  And molder in dust away!

—*Longfellow.*

Appreciation Study

1. Find the stanza that tells about the plot against the prison keeper.
2. Find the place that tells about the bandits rushing in from every direction. How were they able to get within the castle walls? What is the *castle?* What are the *walls?* Who are the *bandits?*
3. What is the *turret* that swings round and round?
4. Read the lines that tell with what weapons they fight the prison keeper.
5. Who finally wins the victory?
6. Read the lines that tell what is the *dungeon.*
7. When would the walls of this dungeon "crumble in dust away"?
8. After you have studied the poem with your teacher, read it through and see if you really understand it all. Try to read each line at a glance.
9. How many of you can learn the first stanza in two minutes? If you memorize two stanzas a day, you will be ready to recite the whole poem one week from to-day.

Finding My Cornet (o)

Did you ever ask God to help you find something you had lost? Did He help you? God loves to do things for those who serve and honor Him. This story tells about one of our missionaries in Burma who lost his cornet, which he was taking to a meeting, and how God found it for him. Find Burma on the map. Read Isaiah 65:24 and 1 John 5:14, and then as you read the story, see if you can tell how God fulfilled to this missionary the promises in these texts.

"One, two, three, four, five, six, seven, eight."

"There's one more piece, porter*—a basket!"

"No, sir! Your ticket says eight pieces. That's all you put in."

"But the basket! It has my cornet* in it, porter."

"Well, I'm sorry for you, mister, but it isn't usual to expect more out of a cloakroom than you put in. You'd better inform the police."

"Then is it really truly lost?"

The awful truth that the porter's statements were correct made me feel sick all over. No, stopping to think, I couldn't remember seeing the basket when we got off the train in the morning. My cornet was lost!

Here we were on our way to the Burma meeting. The good pastor* over there wanted some help with the music. But now it was gone. Gone! The cornet that had inspired the jungle* band, and had played in a hundred villages—*gone!* I was surely disheartened.*

I informed the police. I informed the station master. I searched the station and the lost luggage* room. I asked every coolie* within hearing distance if he had seen my basket. Not a soul had seen such a basket all day long. Neither had I. That was just the whole trouble. The basket was lost, I tell you, and my cornet was *gone!*

Lifelessly I put my eight pieces of luggage into the cart, and directed the driver to the mission house. I felt hopelessly dejected.* All at once the thought flashed into my mind, Why not pray? It was then just 3:30 in the afternoon. So right there, in that old cart rumbling off down the road, mingling with the thousand sounds and voices common to an Eastern street, I prayed.

I told the Lord that that cornet was just as much His as it was mine. I told Him that it was just as good a preacher as I was. Then as we talked the situation over together, I dared to ask Him that if it could glorify His name, if it could benefit His cause, to please have it sent back that evening, as I wanted to take it to the meeting the next day.

Talking it all over with the Lord lifted my burden, and made me feel sure that God was now going to take matters into His hands. Maybe He would teach me a severe lesson. But I felt safe in the hands of the Lord, because He always works things out for our good. In this frame of mind I completed the journey to the mission house, where my wife, sharing my disappointment and hope, helped me get things ready for the night.

Now listen! While we were thus engaged, at five o'clock in the afternoon, there was a knock at the door. I opened the door and a total stranger stood before me with my basket in his hand! A friend of his, traveling in the ladies' compartment* with my wife, had by mistake taken it with *her* luggage. She had remembered my wife's name, and in conversation had learned that we were Seventh-day Adventists. The stranger had quite a time finding us. First, he went to the church, then to the pastor's home, then to the office, and finally to the mission house where we were staying. He declared that his friend had given him no peace till, at 3:30, he had started off in a cart to hunt us up.

But why did our friend wait till 3:30 before starting out to hunt us? Just what was it that made him start that afternoon at exactly 3:30?

—*Eric B. Hare (adapted).*

DICTIONARY EXERCISE

The following are some of the new words you have had in your reading lessons since you made your "word book." Copy them under the right letter in your "word book," dividing them into syllables.

rogue	occupation	banditti
compartment	Allegra	disheartened
nursery	grave	dungeon
Hiawatha	raid	porter
Priscilla	turret	jungle

After you have copied them, find them in the dictionary in the back of your reader, and see how many you divided correctly into syllables.

Mark the accented syllable in each word.

Mark the sounds of *a, e, i, o,* or *u* in each accented syllable.

Try a race with your classmates on finding all fifteen words in your dictionary, and see who finds them first.

Four Sunbeams (298)

1. Four little sunbeams came earthward one day,
   Shining and dancing along on their way,
     Resolved that their course should be blessed.
   "Let us try," they all whispered, "some kindness to do,
   Not seek our own pleasure all the day through,
     Then meet in the eve at the west."

2. One sunbeam ran in at a low cottage door,
   And played hide and seek with a child on the floor.
     The baby laughed loud in his glee,
   And chased with delight his strange playmate so bright,
   The little hands grasping in vain for the light
     That ever before them would flee.

3. One crept to the couch where an invalid* lay,
   And brought him a dream of the sweet summer day,
     Its bird song, and beauty, and bloom;
   Till pain was forgotten, and weary unrest,
   And in fancy he roamed through the scenes he loved best,
     Far away from the dim, darkened room.

4. One stole to the heart of a flower that was sad,
   And loved and caressed* her until she was glad,
     And lifted her white face again;
   For love brings content to the lowliest lot,
   And finds something sweet in the dreariest spot,
     And lightens all labor and pain.

The sunbeams sinking softly down to rest.

5. And one, where a little blind girl sat alone,
   Not sharing the mirth of her playfellows, shone
   On hands that were folded and pale,
   And kissed the poor eyes that had never known
   sight,
   That never would gaze on the beautiful light
   Till angels have lifted the veil.

6. At last, when the shadows of evening were falling,
   And the sun, their great father, his children was
   calling,
   Four sunbeams sped into the west.
   All said, "We have found that in seeking the
   pleasure
   Of others, we fill to the full our own measure."
   Then softly they sank down to rest.
   —*St. Nicholas.*

Appreciation Study

1. In the last stanza, why is the sun called the "father," and the sunbeams the "children"? Why does it seem fitting for the father to call his children home at night?
2. What is the secret of true pleasure taught by the sunbeams?
3. How does the last line in this poem make you feel?
4. Read Luke 6:38, and tell how this poem expresses the thought of that verse.
5. If you were to draw pictures for stanzas 2, 3, 4, and 5, what would you put in each one?

Table Manners ^(o)

As you read these lines, find the lesson we may learn from the blue jay; from the sparrow; from the chickadee. How many of these birds do you know?

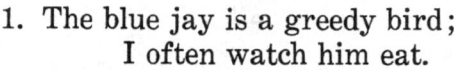

1. The blue jay is a greedy bird;
    I often watch him eat.
   When crumbs are scattered from our door, he
    snatches all the treat;
   He drives the smaller birds away, his manners
    are so rude—
   It's quite a shocking thing to see him gobble down
    his food!
   And sometimes, when I'm not polite, I hear my
    mother say,
   "Why, now I see a little boy who's eating blue jay
    way!"

2. The sparrows are a noisy set, and very quarrel-
    some,
   Because each hungry little bird desires the larg-
    est crumb.
   They scold and fight about the food,
    all chirping, "Me! Me! Me!"
   And sometimes, when we children are inclined to
    disagree
   About the sharing of a treat,
    my mother says,
    "Why, you
   Are acting now the very way
    the silly sparrows do!"

3. And jolly little chickadees are perfectly polite;
   They never snatch, they never bolt, they never,
       never fight;
   They hold the crumbs down daintily with both
       their little feet,
   And pick off tiny little bits—
       we love to watch them eat!
   And when my sister's good at meals,
       my mother says, "I see
   A little girl who's eating
       like a darling chickadee!"

—*Selected.*

The Brave Tiger Mother ^(S)

This story happened in India. Find India on the map. As you read, find out what this tiger mother did that made her worthy to be called brave?

1. Some years ago
a number of English officers in India
went out to hunt.
On their way home, after their day's sport,
they found in the jungle* a little tiger kitten,
not more than a fortnight* old.

2. They took it with them;
and when they reached their tent,
the kitten was given a tiny dog collar and chain.
It was then tied to the tent pole,
around which it played and frisked
to the delight of all who saw it.

3. Just at evening, however,
about two hours after the capture,

the people in the tent were checked
in the midst of their pleasure,
by a sound that caused the bravest heart to fear.

4. It was the roar of a tiger!
In an instant,
the little kitten became every inch a tiger.
It strained its chain with all its baby strength,
while it replied with a loud wail
to the terrible voice outside.
The company in the tent were terrified,
there was something so unexpected
and so wild in the roar.

5. Suddenly, into the very center of the tent
there leaped a huge mother tiger!
Without noticing the men there,
she caught her kitten by the neck,
and by one jerk snapped the chain that bound it.

Then, turning to the tent door,
she dashed off at full speed,
bearing her young one away in triumph.
All honor to the brave tiger mother!

Ratu Meli at Home [S]

Have you ever heard of Ratu Meli,[*] the Fijian[*] chief who visited the United States in 1926? Perhaps you have seen him and heard him tell of his joy in knowing Jesus and of the truth that Jesus is soon coming. While he was in America, he saw many things that were a great wonder to him.

"I have come to a country," he said, "where everything seems to go with electricity.[*] Your washing machines wash your clothes by electricity. You sweep your floors by electricity. At one of our schools, I saw how they even wash dishes by electricity. We need nothing like that in Fiji, because for dishes we use only leaves of trees. The great daily paper printing presses are very wonderful. But the radio amazes me most of all. When I was in California, I saw a picture brought across the ocean by radio! It was published in the paper. I can't understand this. It is wonderful! Daniel 12:4 is certainly fulfilled."

Ratu Meli never tired of telling how God's word has made his people free—free from cannibalism,[*] free from the evils of heathenism.

"In Fiji old things are done away," he said. "The warlike ways of the people have passed away. Fiji suffered very much bondage through false gods and heathen chiefs. But I want to tell you that now we have come to a new time. Through the Bible the bondage of the past has gone and we are free.

"I have heard that some of you in America whose skin is the same color as mine were once slaves. Was there not a great President you had in this country that made you free—Mr. Lincoln? Do you forget that? No; you never forget it. I hear you sing songs that have to do with that freedom.

"In the time of Jesus, people said, 'We are not slaves, we are the children of Abraham.' But Jesus said, 'You *are* slaves because you are *sinners*, and every one that sins is a slave!' For many years in Fiji, we were the slaves of sin. But this Book has brought the truth to us—this Book that says, 'Ye shall know the truth, and the truth shall make you free.' Can we, down in Fiji, forget our deliverance from the bondage* of sin? Can we forget this Book that made us free? Can we forget Jesus? No! *Never* can we forget.

"I will show you some of the things of the old days in Fiji. This is a spear with which we pierced men to kill them. Here is a club. With this club we also killed men, and after that they were baked and eaten. How joyful our hearts are to-day that Fiji has turned away from these terrible deeds. Doesn't God say *His word* is like a sharp two-edged sword? Doesn't He say it is like a hammer that breaks rock in pieces? The *word of God*, the *Bible*, is our *new* club,—God's club that kills sin. It is very fitting that all of us should get into boats and go to every part of the world and tell the people that this is the powerful word by which they may be made free."

On his way to America from Fiji, Ratu Meli visited different parts of Australia. Wherever he went, he took notes about what he saw, so that when he should return to Fiji, he could tell the people of his homeland about the wonders of the great wide world.

"It will take me a year and a half to write up all I saw in Australia," he said; "but now that I have come to America, I don't know when I shall *ever* get through with it. I think when the next General Conference comes, four years from now, I shall still be telling it."

In one of the last talks Ratu Meli gave while he was in America, he said, "You have expressed very much joy in meeting me since I have come here. But there is greater joy than this just a little while from now, when Jesus comes and we all go up in the cloud. That joy will be greater because you will see people saved not only from Fiji but from all different lands.

"Every day we have had a great feast on our table here, and a great big drink from the cup of salvation. Every day my spirit has been filled with joy. It is fitting that I should say, 'Truly God's work is good.'"

When Ratu Meli sailed from San Francisco for his island home, a number of his American friends were at the pier.* As the ship started to move, some one on shore began singing that good old song, "God

Ratu Meli and his Fijian band

Be With You Till We Meet Again." The chief joined in the song as he stood on the deck, waving farewell with his handkerchief and drying the tears that rolled down his cheeks. He afterwards said he felt as Sister White felt after God had shown her the beauty and wonders of heaven. It seemed to her that she could never go back to this dark world again. So he felt that he almost desired to stay with the brethren in beautiful and wonderful America.

He took home a number of band instruments that had been given to him. These musical instruments were given to the students in our schools in Fiji, and they are learning to play. When the instruments were unpacked, they came to a very large one with a big mouthpiece. Some one said, "That must be the one *you* are going to blow, Ratu Meli." This made them all laugh. The picture on page 230 shows Ratu Meli with two of the teachers sitting in the middle of a group of young Fijians, their instruments in their hands. They have sent us their word of gratitude for these gifts to the school.

Many people who saw and heard Ratu Meli speak while he was in America, felt a new interest in foreign missions. They felt that it was truly a great privilege to give money so that many more who have never known the true God may know the joy of obeying Him, and be ready to meet Jesus when He comes.

Comprehension Test

1. Find Fiji on the globe or map. Is it one of the South Sea Islands?
2. What direction is it from Pitcairn? from the Society Islands?
3. Name some of the wonderful things that Ratu Meli saw in America.
4. When were the black people of the United States set free? Who was President at that time?
5. How are we made free from sin?
6. What does the Bible say that God's word is like?
7. How did Ratu Meli say the heathen life differed from the Christian life?
8. What did he say will be the Christian's chief joy in the new earth?
9. How did he feel when he sailed away from America?
10. What song was sung as he was sailing away?

Silent Reading Test

This lesson is your eighth silent reading test. The test is in your "Reading Tests and Scores" pad.

What the Snowflakes Did [255]

Read this poem until you find out what the snowflakes did, and the lesson they teach us. What are the "threads of iron" in stanza 1? What are the "iron horses" in stanza 4?

---

1. Over the great broad prairie*
    The snowflakes, soft and light,
  Began in early morning
    To carpet the ground with white.
  Softly they fluttered downward,
    And some of them paused to rest
  On two little threads of iron,
    That tie the East to the West.

2. But one little snowflake whispered,
    "Alas! how small am I!
  On this cold, hard bed of iron,
    What can I do but die?"
  Her sister snowflake answered,
    "Yes, I know that we are small;
  But that needn't worry you, sister;
    We've nothing to do but fall!"

3. Then every listening snowflake
    Went steadily on and on,
  Falling and falling and falling,
    Till the wintry day was gone;

And then—why, the rails were hidden,
   And everywhere the eye
Saw only the spotless snowdrifts
   Under the cold gray sky.

4. In vain the panting engine,
     With snort and scream, essayed*
  To pass; the tiny snowflakes
     A giant barrier* made!
  Came hurrying men and engines,
     While frantic whistle blew,
  Till at last eight "iron horses"
     The train in safety drew!

5. Now if every little snowflake
   Had paused, that stormy day,
To muse* and sigh despondent*—
   To melt upon its way—
They never could have wrought the chain
   That link by link they threw
Around that monster engine,
   And held it captive too.

6. This story of the snowflakes
   Is more than idle verse—
  It points you to a moral,
     Which I need scarce rehearse:*
  That any thought, word, action,
     However light and small,
  May aid you in your heavenward way,
     Or bind you here in thrall.*

          —*Author Unknown.*

A Rich Poor Boy [O]

Did you ever wish you were rich? Maybe you *are* rich. Read this story, and then decide. The boy in this story was very rich, but he thought he was poor. Read the story, and find out how much the boy was really worth, and what he had that made him so rich.

"I wish I were rich and could have things like *some* of the boys that go to school," said Ben.

"Ben," said his father, turning around quickly, "how much will you take for your legs?"

"For my legs?" said Ben in surprise.

"Yes! What do you use them for?"

"Why, I run, and jump, and play, and—oh, ever so many things."

"That is so," said the father. "You would not take ten thousand dollars for them, would you?"

"No, indeed!" answered Ben, smiling.

"And your arms—you would not take ten thousand dollars for them either, would you?"

"No, sir!"

"And your voice. They tell me you sing quite well, and I know that you talk a little bit. You would not part with *that* for ten thousand, would you?"

"No, sir!"

"Your hearing and your sense of taste are better than five thousand dollars apiece at the very least; don't you think so?"

"Yes, sir."

"How about your health? If you had ten thousand dollars, would you be willing to be an invalid?"

"No, indeed!"

"Your eyes, now. How would you like to have fifty thousand dollars and be blind the rest of your life?"

"I would not like it at all."

"Think a moment, Ben! Fifty thousand dollars is a large sum of money. Are you very sure you would not sell them for so much?"

"Indeed I am!"

"Then they are worth that amount, at least. Let us see now," his father went on, figuring on a sheet of paper. Legs ten thousand, arms ten, voice ten, hearing five, taste five, good health ten, and eyes fifty. That makes a hundred thousand. You are worth one hundred thousand dollars at the very lowest figure, my boy. Now run and play, jump, throw your ball, laugh, and hear your playmates laugh too. Look with those fifty-thousand-dollar eyes of yours at the beautiful things about you, and come home with your usual appetite for dinner, and think how *rich* you really *are*."

—*Sunday School Visitor.*

They Two [222]

1. They are left alone in the dear old home,
   After so many years,
   When the house was full of frolic and fun,
   Of childish laughter and tears.

They are left alone, they two—once more
    Beginning life over again,
Just as they did in the days of yore,
    Before there were nine or ten.

2. And the table is set for two these days;
    The children went one by one
Away from home on their separate ways
    When the childhood days were done.
How healthily hungry they used to be!
    What romping they used to do!
And mother—for weeping—can hardly see
    To set the table for *two*.

3. They used to gather around the fire
    While some one would read aloud,
But whether at study, or work, or play,
    'Twas a loving and merry crowd.
And now they are two that gather there
    At evening to read or sew,
And it seems almost too much to bear
    When they think of the long ago.

4. Ah, well! Ah, well! 'tis the way of the world!
    Children stay but a little while
And then into other scenes are whirled,
    Where other homes beguile;*
But it matters not how far they roam,
    Their hearts are fond and true;
And there's never a home like the dear old home
    Where the table is set for two.

—Author Unknown.

Comprehension Test

1. How many children were there in the family that this poem tells about?
2. Find six words that tell what kind of children they were.
3. Why does the mother weep when she sets the table for only two? Who are these two?
4. Read the lines that tell where the children have gone.
5. What two pictures do you see in stanza 3?
6. Try to read each line of this poem after one glance.

Stories of George Washington ^(S)

Girls may read Part I, and boys may read Part II. Study your part until you can tell it or read it well to the rest of the class. Give your story a good name. How long does it take you to read your part? What do you think is the best part for oral reading?

I. _____ (351 words)

George Washington is called the father of his country. Do you know why? It is because he did so much to make this country free and happy. He was the first President of the United States. He was said to be "first in war, first in peace, and first in the hearts of his countrymen." Although more than a hundred years have passed since he died, his memory is still held dear.

He was a great man, not only in great things, but

in little things. Many interesting stories are told of his truthfulness. Every one has heard the story of George and the cherry tree. Here is another story that shows the same thing.

Early one morning, a wild colt was racing and capering* about one of Mrs. Washington's fields. Nobody was able to manage him.

"Boys," said George to some of his friends, "I am bound to break that colt."

It was a dangerous thing to try, but the boys agreed to help him all they could. They ran after the colt until they caught him. Then they put a bit into his mouth, and held him while George mounted. Away flew the horse, back and forth across the field.

Then he stopped short. He reared and backed. He tried his best to unseat his rider, but in vain. With one last effort, the frightened animal made a great leap. This broke a blood vessel, and the noble horse fell to the ground—dead!

The boys had not expected this, and they were very sorry. They went home trembling with fear. George's mother, knowing they had come from the fields, began to ask about the horses.

"Did you see my sorrel* colt?" she asked.

The boys looked at one another in silence. For a moment, no one dared to speak. Then George said, "The sorrel is dead, mother. I killed him."

His mother looked grieved, but said nothing. Then George told the whole story. When he had finished, she said gently, "I regret the loss of my sorrel, but I rejoice in my son, who always speaks the truth."

II. _____ (237 words)

When Washington was in camp with his army, he walked out one morning to see what was going on. It was winter, so he put on a long overcoat, which hid his general's uniform. He passed a place where a corporal* was directing some of the men in making a breastwork of logs. They were just raising a very heavy one as the general came up.

"Heave, ho!" cried the little corporal. "Up with it, men!" But he did not offer to help, because he was the corporal.

The men lifted with all their might, but they could not move it any farther. In a moment more it would have fallen. But Washington stepped forward, put his strong shoulder under it, and the log was soon put into its place. Then, turning to the corporal, he asked, "Why don't you help your men with this heavy lifting?"

"Why *don't* I?" said the little man. "Don't you see that *I* am the *corporal?*"

"Oh, indeed!" said Washington, as he unbuttoned his overcoat and showed his uniform. "Well, *I* am the *general*, and the next time you have any heavy lifting to do, send for me."

The little corporal was very much ashamed of himself, when he saw that it was General Washington who stood before him. But it was a good lesson for him. And there are still men who may learn a good lesson from this story.

Thought Questions

I. Who did George say had killed the colt? Had he really intended to kill the colt? Why didn't he say, "*We* killed him," or "The colt dropped dead," or something of that sort? What did Adam say when he had eaten of the forbidden fruit? Genesis 3:12. What did David say when he had sinned? Psalm 51:3, 4. What did God say of David? Acts 13:22. Which did the mother prize the more, the colt or the truthfulness of her son?

2. Which showed true nobility, Washington or the corporal? What does this story teach? What did Jesus say about being great? Matthew 20:27. What noted city was named after George Washington? On what day in February was Washington born?

Stories of Abraham Lincoln (S)

Here are three stories of Lincoln. Read them all, then choose the one you like best, and tell it or read it to the rest of your class. Give your story a name. From "Lincoln's Sayings" find one that best fits your story, and memorize it.

I. ⎯⎯⎯⎯⎯⎯⎯⎯

On the next page is the picture of a log shanty built on a lonely farm in Kentucky over one hundred years ago. Here Abraham Lincoln was born February 12, 1809. The house was without windows or floor. No one would have guessed that the child in such poverty* would some day be one of the world's great men. But from his life we shall learn that true greatness does not depend on riches or great opportunities.*

When Abraham was seven years old, his father moved the family to southern Indiana. Here they built a rude shed to shelter them. One side of the house was left open, because there were no doors and windows. After a time, the father built a new log

This is the log shanty where Abraham Lincoln was born.

house. This house had four sides, a door, and a chimney. For furniture there was a table and a few stools, and these were homemade. Abraham slept on a bag of leaves in the loft, or attic.* He reached the attic by climbing a ladder.

Although at this time Abe was only seven years old, he was a very tall, long-legged little boy. His mother made his shirts of coarse cloth dyed with colors that she made herself from barks and roots. His trousers were made of deerskin. He wore moccasins* on his feet. On his head he wore a cap of coonskin* with the tail hanging down behind. Wasn't that a fine handle to carry it by?

II. ──────────────

Young Lincoln once borrowed a book on the life of Washington. He promised to take good care of it. He carried the treasure home in the bosom of his shirt. He read in bed late that night by the light of a rag dipped in tallow. When he finished reading, he put the book on a ledge, between the logs. During the night a storm arose, and the book became soaking wet.

Abe hardly knew what to do. When he took the book home, the owner pretended to be very cross about it.

"I am very sorry, sir," said Abe. "I have no money, but I will willingly work to pay for it."

"You may pull corn fodder* for three days, then," said the owner.

"Does that pay for *the book* or for *the damage* done to it?" asked the young book lover.

"The book isn't worth much now," said the man. "The bargain is that you pull fodder three days, and the book is yours."

This was the first book Abe ever bought. He was so happy to get it for his very own that he was almost glad it got wet. At the end of the first day's work, the man told him he might take the book. But Abe would not take it until he had finished paying for it. The man felt that there was a boy who could be trusted anywhere. As Abe read the life of the great Washington, his heart was stirred with a deep love for his country. He never forgot what a price had been paid for its freedom.

III. ─────────────

Lincoln was honest in all things great and small. A woman once overpaid him by six cents. He did not discover the mistake until she was gone. Then he walked six miles to repay her.

In one place where Abraham Lincoln lived when he was a boy, there was a great deal of drunkenness.

Almost all the men drank more or less liquor. Mrs. Lincoln felt very anxious about Abe. She could not bear to think that he would ever be a drunkard. One day she had a long talk with him about the evils of drink.

"Men become drunkards because they *begin* to drink," she said. "If you never *begin* to drink, you will never be a drunkard."

After Mr. Lincoln became President, he told a friend that the reason he had never used liquor was this talk with his mother. From that day to his death we are told that he never touched intoxicating* liquor of any kind.

At the age of seventeen years, Abraham was nearly six feet four inches tall. In strength he was almost a giant. He could lift a barrel of flour into a wagon.

When Abraham was nearly twenty-one years old, his father moved again, this time to Illinois. For two weeks they traveled through the woods with ox teams. In Illinois Abraham helped his father build a log house. He also helped to split rails enough to fence in fifteen acres of land for a cornfield. A man who worked with Lincoln said that Abraham was the roughest-looking fellow he ever saw, but that he knew more than anyone else. This man also said: "He can split more rails in a day than any other man. He is as strong as an ox, and never becomes tired." Sometimes he was called "the rail splitter."

Once when he needed a pair of new trousers, he made a bargain with a woman to weave him some coarse cloth, and dye it brown with walnut bark. For each yard, he agreed to pay her four hundred good fence rails. In this way he paid for all his clothes.

Thought Questions

1. How does the life of *Abraham Lincoln* show that greatness does not depend on riches? on great opportunities?

2. How did his home differ from yours?

3. What shows that he was studious? that he was industrious? that he was honest? that he respected his parents?

Lincoln's Sayings

All that I am, all that I hope to be, I owe to my angel mother.

God must like common people, or He wouldn't have made so many of them.

It is no pleasure to me to triumph over anyone.

Gold is good in its place; but living, brave, and patriotic* men are better than gold.

I have not willingly planted a thorn in any man's bosom.

I am nothing, but truth is everything.

When you can't remove an obstacle, plow around it.

I do not question the *motives* of anyone opposed to me.

Come what will, I will keep faith with friend and foe.

The reasonable man has long since agreed that intemperance is one of the greatest, if not *the* greatest, of all evils among mankind.

I am not bound to win, but I am bound to be true. I am not bound to succeed, but I am bound to live up to the light I have. I must stand with anybody that stands right; stand *with* him while he *is* right, and *part* with him when he goes *wrong*.

What Words Do [152]

Listen as your teacher reads this poem to you, then try to read it as well as she did.

---

1. One day, a harsh word, rashly said,
   Upon an evil journey sped.
   And like a sharp and cruel dart,
   It pierced a fond and loving heart;
   It turned a friend into a foe,
   And everywhere brought pain and woe.

2. A kind word followed it one day,
   Flew swiftly on its blessed way;
   It healed the wound, it soothed the pain,
   And friends of old were friends again;
   It made the hate and anger cease,
   And everywhere brought joy and peace.

3. But yet the harsh word left a trace
   The kind word could not quite efface.*
   And though the heart its love regained,
   It bore a scar that long remained.

4. Oh, if we could but learn to know
   How swift and sure *one word* can go,
   How we would *weigh* with *utmost* care
   Each thought before it sought the air,
   And only speak the words that move
   Like white-winged messengers of love!
   —*Author Unknown.*

Comprehension Test

1. Read the lines that tell what evil, harsh words do.
2. Read the lines that tell what good, kind words do.
3. Read the lines that tell where the "scar" was that the harsh word left.
4. What is meant by a thought that "sought the air"?
5. What kind of words are like "white-winged messengers of love"?
6. Read the whole poem. Try to read each line at a glance.

The New Skates [O]

Do you know of a noble deed that any boy or girl has done? Read and find at least one noble thing the boy in this story did. What good lesson had he learned about spending money?

"Oh, ho!" shouted Tom Slade, as he balanced himself on his heels, and came up to the bank where Ned was buckling on his sister Clara's skates. Just then he spied a new pair on *Ned's* feet. "Oh, ho!

New skates the last of *January!* Why didn't you wait till *June?*"

"I should, I suppose, if I hadn't got money enough before," said Ned smiling.

"*My!* aren't they *beauties!*" said Tom. "But, Ned, why didn't you get them in *some season?* Here you have been sliding around on your *boots* all winter, and *now* the ice will break up in three weeks."

"They will be just as good for next winter. I did not have the money of my own to buy them any sooner, and father does not allow me to go in debt for anything, and that is the reason I have been without all winter."

"It is not *all* the reason, Ned Devitt," said Clara. "You had money enough before Christmas, if you had not done something else with it."

"What else could he do to give up *skates?*" cried Tom.

"No matter what I did," said Ned.

"Yes, it is," persisted* Clara, "and I shall tell. He had the money all ready, and was just going to buy them, when our washerwoman's boy came with his toes all out of his shoes, and couldn't go to school. Ned said shoes were more needed than skates, and he went off and bought that boy a pair of shoes, and that is why he did not have his skates sooner!"

Tom's eyes shone as he gave a long, low whistle.

"I could not have done it," he said, "but it certainly was good in you."

By that time Clara's skates were fastened on, and the merry trio* darted down the pond as swift as arrows.

Ned enjoyed his skates all the more that day, and for all the rest of the winter, from the fact that they were truly his own. Skates that are not paid for do not belong to the skater, but to the merchant, or to the one who lent the money to purchase them. Debt is a bad thing, and it would be better never to skate than to use skates covered with debt.

All the rest of the winter Ned was something of a hero* in the eyes of his companions. While, as Tom said, *they* might not have been equal to the task of making the sacrifice that Ned made, they were all able to see that it was a noble thing to do, and they admired him for the unselfish deed.

—*The Youth's Instructor (adapted).*

Rules for Good Behavior

Read these rules for good behavior, and then copy five that you think *you* most need to watch in *yourself*. Then see if you can keep from breaking them for at least one week.

1. I will not be ashamed to do right anywhere.
2. I will not do anything that I would not be willing for everybody to know.

3. I will not go in the company of boys who use bad language.

4. I will not have the sulks and pout whenever I cannot have my own way about everything.

5. I will not loaf over a lesson just because it is hard.

6. I will not be mean to little boys who have no big brother for me to be afraid of.

7. I will learn to be polite to everybody.

8. I will never make fun of children because they are not dressed nicely.

9. I will try to learn something useful every day; and whenever I see a man making anything, I will watch to see how he does it.

10. I will keep my hands and face, my neck and ears clean, and my hair brushed, without having to be *told* to.

11. I will be respectful to old people, and behave so that my parents will not be ashamed of me.

12. I will be in earnest about everything. I will work with all my might. I will study with all my might, and I will play with all my might.

13. I will read books and papers that will make me want to know something and do something that will help other people.

14. I will not tell lies, nor steal.

15. I will pray every day, and I will ask Jesus to make me a good boy (or girl), and show me how to prepare for heaven.

—*The Youth's Instructor (adapted).*

Giving to Missions (O)

This story tells how a boy named Phil kept an account of all the money he spent, and what it helped him to see. It tells three ways of giving to missions. Read, and find out what these three ways are. Then decide which you think is the best way.

"Yes, I always give for missions and everything else," said Phil. "I give something every Sabbath; don't you?"

"Why, no; I give *five or ten cents* when I think I can *spare* it, when I have a good deal of money, and don't want it for anything," said Tom.

"*I* give whatever father and mother give me for it," said James.

"Oh, *I* always give *my own* money!" said Phil. "I don't think it's any giving at all unless you do *that*."

"Yours is the best way, I'm sure," said Tom, soberly. "What *you* give is just so much out of what you would like to spend on yourself."

"Yes," said Phil, feeling very self-denying.

"I'm going to try your way," said Tom; "and I'm going to keep an account and see what it will amount to."

The three boys were on their way home from church, where they had heard from a missionary some very interesting accounts of his work. He had deeply stirred the sympathies of his young hearers as he told of lives wretched and degraded in this world and with no hope of any other.

Many went away with the solemn feeling that in

some way they would be held answerable if they did not hold out a helping hand to those in such great need.

Little societies were formed among the children, for they thought it would be pleasanter to put their gifts together than to offer them separately. Several boys came to Phil's house on the next afternoon to talk it over. Phil put down their names in his account book as the first members of their society.

"What's this, Phil?" asked his uncle, picking up the book that evening after supper.

"Oh, that's my account book, uncle. I brought it down to write the names for our missionary society."

"May I read it?"

"Certainly you may. I am simply trying to work up the idea of liberal giving among the boys."

"A most excellent idea," said his uncle. "Let me see—bananas, twenty-five cents; soda water, ten cents; peanuts, twenty-five cents; bat, thirty-five cents; candy, fifteen cents; baseball cap, seventy-five cents; Sabbath school, six cents—"

"Oh, stop, Uncle George! That's when I was visiting at Cousin Tom's, and I promised mamma I'd put down every cent I spent."

But Uncle George seemed not to hear, and went on: "Peanuts, fifteen cents; bananas, twenty-five cents; getting shoes mended, forty cents; missionaries, five cents; soda water, ten cents; bananas, twenty-five cents; getting bat mended, fifteen cents; lemonade for the boys, fifty cents; collection in Sabbath school, two cents—"

"*Please*, give me the book, uncle."

"I am glad you don't forget your charitable* duties, Phil," said his uncle, giving up the book with a mischievous smile.

Phil took it in some confusion. He had heretofore thought but little more of his spendings than to remember his mother's wish, that he should keep an account of what she gave him regularly. Now, in looking over his record, he was astonished.

"Well, well!" he exclaimed, as he added up one page, "two dollars and ninety cents for eating and play, and seventeen cents for giving, and *I* bragging to the boys what a good thing it was to *give regularly and liberally!*"

Phil was a boy who meant to do right, and his heart troubled him as he ran over the long list. He thought of the bread of life which that money might have carried to starving souls.

At last he got up and stood before the glass.

"Now, young man," he said, shaking his head at the boyish face he saw there, "you know very well that a quarter for peanuts doesn't look any larger to you than a pin's head, and that a quarter for missions looks as big as a cart wheel. But all that must stop. You've got to turn over a new leaf. This book isn't going to hold any more account of dollars for self and cents for Jesus."

Something to Do. Look over Phil's account as his uncle read it, and decide how much you think he *should* have given to missions.

Suppose you keep a strict account of all the money you spend from now till the close of the school year, including what you give to Jesus, and see what *your* record will be.

In the Time of Trouble ⁽²⁴³⁾

This psalm contains promises to those who trust God. How many promises can you find? Which one do you like best?

As you read orally, see how many of the lines you can read at one glance.

1. He that dwelleth in the secret place of the Most High
   Shall abide* under the shadow of the Almighty.
   I will say of the Lord,
   He is my refuge* and my fortress;*
   My God; in Him will I trust.

2. Surely He shall deliver thee from the snare* of the fowler,*
   And from the noisome* pestilence.*
   He shall cover thee with His feathers,
   And under His wings shalt thou trust:
   His truth shall be thy shield and buckler.*

3. Thou shalt not be afraid for the terror by night;
   Nor for the arrow that flieth by day;
   Nor for the pestilence* that walketh in darkness;
   Nor for the destruction that wasteth at noonday.

4. A thousand shall fall at thy side,
   And ten thousand at thy right hand;
   But it shall not come nigh thee. . . .

5. Because thou hast made the Lord, which is my
     refuge,
   Even the Most High, thy habitation,*
   There shall no evil befall thee,
   Neither shall any plague come nigh thy dwelling.
   For He shall give His angels charge over thee,
   To keep thee in all thy ways.
   They shall bear thee up in their hands,
   Lest thou dash thy foot against a stone. . . .

6. Because he hath set his love upon Me,
   Therefore will I deliver him. . . .
   He shall call upon Me, and I will answer him:
   I will be with him in trouble;
   I will deliver him, and honor him.
   With long life will I satisfy him,
   And show him My salvation.

   —*Psalm 91.*

The Broken Flowerpot (O)

This story tells how an ivory domino box suddenly turned into a beautiful geranium in a lovely blue-and-white flowerpot. Read and find out how this was done. Give each part of this story, I to VII, a name or subject that fits it.

I. _____

My father was seated on the lawn before the house, his straw hat over his eyes, and his book on his lap. Suddenly, a beautiful blue-and-white flowerpot, which had been set on the window sill of an upper story, fell to the ground with a crash, and the fragments flew about my father's feet.

"Dear, dear!" cried my mother, who was at work on the porch, "my poor flowerpot, which I prized so much! I would rather the best tea set were broken! The beautiful geranium I reared* myself, and the dear, dear flowerpot that you bought for me on my last birthday! That naughty child must have done this!"

I came boldly out of the house and said rapidly, "Yes, mother; it was I who pushed out the flowerpot."

"Well," said my mother, "I suppose it was an accident. Take care in the future, my child. You are sorry, I see, to have grieved me. There is a kiss— don't fret!"

"No, mother, you must not kiss me. I do not deserve it. I pushed out the flowerpot on purpose."

"Ah! and why?" asked my father.

"For fun!" said I, hanging my head. "Just to see how you would look, father; and that is the truth of it."

My father dropped his book, stooped down, and caught me in his arms.

"My boy," he said, "you have done wrong, but you shall remember all your life that your father blessed God for giving him a son who spoke the truth in spite of fear."

II.

Not long after this, a gentleman gave me a beautiful large domino* box in cut ivory, painted and gilded. This domino box was my delight. I was never tired of playing dominoes with the old nurse, and I slept with the box under my pillow.

"Ah!" said my father one day when he found me in the parlor, arranging the ivory pieces, "do you like that better than all your other playthings?"

"Oh yes, father!"

"You would be very sorry if mother were to throw that box out of the window and break it, just for fun."

I looked pleadingly at my father, but made no answer.

"But perhaps you would be very glad," he went on, "if suddenly it should turn into a beautiful geranium in a lovely blue-and-white flowerpot. Then you could have the pleasure of putting it on mother's window sill."

"Indeed I would," said I, half crying.

"My dear boy, I believe you; but good wishes do not mend bad actions. Good actions mend bad actions."

So saying, he went out and shut the door. I cannot tell you how puzzled I was to make out what my father meant.

III.

"My boy," he said next day, "I am going to walk to town. Will you come? And, by the way, fetch your domino box. I should like to show it to a person there."

"Father," I said by the way, "how can my domino box be changed into a geranium in a blue-and-white flowerpot?"

"My dear," said my father, putting his hand on my shoulder, "that will depend on what is here," and he touched my forehead, "and what is here," and he touched my heart.

"I don't understand, father."

"I can wait until you do, my son."

IV. ─────────────

My father stopped at a nursery,* and after looking over the flowers, paused before a large double geranium.

"Ah, this is finer than the one your mother was so fond of. What is the price of this, sir?"

"Only seven shillings and sixpence," said the gardener.

My father closed his pocketbook. "I can't afford it to-day," he said gently; and we walked out.

V. ─────────────

On entering the town we stopped again, this time at a china warehouse.

"Have you a flowerpot like the one you sent me some months ago? Ah, here is one, marked three shillings and sixpence," he said to the storekeeper. Then, turning to me, he continued, "Well, my boy, when mother's birthday comes again, we must buy her another. That is some months to wait. And we can wait, my boy. For truth that blooms all the year round is better than a poor geranium, and a word that is never broken is better than a piece of china that is easily broken."

My head, which had been drooping before, rose again, but the rush of joy at my heart almost choked me.

VI.

"I have called to pay a little bill," said my father, entering a shop where all kinds of pretty toys were sold. "And, by the way," he added, "my little boy can show you a beautiful domino box."

I held up my treasure, and the shopman praised it highly.

"It is always well, my boy," continued my father, "to know what a thing is worth, in case one wishes to part with it. If my son gets tired of his plaything, what will you give him for it?"

"Why, sir," said the shopman, "I think we could give eighteen shillings for it."

"Eighteen shillings!" said my father. "You would give that? Well, my boy, whenever you do grow tired of your box, you have my leave to sell it."

My father paid his bill, and went out. I lingered a few moments, and joined him at the end of the street.

VII.

"Father, father!" I cried, clapping my hands, "we can buy the geranium! We can buy the flowerpot!" And I pulled a handful of silver from my pocket.

"I *thought* the good angel in your mind and heart would win the victory," said my father proudly.

How overjoyed I was, when, after placing vase and flower on the window sill, I took my mother by the hand, and made her follow me to the spot.

"It is his doing and his money!" said my father. "Good actions have mended the bad."

—*Edward Bulwer-Lytton.*

The Thermometer [S]

As you read this lesson, do the experiments given, and see for yourself how a thermometer works.

You have all seen a thermometer,* and I dare say you can tell what it is used for. The word "thermometer" comes from two words, *thermo* and *meter*. *Thermo* means *heat*. *Meter* means a *measure*. The thermometer, then, is something that measures heat.

Look carefully at a thermometer. You will see that it is made up of a little glass tube with a round bulb at the bottom. This bulb contains a liquid called mercury.* Many years ago, linseed* oil was used instead of mercury.

The thermometer was invented about three hundred years ago, but it is not known by whom. A German, whose name was Fahrenheit,* was the first to use mercury. For this reason most thermometers are called Fahrenheit thermometers.

By the side of the little tube that holds the mercury, you will see a great many short lines. Some of these lines are numbered. Find on the thermometer the line that is numbered zero. From this line notice that the numbers increase by tens. The number next to the line at the top of the mercury tells how hot or how cold the weather is; for the mercury rises with the heat and lowers with the cold.

If you look at a thermometer early in the morning, the mercury will be lower than at midday. Why is this? Hold the thermometer in very cold water, and see what happens. Now put it in warm water or hold it near the fire. What change do you notice?

Hold the thermometer in melting ice. See the mercury fall lower and lower. At last it reaches the little line above zero marked thirty-two degrees. This is called the "freezing point." When you see the mercury standing near the freezing point, you will need to protect your house plants. If you do not, the frost may nip their tender leaves.

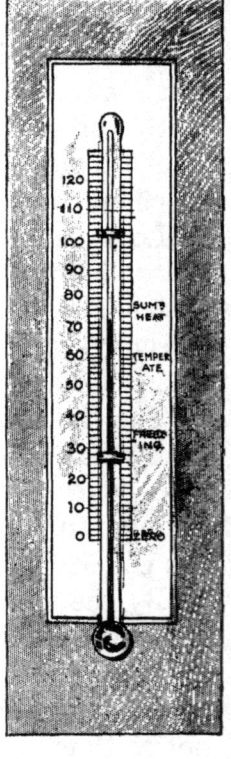

Some thermometers are called fever thermometers. They are used by doctors and nurses to find out the amount of heat in the body. Perhaps you have sometimes had your temperature* taken by a doctor. The normal, or healthy, temperature of the body is ninety-eight and six-tenths degrees. Can you find where this is marked on the thermometer?

Place the thermometer in a basin of water. Heat the water until the mercury rises to the number ninety-eight and six tenths. On the thermometer this is called "blood heat." It is the same as the normal temperature of the body. When the heat of the body is greater than this, the person has fever.

"But *why* does the mercury rise and fall?" you ask. Why does the water in the teakettle boil over when it becomes hot? And why does fruit that is canned when boiling hot occupy less space when it becomes cold? We know that heat expands,* or increases the size of anything. We also know that cold contracts,* or causes a thing to become smaller. When the mercury in the thermometer expands, it must rise, as it cannot go lower.

Air also expands when it becomes warm. Without this law, which the wise Creator has made, there would be no gentle breezes to cool the hot summer days. Without it, there would be no circulation* of heat to warm the cold days of winter. If you sat near the fire, you would be burned with the heat. If you moved away from the fire, you would suffer with the cold.

In this and in many other ways God has written to us the message of His love and thoughtful care. In everything that He has made, and in all the ways that He works, He is planning for the comfort of His children. Is He not good, and is He not worthy of all our love?

Comprehension Test. Put the right word or words where the blanks are.
1. "Thermometer" is composed of the words ——— and ———, which mean ——— and ———.
2. The thermometer was invented ——— years ago.
3. ——— was first used in it.
4. ——— first used mercury.
5. This man lived in ———.
6. On a hot day the mercury ———.

7. On a cold day it ———.
8. Freezing point is ———.
9. The normal temperature of the body is ———.
10. If the body temperature is above normal, the person has ———.

Fill out this chart during the week. (Try to judge of the temperature before looking at the thermometer.)

Temperature	Mon.	Tues.	Wed.	Thur.	Fri.

At 8:30 outdoors
At 8:45 in the schoolroom
At 11:45 in the room
At 12:00 outdoors
At any convenient time:
  On the floor
  Five feet from the floor
  Near the fire
  In corner farthest from fire.					

Reading Tests and Scores for the Fourth Period

You are now in the last half of the fourth grade. How are you getting along with your reading goals? Make up your mind that by the time you complete your fourth grade, you will reach a high score in silent reading, in oral reading, and in memory reading. You can do it, if you keep trying.

What three tests are there in *silent* reading?
What four things should you strive for in *oral* reading?
How much *memory* reading will give you a score of 100?
You are now ready for the tests your teacher will give you.

FIFTH PERIOD

A School of a Century Ago ^(S)

This school was in New York City. Find New York City on the globe or map. Find out from this story how this school of one hundred years ago was different from your school to-day.

1. Imagine you are living one hundred years or more ago. Let us take a stagecoach, for there are no railroad trains, and go to New York City. Here we shall visit one of the best schools in the United States.

2. Are you surprised to find such a small city? There are only a few cities of any size in the whole United States. Even Chicago is only a few log houses. The people who live there are often attacked* by wild Indians. In New York State there are large tribes of Indians, who sometimes give trouble to the white people. In the United States at this time, there are only twenty-four states. Hardly anything is known of the vast country west of the Mississippi* River.

3. It is late in the evening when we reach New York City. We could not send a telegram, or even telephone to our friends, for there is not a telegraph or a telephone in all the world. Nor can we take an electric street car, for no one has yet dreamed of such means of travel. But we can *walk* to the home of our friends. Only don't you wish the streets were lighted with good electric lights? Maybe we can borrow a lantern somewhere. But no! People do not know

A SCHOOL OF A CENTURY AGO
Match each picture with the paragraph in the story that tells about it.

what kerosene is. Oh, good! the great round moon is coming up! This lamp of heaven is no new invention. Now we shall soon be with friends. There in the window is a lighted candle to let us know that they are expecting us.

4. In the morning we feel quite rested after our long stage ride, even though we slept on a bed of straw with no comfortable springs under us. But we were more fortunate than the children in whose home we are staying, for they all slept on the floor to give their guests the best place in the house. Don't you wonder how the mother ever gets the sewing done for this family of children, without a sewing machine? No one has ever heard of a sewing machine.

5. This morning we shall go with the children to visit their school. When we reach the schoolroom, we find several hundred children in the room, with only one teacher! How can one teacher ever find time to teach so many children? Keep your eyes open, and we shall soon see.

6. The children do not have single seats and desks as most school children have to-day. They sit on long benches without backs. These benches face a long, narrow table with a slanting top. In this way a large number can be seated in the room. Some schools have as many as eight hundred children under one teacher. The teacher cannot teach all the classes,—of course not. It is the teacher's business to keep order,—and the order is very good.

Here are some good mottoes that the school has chosen:

"A place for everything, and everything in its place."

"Let every child at every moment have something to do."

It would take too much time for this army of children to pass down a cloakroom and hang up their hats. So each child's hat is fastened by a string around his neck, and hangs on his back.

7. Quickly this large school begins its work. The children are in groups of ten. One in each group is called a monitor.* It makes us think of our Sabbath schools. The monitors are chosen from the older children. They wear a leather ticket, or badge, on which is lettered "Monitor of the First Class," "Monitor of the Second Class," and so on.

On the wall, around the large room, near each long bench, hang a blackboard and a reading chart. Small groups of children stand around one of these blackboards or charts when they recite to a monitor.

8. These monitors not only hear the children recite, but they do most of the other work of the school. When a new child comes to school, a monitor tells him in what class to go. When a child is absent, a monitor finds out why. A monitor rules the writing paper, for ruled paper, what little there may be, costs altogether too much for common use. Only the older ones are given this paper. A monitor has charge of the slates and books.

9. Do you see that group of little children learning to write? They are writing in the sand, so it is very easy to erase a mistake. But the sand is not out-

doors on the ground. Oh no! It is spread in a thin layer on the desk. This saves paper. It saves pens—quill pens, I mean—and pencils, too, for the children write in the sand with pointed sticks. It is then erased by passing a long straight stick across the sand.

The children are taught spelling, reading, and writing, and they learn these very well. Up to about this time, many people did not want to have the children taught arithmetic. Perhaps they thought the little monitors could not teach arithmetic; and where would they get money enough to hire men and women to do all this extra work? But some of the best schools, like this one in New York City, have classes in arithmetic once or twice a week for *some* of the pupils. And a few of the brightest pupils even study *geography!*

Do you not think we have spent an interesting day in this school of one hundred years ago? It is now time for the children to go home. At a given signal, all hats are quickly lifted from the children's backs and placed in position on their heads. Then, together they march out of the room.

Comprehension Test

1. How did people travel long distances one hundred years ago?
2. How many states were there in the United States then? How many are there now?
3. In what state is New York City? Chicago?
4. Find *your* state on the map.
5. Find the part of the United States that was hardly known then.

6. Why could not people send messages to their friends quickly?
7. What did people use for lights in their homes?
8. How were the streets of a city lighted?
9. What kinds of beds did people sleep on?
10. How did people do their sewing?
11. How many children did one teacher sometimes have in school?
12. What kind of desks were in the room?
13. What were some of the school's mottoes?
14. Where did the children hang their hats?
15. Who helped the teacher, and what did they do?
16. What did the children study?
17. On what did they practice writing?

"The Mother of a Thousand Daughters" (S)

Do you know any missionary who ever went to China or Japan or India or any other part of Asia? This story is about a lady missionary who went from New York City to Ceylon, an island near India. Before you read the story, trace her journey on the map or globe. What two oceans did she cross?

This story is told in 512 words. See if you can read it in four minutes or less, and find out who this missionary was and why she was called "The Mother of a Thousand Daughters."

Eliza Ag'new was a bright little girl who went to one of the schools in New York City a little more than one hundred years ago. And *she* studied *geography!* How she did enjoy it! It was so interesting to learn about this great, wide, wonderful world!

Eliza often heard people talk about the heathen

across the sea. A few self-sacrificing* men and women had even gone from the United States to India and other lands where there were millions of heathen who had never heard of the Saviour.

When Eliza read in her geography about these distant lands, she thought about these poor people who had no one to teach them of God. Oh, if she could only go and help them! She thought about them so much and so earnestly that at last she made up her mind to go to some heathen land as a missionary as soon as she was old enough. And this resolve, which she made when she was only eight years of age, she never forgot.

In one of her geography lessons she studied about the island of Ceylon.* She found it on the map. It was a long way from New York. In order to reach this island one would have to sail across two oceans. She learned that along the coasts of Ceylon people fished for pearls. Eliza knew what was meant by "the pearl of great price." She knew what Jesus meant when He said, "Follow Me, and I will make you fishers of men."

Eliza completed her study of geography long before she was old enough to go away from home as a missionary. But she did not give up her plan. When the Lord opened the way, she sailed away to the island of Ceylon. It took a long time to make the trip, and it cost a good deal of money. Although she lived to be quite an old lady, she never saw her home in America again. Ceylon was her home the rest of her life.

When she reached Ceylon, she made up her mind to "fish for pearls." But the pearls she wanted to get were the souls of the girls in a town called Oodooville.* She started a school for these girls, and for forty-one years she was the principal of this school. In some cases the children and even the grandchildren of her first pupils attended the school.

She was very, very happy in her work of "finding pearls." It is said that every girl who took the full course in the school became a Christian. She had the joy of seeing six hundred girls accept Christ as their Saviour. Many of these became missionary teachers and Bible workers.

Miss Agnew was so gentle and loving and good that the girls all called her "Mother." And she really was a mother to them. They felt that they were her daughters. Altogether she taught a thousand girls in her school. This is why this good missionary is called "The Mother of a Thousand Daughters."

Between Two Angels [266]

When you read this poem, see how well you can bring out the thought by the tones of your voice. If you were to draw a picture to illustrate the poem, what would you put in it?

1. There stood in a garden a child, sweet and fair,
   Watching some fruit that hung ripening there;
   Two anxious angels were watching above,
   One gazing in *hatred*, the *other* in *love*,—

One angel of *darkness*, the *other* of *light*,
One clothed in *black*, the *other* in *white*.
The child never *dreamed* that the angels were there;
He just *longed* for the *fruit*, so rich and so rare.

2. "How I *should* like that big apple so red!
But I cannot forget what my dear mother said,—
That doing the things I'm forbidden to do
Would make *me* unhappy, and grieve *her* heart, too."
"Take it," the dark angel whispered, "and eat;
It is not very often you get *such* a treat.
There is no one to *see* you, and no one to *tell*."
So up went a hand; it could reach the fruit well.

3. *Again* there's a whisper, sweet, gentle, and low,
The little child listened. The voice said, "You know
Your dear mother told you, though no one *was* nigh,
That *Jesus* could see you from heaven on high."
The child paused a moment, then said as he smiled,
"*I'll not be a thief; I'll be a good child!*"

4. A rustling sound stirred the soft summer air—
One angel was *gone*, but *one* was still *there*;
The angel of darkness had taken its flight;
The child was alone with the angel of light.
In this little story we plainly can see
An everyday lesson for *you* and for *me*;
If we listen to Conscience, the angel of light,
We shall conquer Temptation, the angel of night.

—*Author Unknown.*

DICTIONARY DRILLS

Here are a few more sounds and marks that you will need to know in order to understand your dictionary. How many of these have you learned before?

ç (=s), as in çent
ȩ (=k), as in ȩut
ph (=f), as in phone

gh (=f), as in laugh
çh (=sh), as in maçhine
ȩh (=k), as in ȩhorus
ch, as in chair

Which sound of *c* is like *s*? Which one is like *k*?
Which sound of *ch* is like *sh*? Which one is like *k*?
When *ch* is not marked, how does it sound?
What two letters together sound like *f*?

Divide the following words into syllables, and mark the accented syllable. Then mark each *c* and *ch:*

city	electric	comfortable	classes
coach	car	pencil	recite
school	twice	across	comes
Chicago	candle	benches	costs

Watch for the words in your reading lessons that are starred. First, try to guess what the word means. Then find it in the dictionary, and see if you guessed right.

The Sunshine Basket [S]

Did you ever make a "sunshine basket"? If not, perhaps you would like to sometime. This story will suggest what to put into one, and what to do with it when it is made.

How does this story prove that "it is more blessed to give than to receive"?

Jennie Grant lay on a cot near the window. She had been lying in that same place for many weeks. One of her legs was shorter than the other, and the doctor had fastened a heavy weight to it in order to make it grow. But she must lie still all the time.

Every morning before her father went to his work, he moved her cot close to the window so she could look out. There was not much to see, for the buildings were high. But she loved to watch the swallows against the sky, and there was a flock of doves that often alighted on the roof across the way. Still she became very tired with nothing to do and no one to play with.

One day, Mrs. Brightly came to see if she could help her. On the way home she was busy thinking about Jennie. Suddenly she said to herself, "I know what I'll do. There are my two little sisters who have plenty of money and hardly ever think of anyone but themselves, and there are some other little neighbors. We will have a little 'Sunshine Band,' and make a sunshine basket for Jennie. It will make her happy, and the children will enjoy doing something for some one who needs help. They will find that 'it is more blessed to give than to receive.'"

She wrote notes to the girls, asking them to come to her house Monday afternoon. Then she told them the plan. They decided to fill a pretty basket to stand by Jennie's bed, and take it to her on her birthday. Everything was to be put in packages, so her pleasure would last a long time, and everything was to be something for Jennie to do. Week after week they met and worked on the articles for the basket. They enjoyed it so much that they could hardly wait for Jennie's birthday to come.

In the basket was a little jointed doll, and in the box with her were bits of bright silk and muslin, a little needlebook, thread, needles, and scissors, so that Jennie could make doll's clothes. In another package were a box of paints and a book of pictures to color. They knew that Jennie would like to do something for some one else, so they made some little books of cambric,* and all the girls brought pictures for Jennie to cut out and paste in the books. When the books were made, they were to be sent to the hospital for sick children. One girl brought some sheets of paper dolls for her to cut out. Another brought a puzzle to be put together. They wrote a note to go with each package.

One bright morning when Jennie opened her eyes, she remembered it was her birthday. The first thing she saw was a big basket beside her bed, and on top a label that said, "Reach in and take out a package when you don't know what else to do. From 'The Sunshiners.'"

Just then Jennie's mother came in with her breakfast.

"Oh, mother!" exclaimed Jennie, "how can I wait till after breakfast before I reach in my hand? What do you suppose is in the basket?"

I am afraid Jennie did not eat much breakfast, but she waited until mother had washed her face and brushed her hair, and father had moved her cot to the window.

At last the time came when she had "nothing to do." Then she put her hand under the cover of the basket and felt of the bundles. She took out the first one she felt; and which do you suppose it was? It was the little box that held the doll. On the top it said, "I am little orphan Arabella,* and I am looking for a mamma to dress me."

Jennie had a delightful time cutting out patterns and making clothes for little orphan Arabella. She did not open any more of her bundles for a day or two, for she wanted to make them last. And they did last for several weeks.

The girls enjoyed their giving so much that they decided to be "Sunshiners" all the year round, and they asked Jennie to be a member of the society. She could think of nice things to do quicker than any of them. Months later, when the weight was taken off her foot and she was able to walk, she was always finding some one to help and make happy, as every true "Sunshiner" should.

—*Adapted.*

Duty and Inclination [O]

1. "Stay at home," said Inclination,*
   "Let the errand wait."
   "*Go at once!*" said Duty sternly,
   "Or you'll be too late."

2. "But it *rains*," whined Inclination,
   "And the wind is keen."*
   "*Never mind all that,*" said Duty,
   "Go, and brave it, Jean."

3. Jean stepped out into the garden,
    Looked up at the sky;
   Clouded, shrouded,* dreary, sunless,
    Rain unceasingly.*

4. "Stay," again moaned Inclination,
    But it was in vain;
   Forth went Jean, with no more waiting,
    Out into the rain.

5. You will smile if now I tell you
    That this quiet strife,
   Duty conquering Inclination,
    Strengthened all her life.

—Author Unknown.

Comprehension Test

Did Inclination ever talk to you? What did she say? What did Duty say? Which voice did Jean listen to? What effect did this have upon her future life?

Longfellow's Armchair (O)

It was in Cambridge,* Massachusetts,* on a day in February* over fifty years ago. Groups of happy school children were eagerly discussing some subject in which they were greatly interested.

"Mr. Longfellow's birthday is the twenty-seventh of this month. He will then be seventy-two years old. Let's get him a present. I believe he will like it," said one of the boys.

"We couldn't ever get anything *good* enough for

such a great poet as Mr. Longfellow, could we?" said another boy, doubtfully.

"Why, *of course* we could! If *we* gave it to him, he'd like it anyway, because he likes *children*," said another. "Haven't you ever read his poem, 'The Children'?"

"He wrote another poem about children, too. It is called 'The Children's Hour.' No one could read *that* without knowing he liked children," said another.

"Well, if that point is settled," said one of the older boys, "let's decide what the present shall be. Why wouldn't a nice easy chair be all right?"

"That's just the *thing!* He would appreciate *that*, I know," said all the children heartily.

"I'll tell you what *I* think," said the teacher whose advice the children had asked. "You know the great chestnut tree near the blacksmith's shop has fallen down. Mr. Longfellow thought much of that old tree. You could get the cabinetmaker* to make a chair of some of that wood."

Every one was pleased with that idea, and so the chair was made. And a fine chair it was, too.

At last the eventful day came, and the chair

was placed in Mr. Longfellow's study. You can imagine how surprised and how happy he was when, after breakfast, he went to his study and found this beautiful gift from the children. He thanked the children by writing them a poem, which he named "From My Armchair."

In the poem he called the chair a throne,* and he said it made him feel like a king. It was so long before this that he had written the poem about this chestnut tree where "the village blacksmith" worked, that he said the chair seemed like a "whisper of the past," and made him feel young again. He said that their love had given life to the dead wood, so that its branches had blossomed again in song.

Only three years after this the gentle poet died. This was a cause of general mourning, for he was beloved by all. Even those who never saw him were sad, because they had learned to love him by reading his beautiful poems. Abraham Lincoln once heard a poem of Longfellow's that filled his eyes with tears. At first he could not speak. Then he said, "It is a wonderful gift to be able to stir men like that."

Comprehension Test. Where the blanks are, put a word or words that will make the sentence true.
1. Mr. Longfellow lived in the State of ———.
2. His birthday comes on ———.
3. Some of the poems he wrote are ———, ———, ———.
4. I like his poem ——— best.
5. The "song" that "blossomed" out of the branches of the dead chestnut tree is named ———.
6. What are the words carved on the chair? From what poem are they taken?

From My Armchair ⁽²⁵⁸⁾

1. Am I a king, that I should call my own
   This splendid ebon* throne?
   Or by what reason, or what right divine,*
   Can I proclaim it mine?

2. Only, perhaps, by right divine of song
   It may to me belong;
   Only because the spreading chestnut tree
   Of old was sung by me.

3. Well I remember it in all its prime,*
   When in the summer time,
   The affluent* foliage* of its branches made
   A cavern* of cool shade.

4. There by the blacksmith's forge beside the street
   Its blossom white and sweet
   Enticed* the bees, until it seemed alive,
   And murmured like a hive.

5. And when the winds of autumn, with a shout,
   Tossed its great arms about,
   The shining chestnuts, bursting from the sheath,
   Dropped to the ground beneath.

6. And now some fragments of its branches bare,
   Shaped as a stately chair,
   Hath by my hearthstone* found a home at last,
   And whisper of the past.

7. I see again, as one in vision sees,
   The blossoms and the bees,

And hear the children's voices shout and call,
And the brown chestnuts fall.

8. I see the smithy with its fire aglow,
I hear the bellows blow,
And the shrill hammers on the anvil beat
The iron white with heat!

9. And thus, dear children, have ye made for me
This day a jubilee,*
And to my more than threescore years and ten
Brought back my youth again.

10. Only your love and your remembrance could
Give life to this dead wood,
And make these branches, leafless now so long,
Blossom again in song.

—*Henry Wadsworth Longfellow.*

Comprehension and Appreciation Study
1. What does Longfellow call this armchair in stanza one?
2. Read the stanza that tells why he has a right to call the chair his.
3. Have you ever seen a "cavern of cool shade" made by a tree?
4. When did the chestnut tree murmur "like a hive"?
5. What were the tree's "great arms"?
6. How did the tree "whisper of the past"?
7. When is an iron "white with heat"?
8. Read the stanza that tells how old Longfellow was at this time.
9. What kind of "blossoms" did the "dead wood" of the tree now bear?
10. How long does it take you to find in the dictionary the nine starred words?

Saved From a Panther (S)

Did you know that some wild beasts will not attack a person who is singing? That is really a fact, as you will find by reading this true story. The story tells how God heard the prayer of two little girls, and protected them from a panther when they were walking home through the woods one evening in Pennsylvania. As you read the story silently, see if it makes you think of some promise in the Bible.

Practice reading paragraphs 4 to 10 orally. Try singing, instead of reading, the words of the song, as these children sang them.

---

1. Near the summit of a mountain in Pennsylvania* was a small place called Honeyville. It consisted of two log houses, two shanties, a rickety old barn, and a small shed, surrounded by a few acres of cleared land. In one of these houses lived a family of seven,—father, mother, three boys, and two girls. The mother and her two little girls, Nina and Dot, were Christians, and their voices were often lifted in praise to God as they sang from an old hymn book which they dearly loved.

2. One morning in the late autumn, the mother sent Nina and Dot on an errand to their sister's home three and one-half miles away. The first two miles took them through dense woods, while the rest of the way led past houses and through small clearings.* She told them to start on their return home in time to arrive before dark, as many wild beasts—bears, catamounts,* and sometimes even panthers*—were prowling around. These animals were hungry at this time of the year, for they were getting ready to

"hole up," or lie down in some cozy cave or hole for their long winter's nap.

3. The girls started off, merrily chasing each other along the way. They arrived at their sister's in good time, and had a jolly romp with the baby. After dinner, the sister was so busy and the children were so happy in their play that the time passed unheeded* until the clock struck four. Then the girls were hurriedly started for home, in the hope that they might arrive there before it became very dark. The older sister watched until they disappeared up the road, anxiously wishing some one were there to go with them.

4. The girls made good time until they entered the long stretch of woods.

"Oh, I know where there is such a large patch of wintergreen berries, right by the road!" said Nina. "Let's pick some for mamma." So they climbed over a few stones and logs, and, sure enough, the berries were plentiful. They picked and talked, sometimes playing hide and seek among the bushes.

5. When they started on again, the sun was sinking low in the west, and the trees were casting long, heavy shadows over the road. When about half the distance was covered, Dot began to feel tired and afraid. Nina tried to cheer her.

"Over one more long hill, and we shall be home," she said.

But now they could see the sun shining only on the tops of the trees on the hill, and in the woods it was already twilight.

6. They had often played "trying to scare each other" by one saying, "Oh, I see a bear or a wolf up the road!" and pretending to be afraid.

So Dot said, "Let's scare each other. You try to scare me."

Here are some of pussy's wild relatives. Which is the catamount? the panther? Why are they fierce? Will they ever be different? Do you know any other wild relatives of the cat?

"All right," Nina said. Then pointing up the road, she said, "Oh, look up the road by that black stump; I see a—"

She did not finish; for suddenly from almost the very spot where she had pointed, a large panther stepped out of the bushes. He turned his head first one way and then another. Then, as if seeing the girls for the first time, he crouched down, and, crawling, sneaking along, like a cat after a bird, he moved toward them. The girls stopped and looked at each other. Then Dot began to cry.

"O Nina! let's run!" she said, in a half-smothered whisper.

These kittens do not look as if they were a close relative of the panther, do they? But did you ever watch a cat sneak along after a bird, or a mouse, or other small animal? It surely *acts* very much like its savage relatives.

But Nina thought of the long, dark, lonely road behind, and knew that running was useless. Then she thought of what she had heard her father say about showing fear.

"No, let's pass it," she said as she seized her little sister's hand, "God will help us." And she started up the road toward the panther.

7. When the children moved, the panther stopped, straightened himself up, then crouching* again, he moved slowly, uneasily, toward them. When they had nearly reached him, and Nina, who was nearer,

saw his body almost rising for the spring, there flashed through her mind the memory of hearing it said that a wild beast would not attack anyone who was singing. What should she sing? In vain she tried to recall some song. Her mind seemed a blank. In despair she looked up, and breathed a little prayer for help. Then she caught a glimpse of the last rays of the setting sun touching the tops of the trees on the hill, and she began to sing:

> "There is sunlight on the hilltop,
> There is sunlight on the sea."

Her sister joined in. At first their voices were faint and trembling, but by the time the children were opposite the panther, the words of the song rang out sweet and clear on the evening air.

8. The panther stopped, and straightened himself to his full height. His tail, which had been lashing and switching, became quiet, as he seemed to listen. The girls passed on, hand in hand, never looking behind them.

> "Oh, the sunlight! beautiful sunlight!
> Oh, the sunlight in the heart!"

9. How sweet the words sounded as they echoed and reëchoed* through the woods. As the children neared the top of the hill, the rumbling of a wagon fell upon their ears, so they knew that help was near. But still they sang. When they had reached the top, there was the wagon. Then for the first time they turned and looked back just in time to catch a last

glimpse of the panther as he disappeared into the woods.

10. The mother had looked often and anxiously down the road, and each time was disappointed in not seeing the children coming. Finally she could wait no longer, and started to meet them. When about halfway there, she heard the music:

> "Oh, the sunlight! beautiful sunlight!
> Oh, the sunlight in the heart!
> Jesus' smile can banish sadness;
> It is sunlight in the heart."

11. At first, a happy smile of relief passed over her face; but it faded as she listened. There was such an unearthly sweetness in the song, so strong and clear, that it seemed like the music of angels instead of her own little girls. The song stopped, and the children appeared over the hill. She saw their white faces, and hurried toward them. When they saw her, how their little feet flew! But it was some time before they could tell her what had happened.

What a joyful season of worship they had that night! and what a meaning that dear old hymn has had to them ever since!

A few days later, a party of hunters killed the panther that had given the children such a fright. But the memory of that thrilling experience will never fade from the mind of the writer, who was one of the children.

—*Nina Case Baierle (adapted)*.

DICTIONARY TIME DRILL

The three sets of words following are starred words taken from reading lessons you have had. See how many words in Set 1 you can find in the dictionary in two minutes.

How many in Set 2 can you find in two minutes?

How many in Set 3 can you find in two minutes?

1	2	3
cabinetmaker	brawny	sexton
February	sinewy	anvil
throne	chaff	catamount
smithy	forge	repose
bellows	panther	Pennsylvania

Honesty Is the Best Policy (S)

Test your silent reading rate on each part of this story.

After reading it silently, try to decide on a good name for each of the four parts. Write these titles down, and in class compare them with the topics your classmates have written. Decide which ones you think are best.

Practice reading Part I as it is phrased.

I. _____ (311 words)

When John Martin was about thirteen years old,
he went to Philadelphia to learn a trade.
He entered as an apprentice with his brother,
who was a coach maker
in the northern part of the city.
One time, he was sent to a drug store
for a half gallon of oil.
He had often been sent on a similar errand,
and had always paid twenty-five cents for the oil.

But it happened that oil had fallen,
and the price was now only twenty cents.
John did not know of this change in price.
    He had taken with him a one-dollar bill
to pay for the oil.
He received in change—
not, as he expected, three quarters of a dollar,
but four Spanish pieces worth twenty cents each.
John was ignorant of their value,
but supposed they were quarters of a dollar.
He thought the druggist by *mistake*
had given him four instead of three.
    He had been taught when a child to be honest.
He knew that he ought to do to others
as he would have others do to him.
He knew that it was as dishonest
to take advantage of another's mistake
as to cheat in any other way.
His first thought, therefore,
was to return one of the coins to the man.
But at the same moment
another thought came to him,—
to give three to his brother, as the right change,
and keep the fourth for himself.
    He closed his hand upon the money,
picked up his jug of oil, and left the store.
On the doorstep he stopped and looked at his money.
There were certainly four pieces,
and he should have but three.
Conscience began to reprove him,
but selfishness got the mastery.

Fearing that the druggist
would discover his mistake and call him back,
John hurried homeward,
thinking of his good fortune.

II. ———————————— (415) words)

The jug in which he carried the oil had no handle, and John had to carry it by a string tied around its neck. This so cut his fingers that, after changing it from one hand to the other several times, he was compelled to stop at the first street corner and rest.

He put down the oil, and seated himself upon a step. He took out the coins to make sure that there was one too many. But, although he rejoiced at his good fortune, John's heart was not at ease. He knew he should have returned one of the pieces to the storekeeper. He knew that in keeping it he was acting dishonestly. He felt that he ought still to turn back and correct his mistake.

But John soon framed a number of good reasons why the fourth piece of money was properly and lawfully his. The druggist ought not to have made the mistake, he said to himself. He ought to lose by his carelessness. To the storekeeper a quarter of a dollar was but a trifle, and would never be missed, while to him it was a large amount. Besides, it was now too late to return. If he did, he would probably be blamed for not returning at first. Then, too, he would be losing too much time, and displease his brother. John entirely convinced himself that he would be wronging his brother of valuable time by returning to correct so trifling a mistake. He proceeded on his way.

But by the time he reached a second corner, his conscience, as well as his jug, began to be very heavy again. He again sat down to rest. He tried to settle the dispute between his conscience and his own evil desires. Again he went on his way, determined to keep the money, but by no means satisfied that he was doing right.

The next corner brought John a third time to a stand. Rest relieved the smartings of his hands, but the cuttings of his conscience were not so easily removed. He thought some minutes. Conscience now spoke louder than ever. But he was ashamed to go back.

He wished he had obeyed his first honest impulse. He felt very unhappy. But he must not delay. He had already been a great while about his errand. He took up his jug. He was undecided whether to go home or to return. He stood one moment, and determined—*to go back!*

III. _____ (311 words)

It was a hard task to trudge back three long squares with a heavy jug without a handle, and more than once he almost determined to give up his honest resolution. But finally, he reached the store and set down his load.

"You have given me too much change," said he, showing the four coins to the storekeeper. "You have given me four quarters of a dollar instead of three."

"And how far had you gone before you discovered the mistake?" asked the storekeeper.

This was a hard question, for John had made the discovery before he left the store. He now imagined that the druggist knew the whole story. But such was not the case. He only knew that, from the time John had left he must have gone some distance, and he wondered how far. Supposing from his silence that he did not understand him, he repeated the question in another way.

"I say, how far, my boy, have you been since you were here?"

"To Callow-hill Street, sir," said John.

"You think there is a quarter too much, do you? Well, you may have that for your honesty."

John thanked him, and put the money into his pocket, without suspecting the joke. He took his burden with feelings far different from those that had filled his bosom half an hour before, and was about to leave the store.

"Stop, my man," said the druggist, "I will not deceive you. You have your right change. The oil is twenty cents, and those four pieces are not quarters of a dollar. They are twenty-cent pieces."

"Here is a quarter," continued the kind storekeeper, taking one from his drawer, "which I will give you. You can notice the difference between them as you go home, and let me advise you always to deal as honestly as you have to-day."

IV. _____ (195 words)

Who can imagine the feelings of the boy when he saw that, if he had carried out his sinful intention, he must have been discovered? He would have handed his brother only three of the Spanish pieces. His brother would, of course, have asked for the rest, and John would have been driven to add falsehood to crime by saying that was all the druggist gave him. That would have stamped his character with untruthfulness as well as dishonesty, and probably he would have been sent to his father in disgrace. As it was, he picked up his jug, and with a light heart and rapid step hastened up the street.

He was so thankful at the happy result that he set out on a run, and did not feel the string cut his fingers until he reached the third corner, where he had made up his mind to return to the store. During thirty-five years that John Martin lived after this event, he never forgot the lesson it taught him, and throughout his life, in private business and in public office, he ever acted under the firm belief that "honesty is the best policy."*

Silent Reading Test

This lesson will be your tenth silent reading test in rate and comprehension.

The test is in your "Reading Tests and Scores" pad.

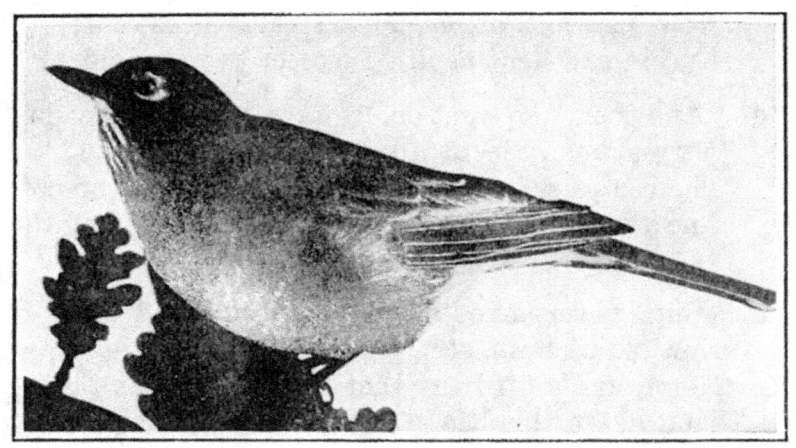

A Robin's Health Lecture [303]

In these verses a robin tells three things that are good for our health. Find them, and find *how* they help us.

1. I heard a bird lecture one morning, this spring,
   And 'twas this that he said almost the first thing:
   "I've been off for a while where the winters are warm,
   But now I've come back, and am preaching reform.*

2. "I have heard other lecturers* say I would find
   It a very hard thing to enlighten the mind;
   But, nevertheless, my success I shall try,
   All over the country, wherever I fly.

3. "Do open your windows, and let in the air,
   I know you'll feel better and look far more fair—

Now, just look at *me*, why, *I never* take cold;
And in excellent health I expect to grow old.

4. "And then," he went on, "I have known in my day
   A great many birds all reared the same way;
   Their cradles were rocked to and fro by the breeze,
   And the roofs of their houses were leaves of the trees.

5. "But I never have known a birdling* to droop,
   Nor, old as I am, seen a case of the croup—
   Nor heard a bird say that so sore was his throat
   That he, for his life, could not raise the eighth note.

6. "And one with dyspepsia,* too gloomy to sing,
   That we should consider a *terrible* thing;
   Consumption has never unmated a pair"—
   Here the bird commenced warbling an ode* to fresh air.

   * * * * *

7. "We lave* in the brook, and we drink nothing strong;
   If I'd time I would sing you a 'cold-water song,'
   And when earth's great lamp has gone out in the west,
   You'll find our lays* hushed, and our bodies at rest.

8. "We birds are so happy! But I must not stay,
   For sev'ral appointments await me to-day,"
   Then he stepped back and forth on the limb of a tree,
   And flew out of sight, wishing long life to me.

—*Author Unknown.*

The Horse That Carried Double (S)

Did you ever see a gray horse with a green tail? This story tells about a horse like that. After reading it silently, practice paragraphs 3, 5, 9, and 11 orally. Now for the story.

---

1. On a certain mild afternoon in the early spring, you might have seen two little travelers on the Fancy Hill Road; and if you belong to our town, you would have known them at once for Susie and her little brother Daniel. In fact, several persons did recognize them, and stopped to ask what they were doing by themselves so far from home.

"We are going to meet papa," was the answer they made in proud tones. "Mamma lets us. He's coming from the bridge in the sulky,* and we'll ride back with him."

2. And on they went in the sweet afternoon sunshine, hunting in fence corners for dandelions, counting the soldier blackbirds with their red shoulder badges, and pretending to hear lions roaring in the woods.

Somehow, papa was longer coming than they had expected. But then, children always do expect things to happen at once. It was not early when they left their own doorstep. It seemed to be getting late very, very fast. Still no sulky with a long-tailed bay* horse hitched to it came in sight.

3. Daniel's short steps began to lag now. He really had gone a long way for such a little boy.

"I don't believe papa is ever tomin'," he whimpered.

"Oh yes! he is," said the brave little sister. "Mamma said so. Maybe he's just round that bend in the road."

4. She coaxed Daniel to the bend, but papa was not there. Although they could see a long way down the dim road, there was neither man nor horse on it.

It was quite dusk* now, and Susie was afraid to go farther down that dark, empty road. They sat down on the roots of a friendly old oak tree, and waited. Oh, how late and lonely it was! And a little screech owl above them screamed so mournfully that it made the cold chills run down their tired little backs.

5. "Come, brother; we must turn back," said Susie, getting up bravely. "Papa isn't coming, after all. Something has kept him. We must go home."

But now Daniel made a more dismal noise than the owl.

"I tan't walk so far! I'm tired! My legs hurt!" sobbed the baby.

For one bad quarter of a minute Susie thought she was going to break down and cry too, it was so gloomy. But the responsibility for the smaller and weaker one kept her up. The sister love in her heart made her strong.

"Oh, Dannie!" she cried, with a womanly pretense* of joy, "I'll get you a *horse* to ride, and then you won't get tired."

6. Fortunately some wood hauler had dropped by the roadside a small, green tree, only a few feet long, with a bunch of leaves at the end. Daniel was persuaded to bestride this "horsey." They named it Rob Roy, after the long-tailed bay. Then Susie set herself to brighten the way with many a treasured bedtime story.

When the story came slowly, little Daniel's legs began to ache. But when it rose again on the wings of tired Susie's memory, the ground was covered without the child's knowing it. So they went along the road, which was now very dark.

7. Do you wonder what had become of papa? Why, my dears, there are *two* roads from the bridge, and papa had taken the *other* one. He stopped on the way too, and was late getting home, and you may well believe he found mamma in a terrible fright about the children.

8. Rob Roy—the real, live Rob Roy—had never been made to spin over that Fancy Hill Road so quickly as he spun now. No doubt he knew that something was wrong when there were no children at the gate to rub his nose and give him an apple.

The two little tramps were halfway home when papa met them. Glad? I don't know who was the more happy, papa or the children. Oh yes! I do, too; for their *little* hearts could not have held the thankfulness that filled papa's *big* heart.

9. And *now Susie* broke down and cried!

"How funny!" said Daniel, staring at her. "I cwied when we were lost, and Susie cwies when we are found."

10. But papa seemed to think the tears were all right, and he kissed each one as it fell. He called Susie the bravest little woman in town. For Daniel had insisted on taking the gray horse with the green tail into the sulky, and papa was hearing from him the wonderful tales that Susie had fed this new horse's rider. He saw right down into the brave little heart, and understood all about it.

11. "Were you very tired, little daughter?" he asked tenderly.

"No, papa," she said, smiling away her tears. "The stories kept me from thinking about it. Only it was so hard to *remember* them all."

"Ah!" said papa, with another kiss, "the gray horse with the green tail carried double, then. Most unselfish deeds do."

If you know what he meant, it is a good deal more than Daniel did. But Susie was smiling in a wise way.

—*Elizabeth Preston Allan (adapted).*

Comprehension Test

1. How was it that this horse "carried double"?
2. What was the gray horse? What was its green tail?
3. Why are the blackbirds called "soldier blackbirds"? Have you ever seen any birds like these?
4. Tell all the ways that Susie managed to keep her baby brother encouraged.
5. Do you think *you* could have been as brave and thoughtful as Susie was?
6. What different things made the road seem lonely and dismal?
7. Who was more glad when papa found the children, papa or the children? Why?

The Lilac's Dinner [116]

1. The sun shone warm, and the Lilac said,
    "I must hurry and get my table spread,
    For if I am slow, and dinner late,
    My friends, the Bees, will have to wait."

2. So delicate lavender glass she brought
    And the daintiest china ever bought,
    Purple tinted, and all complete;
    And she filled each cup with honey sweet.

3. "Dinner is ready!" the Spring Wind cried;
    And from hive and hiding far and wide,
    While the Lilac laughed to see them come,
    The little gray-jacketed Bees came; "Hum-m!"

4. They sipped the sirup from every cell,
    They nibbled at taffy and caramel;*
    Then, without being asked, they all buzzed, "We
    Will be very happy to stay to tea."

—*Clara Doty Bates.*

Appreciation Study

1. What is the "table" the Lilac spreads?
2. What is the "lavender glass"? the "purple-tinted china"?
3. Who were the Lilac's guests?
4. What are the Lilac's "taffy" and "caramel"?

DICTIONARY EXERCISE

Learn the following sounds and their markings:

ḡ, as in ḡet
ġ (=j), as in ġem
ṉ (=ng), as in iṉk

ṣ (=z), as in hiṣ
th, as in that
th, as in thin

Divide the following words into syllables, mark the accent, and then mark each *g*, *n*, *s*, and *th*.

desires	thimble	friends	without
was	them	weather	linger
truth	gentle	generous	gray
truths	finger	glass	displease
throw	nose	with	these

How Frogs Grow (S)

Did you ever gather the eggs of frogs or toads and watch them grow? If not, you will surely want to after you read this story.

Perhaps you already know that the funny little polliwogs in our ponds and ditches turn into frogs. It is quite interesting to notice the changes that take place before polliwogs can pass from the life of a water animal to that of a real frog that can live on the land.

Does this picture show how *frogs* grow or how *toads* grow? How do you know?

Let us begin with the eggs. These can be found in the water of a quiet pond or marsh in March. They are little black specks not larger than a shot, scattered through a lump of clear jelly. This mass is called "frog spawn." It is generally fastened to sticks and grass in the water near the shore. The jelly holds the eggs together so that they may not drift away. It also provides food for the young animals when first hatched. If you should gather some of this frog spawn in the spring, and put it into a vessel of water with a few water plants, you would have good entertainment for a month or two.

By the tenth day, the round black specks begin to lengthen, and soon to wriggle about. Gradually, the jelly mass disappears, and in about two weeks the young polliwogs, with big black heads, dart hither and thither, rapidly wagging their long flat tails as they swim through the water—a sight with which country children are usually familiar.

When the polliwogs grow a little larger, you can see feathery bunches hanging at the sides of the head. These are outside gills. After a time the wide mouth appears, and the polliwog tries to nibble at the water plants around it. Little by little these outside gills shrink away. The polliwog then breathes by taking water in at the mouth, and allowing it to run out through slits in the neck. In this way the water passes over *inside* gills, the same as in fishes. Indeed, it looks very much like a tiny fish, and not at all like a frog.

Eyes and nostrils* next begin to be seen. Soon two little lumps come on the sides, which will grow some day into hind legs. The front legs do not show until later. When they come, the polliwog is well supplied with limbs, having four legs and a broad swimming tail. The odd creature will now be found spending much time near the surface, with its mouth out of water, for it is trying another plan for breathing.

While these changes have been taking place on the *outside* of the animal, still more important changes have been going on within its body. Lungs have been growing. As the polliwog gets used to breathing with the new lungs, the blood gradually changes its course and rushes to them to be purified, instead of going to the gills as before. In about two months after the eggs are laid, the inside gills are no longer needed, and they shrink away. At first the polliwog had a true fish's heart, with only two rooms, but now a third room grows; so it has a three-room heart.

This active little creature now deserves the name of frog. It swims with its new legs, and takes such long leaps that you must keep close watch, or it will jump out of your pond or vessel, and you can no longer watch it grow. As the tail is no longer needed, little by little, like the gills, it is taken into the body until there is no trace of it left. The young frog really feeds on its tail until the tail is gone.

The frog is now ready to leap boldly on shore, although most of its time is passed in the water, perched on some stick or stone. When cold weather comes, it drops to the bottom of the pond, and spends the winter in sleep.

If you had a skeleton of a frog, you would notice how much longer the hind legs are than the front ones. This helps the frog to leap. The long toes are usually joined with a web to assist in swimming.

The frog has no ribs, so it cannot breathe as we do. Our ribs are raised each time we breathe, and the air rushes in through the nose and mouth to fill the empty space made in our chests. But as the frog has no ribs by which to enlarge its chest, it simply closes its lips, and swallows the air that is in its mouth. A frog has no other way of breathing, and if its mouth is fastened open it will smother.

A frog has teeth in the lower jaw, a smooth skin, and usually webbed toes. It has a naked air sac of skin under its chin. When a frog sings, this air sac swells out like a balloon. It is his bagpipe,* with which he fills the night with music that some one has called "the sweetest sound in nature."

Tree frogs do not differ much from other frogs, except that their toes end in suckers, so that they can easily climb the tree upon which they live. Most tree frogs are green or brown, and look something like leaves or branches of the trees. They are very small, not more than an inch and a half long.

Comprehension Test. Complete these sentences:

1. A cluster of frog's eggs is called ———. These are laid in the month of ———.
2. The purposes of the jelly part are ——— and ———.
3. The outside changes that take place from the time the eggs are laid till the frog is full grown are: 1. ———, 2. ———, 3. ———, 4. ———, 5. ———, 6. ———, 7. ———, 8. ———, and 9. ———.
4. It is about ——— months from the time the eggs are laid until the frog is full grown.
5. A frog breathes by ——— the air.
6. A frog has teeth in its ——— jaw.
7. A frog has ——— skin, and usually ——— toes.
8. The toes of a tree frog end in ———.
9. A frog has ——— under his chin, which swells out when he sings.
10. A frog spends the winter in ———.

Cradles (130)

1. Oh, the many cradles
    Swinging in the breeze,
 Where are warmly sleeping
    The babies of the trees!
 Tiny little leaflets
    Wrapped in softest down,
 Furry pussy willows,
    Alder* tassels brown,

2. Waiting till the sunbeams
    Kiss them in their sleep,

Alder Tassels

And the robin calls them
  From their beds to peep.
Then we soon shall see them
  Dancing in the air,
And we'll find their cradles
  Scattered everywhere.

3. Oh, the many cradles
    Underneath the ground,
  Where the flower babies
    Sleep so sweet and sound!
  Yellow dandelions,
    Daisies tall and fair,
  Above the soft green grasses,
    All are waiting there;—

4. Waiting for the tapping
    Of the warm spring rain,
  Bidding them awaken
    And come forth again.
  Then they'll gayly hasten
    From their beds to spring;
  And to bid them welcome,
    Merrily we'll sing.
        —*Author Unknown.*

Pussy Willows

Appreciation Study

1. How many kinds of cradles does this poem tell about?
2. What are "the babies of the trees"? Find some of them and bring them to school.
3. Do willow trees and alder trees grow where you live? When are their cradles "scattered everywhere"?
4. What calls forth the underground babies? What are the underground babies?

Always Tell the Truth ^(o)

This story shows the truth of Proverbs 28:13. Find out how, by reading first the verse and then this story.

---

1. A boy went to live with a man who was called a hard master. He never kept his boys. They ran away or said that they meant to quit. So half his time he was without, or in search of, a boy. The work was not very hard—opening and sweeping the shop, chopping wood, going errands, and helping generally.

2. At last John Fisher went to live with him.

"John is a good boy," said his mother.

"I should like to see a boy nowadays that has a spark of goodness in him," growled the new master.

It is always bad to begin with a man who has no confidence* in you; because, though you do your best, you will have little credit for it. However, John thought he would *try*. The *wages* were good, and his mother *wanted* him to go.

3. John had been there but three days, when, in sawing a knotty stick of wood, he broke the saw. He was a little frightened. He knew he had been careful, and he knew he was a good sawyer* too, for a boy of his age. Nevertheless, the saw had broken in his hands.

"Mr. Jones will thrash you for it," said another boy, who was in the woodshed with him.

"Why, of course I didn't *mean* it, and *accidents* will happen to the *best* of folks," said John, looking with a very sorrowful air at the broken saw.

4. "That will make no difference to Mr. Jones," said the other boy. "I never saw anyone like him. William might have stayed, only he jumped into a hen's nest and broke her eggs. He dared not tell of it. But Mr. Jones kept suspecting and suspecting, and laid everything that was out of the way to William, whether he was to blame or not, till William could not stand it, and *would* not."

"Did William *tell* Mr. Jones about the eggs?" asked John.

"No," said the boy, "he was afraid. Mr. Jones has such a temper."

"I think he would have better owned up at once," said John.

"You'll find it easier to preach than to practice," said the boy. "*I'd* run away before *I'd* tell him." And he soon went away, leaving poor John alone with the broken saw.

5. The boy did not feel very comfortable or happy. He shut up the woodhouse, walked out into the garden, and went up to his little room under the eaves. He wished he could tell *Mrs*. Jones, but she wasn't sociable.

6. When Mr. Jones came into the house late that night, John heard him. He got up, crept downstairs, and met Mr. Jones in the kitchen.

"Sir," said John, "I broke your saw, and I thought I would come and tell you before you saw it in the morning."

"Why did you *get up* to tell me?" asked Mr. Jones. "I should think *morning* would be time enough to tell of your carelessness."

"Because," said John, "I was afraid if I put it off, I might be tempted to lie about it. I am very sorry I broke it, but I tried to be careful."

Mr. Jones looked at the boy from head to foot. Then, he placed his hand gently and trustingly on his shoulder.

"Never mind the broken saw, John," he said heartily. "I see I can trust you. Go to bed, boy. Never fear. I'm glad the saw broke. It has shown me that you have an honest heart. Go to bed."

7. Mr. Jones was fairly won. Never were better friends than John and he after that. John thinks justice* had not been done Mr. Jones. He thinks that if the boys had treated him honestly and "aboveboard," he would have been a good man to deal with. He thinks it was *their conduct* that made him suspicious. I do not know how it is. I only know that John Fisher finds Mr. Jones a kind master and a faithful friend.

—*Adapted.*

Thought Questions

1. What do you think of the advice of John's friend? Was it honest? Was it truthful?

2. What is meant by being "aboveboard"?

3. Where is a verse in the Bible that says, "When a man's ways please the Lord, He maketh even his enemies to be at peace with him"? How was this fulfilled in John's case?

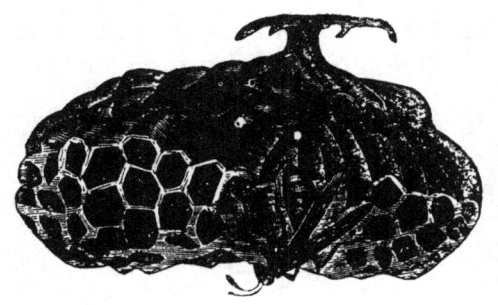

Nature's Teacher [144]

1. Who taught the spider how to make
      Her silken web so light?
   Who gave her such a cunning way
      To take her airy flight?

2. Who told the timid little bird
      To play that she was lame,
   And try to lead me far away
      When near her young I came?

3. Who taught a little mother wasp
      To make her paper nest,
   And work away the summer hours
      Without a thought of rest?

4. How does a little honeybee
      Know how to make her cell,
   And fill it with such dainty food
      To feed her babies well?

5. It was their Maker gave to them
      Such wondrous, skillful ways;

He gave them all some work to do
Through all the summer days.

6. He gives to *us*, my children dear,
More skill of mind and heart;
Then *surely* we should try *our best*
To do as well our part.

—*Florence Bass, in "Stories of Animal Life."*

Appreciation Study

1. Have you ever seen a spider "take her airy flight"? How did she do it?
2. Did you ever see a bird "play that she was lame"? What bird does this way? Why?
3. Have you ever seen a wasp's nest? What is the material in it like?
4. What is the shape of the honeybee's cell?
5. How did God make children different from these creatures?

Only a Few Drops (O)

1. The most interesting event of our family history during my tenth year, was the purchase of a cow. My father had a patch of land about a mile from our house, and he thought that the best use he could turn it to would be to pasture a cow.

2. "And who is going to drive the cow to the pasture, father?" I asked, as he put her into the yard on the first evening after her arrival.

"You, Robert," he replied; and his answer gave me no little sense of my importance. Here I was with a charge* laid upon me,—an important duty which I was to do every day, and which for some time I *did* discharge with pleasure.

3. The weather was pleasant, and the cow was a novelty;* and, above all, my friend, Harry Frazer, had *his* cow to drive half a mile in the same direction. There was one difference between his duties as cow driver and my own, however, that annoyed me.

Harry drove out *his* cow only when the weather was *pleasant*, while *I* had to go in *all* weathers, wet or dry. In fact, there was no one else at *my* home to perform this duty, whereas Harry's father had a stout farm boy in his service, who did such drudgery as *I* had to do *myself*.

4. I did not like the difference between my friend's cow driving and my own. He was older than I, and stronger, too. I thought it a hardship, therefore, that I should have to drive *my* cow when Harry did not drive *his*. Nor did his remarks on the subject tend to lessen my discontent.

"Mother says that she will not have me go out in such weather as this. I am sure if *I* were *you* I *would not go. My* father always sends *the boy*."

For the first time in my life, I began to pity myself, and to think myself hardly used. And the more I thought of it, the harder it seemed.

5. One day, early in October, I awoke at the usual time, and heard the cold rain pattering against the windows. My first thought, I am sorry to say, was a grumbling thought. Two miles in the rain there and back! The thought was quite intolerable.* "I

will not go to pasture to-day for *anyone*," I thought; and I resolved to go to sleep again. But my ill humor had fairly waked me up; and, do what I would, I could not even doze.

6. Another minute and I heard my father's foot on the stairs. He was going out as usual to milk the cow, expecting me to be ready by his return. My heart told me I was wrong. *He* was doing *his* work; and should not *I* do *mine?* But I had resolved to think myself badly used; so to all the whisperings of my better self, I only answered, "To go out *two miles* in weather like *this!* No, *indeed!* It is too much to *expect* of anyone." Presently* I heard him calling me.

7. "Robert, why are you not up? You should have been ready this half hour."

Still I made no answer. Then I heard him coming upstairs. The door opened, and he entered; but I only breathed heavily. He took me by the arm and shook me, and then I saw there was no help for it; I *had* to open my eyes.

8. I went downstairs, still grumbling to myself that it was really too bad. I believe I had a very surly* air when I entered the kitchen, where my mother was waiting to hasten my departure.

"Come, Robert," she said, "put on your shoes, and let us see how fast you can trot."

"*Nobody* can trot fast in such a rain as *this*," I replied, pettishly,* muttering half to myself and half aloud. "I think it is a *shame*. *Harry's* mother would not let *him* go out on such a morning; he can stay at home when he likes." And with that I began slowly to lace my stout shoes, which never before seemed so heavy.

9. Nothing suited me. I dawdled as much as I could over my preparations, and was lingering at the door when my father entered the kitchen. I thought that he had left the house; but there he was, looking as if he read all my ill humor in my face and the turn of my shoulders.

"Are you ill this morning?" he asked.

"No," I replied, "I am not *ill;* but it *rains,* and I *do* think it is hard I should have to go out in such weather as *this.* None of the *other* boys about the place will be out. I am sure that *Harry Frazer's* mother would never let *him* leave home on such a day, and I don't know why *I* should have to go."

10. I said this as if I pitied myself very much; and I expected that he would say, "Well, wait a little, and perhaps it will clear up;" or, "You need not go to-day, the cow will do well enough in the shed for once." I had often known Harry's parents to yield in this way to *his* complaints, and had wished a hundred times that I were as well off as he, and could as readily be excused from disagreeable duties.

11. But, happily for me, my father was a wise and faithful parent, and to my words uttered so piteously, "I don't know why *I* should go," he replied, "But *I do,* my boy."

I looked up inquiringly.

"You will go," he continued, "because it is your *duty,* and because your *father bids* you."

I did not risk a reply, but cast a gloomy look out of doors as I prepared to obey in silence.

"See, now," said my father, in his strong, cheerful tones, "it *is* a bad day, to be sure, but we cannot help it. Be a *man*, Robert, and meet the rain as you must learn to meet *all* your difficulties, when they are in the way of duty. Meet them *bravely* and *cheerfully*. The shower, after all, is only a *few drops* at a *time*. So now, step out *bravely* like a *man*."

12. His words gave me courage, and I felt in a moment what a coward my ill humor had been making of me. "Only a few drops at a time," I said to myself. And the shower seemed actually to dwindle down to a very gentle rain. "Yes," I thought, "I will go without delay, because it is my duty;" and these few brave words seemed to call back all my old willingness.

13. After all, what a noble thing it is for boy or man to do his duty! How it gives him courage to face difficulties! What a joy it gives him in overcoming them! I seized my stick, and walked out manfully into the rain. I whistled to Cuff, our faithful house dog, to go with me, and was soon marching through the mud with as light a heart as if the skies were blue and sunny.

14. A dozen times during my walk I said to my-

self, " 'Only a few drops at a time,'—what does that amount to when one is doing his duty?" And my walk seemed even shorter than usual. As I came home, I passed the Frazer house, and saw Harry lazily standing at the door.

15. "*What!* you've been out to pasture, I suppose," he said. "I'm only just up. You wouldn't catch *me* going out on such a day as this."

"It's nothing if you make up your *mind* to it, Harry,—'only a few drops at a time.' " And I ran on with the feeling that I had gained something by my wet walk.

16. It was my first experience in the art of facing difficulties with a brave heart, from a sense of duty. Nay, more; I had learned how to make light of trials by dealing only with those of the present moment. Often in after life, when troubles thickened about me, and I was tempted to despond,* I recalled my father's cheerful words, "Only a few drops at a time."

—*Adapted.*

Thought Questions

1. What is there in this story which shows that evil, thoughtless words may influence a friend to do wrong?
2. Which boy would you rather be like—Harry or Robert? Why?
3. Which boy's parents would you rather have? Why?
4. Which of these boys do you think made the best man?

The Hero Archer of the Swiss Mountains (S)

The Swiss Mountains are in Switzerland. Find Switzerland on the map before you begin to read. As you read, find out who the hero archer of the Swiss mountains was. What is an archer, and what did this archer do that won for him the name "hero"?

Paragraphs 7, 11, and 12 are good for oral practice.

---

1. Nestled among the mountains of central Europe is a beautiful country called Switzerland.* There are no large rivers in Switzerland, but there are many charming little lakes that reflect on their bosoms the bright blue sky above. Over these hills and by the side of these lakes many a Swiss herds his sheep and cattle, happy and free.

2. But the Swiss people were not always free and happy. A long time ago an army crossed the mountains and tried to rob the Swiss of all that they had.

3. Although these brave people fought long for their homes, they were defeated, and many of them were made slaves. A cruel man by the name of Gessler* then became ruler of the country.

4. Gessler must have been a good deal like Haman, whom the Bible tells about; for one day he hung his hat on the top of a tall pole in the public square, and then gave orders that every one who passed that way should bow down to it.

5. There was one man who would not do this. That man was William Tell. Because Tell would not

obey, he was put in prison. His little son was also put in prison, because he, too, refused to bow to Gessler's hat.

6. One day this cruel Gessler made up his mind to punish Tell still further. He ordered him brought out of prison.

"I hear," he said, "that you can shoot well with a bow and arrow. To-morrow your son shall stand at one side of the public square, with an apple on his head. You shall stand at the other side and shoot the apple with an arrow."

7. "You want me to kill my boy," said Tell in great distress.

"No," said Gessler, "I want you to shoot the *apple;* and if you do not hit it, both you and your boy shall die."

"And what if I *do* hit it?" asked Tell.

"Then both of you shall go free," said Gessler.

8. When the mother of the little boy heard of Gessler's wicked plan, she was in deep trouble. She knew that her husband could send an arrow as straight as a line, but she feared that in his anxiety his hand would be unsteady and that he would fail. And then—oh, awful thought!

9. What do you suppose this noble woman did? What would *you* have done if *your* father and brother were in danger of being put to a cruel death? Ah, yes! This mother had learned of Him who sympathizes with the oppressed,* and to Him she told her trouble. Earnestly that night she prayed that God would save her loved ones.

10. The next day Tell and his son were brought out of prison to the public square. Gessler placed a very small apple on the head of the boy. He then gave Tell the bow and arrow, and ordered him to shoot.

"Don't be afraid, father. I *know* you will hit it," said the boy, as his father took the bow.

11. "The sun shines in my eyes," said Tell to Gessler.

"Say not a word," commanded Gessler. "*Shoot!*"

"May I not have a *straight* arrow?" asked Tell; "this one is *crooked*."

"*Shoot!* I say," Gessler replied angrily.

12. Tell lifted the bow. He drew back the arrow. Then, *twang!* went the arrow, and Tell hid his face from the sight.

A great shout went up from the people who stood round. In another instant Tell felt the arm of his little son around his neck.

"*Father, father! I am safe!* The arrow went right through the center of the apple!" he exclaimed with great joy.

13. Gessler was disappointed, and he would have put Tell back in prison if he had not feared the people. Soon Gessler was driven out of Switzerland, and the people were again free.

Who saved Tell and his son that day from death? Who will be *our* refuge in time of trouble?

Comprehension Test. Underline the word or words in the parenthesis that makes the sentence true.

1. Switzerland has (deserts, lakes, mountains).
2. Gessler was like (Moses, Haman, Paul).

3. Gessler was (cowardly, cruel, generous).
4. William Tell was (accurate, skillful, weak).
5. Mrs. Tell helped by (good deeds, prayer).
6. Tell's son (loved, encouraged) his father.
7. This story illustrates (Psalm 46:1; Daniel 3:6).
8. (Gessler, Tell, Tell's son, Mrs. Tell) was a hero.

God's Wonderful Promises [171]

This psalm is full of wonderful promises. Read the promise for the poor man; for those that fear the Lord; for those who trust God; for those who seek God; for the righteous; for God's servants. Find the lines that tell what the fear of the Lord is. Memorize the promise or stanza that you like best.

1. This poor man cried, and the Lord heard him,
   And saved him out of all his troubles.
   The angel of the Lord encampeth round about
       them that fear Him,
   And delivereth them.
   O taste and see that the Lord is good:
   Blessed is the man that trusteth in Him.

2. O fear the Lord, ye His saints:
   For there is no want to them that fear Him.
   The young lions do lack, and suffer hunger:
   But they that seek the Lord shall not want any
       good thing.

3. Come, ye children, hearken unto Me:
   I will teach you the fear of the Lord.
   What man is he that desireth life,
   And loveth many days, that he may see good?

Keep thy tongue from evil,
And thy lips from speaking guile.*
Depart from evil, and do good;
Seek peace, and pursue* it.

4. The eyes of the Lord are upon the righteous,
And His ears are open unto their cry. . . .
The righteous cry, and the Lord heareth,
And delivereth them out of all their troubles.
—*Psalm 34.*

Reading Tests and Scores for the Fifth Period

You are now ready for your last reading tests for the fifth period. In your *silent reading* test you should be able to read nearly 140 words a minute. See how well you can do in this test. *Think* about what you read so that your comprehension score will be high. What other test is a part of the silent reading test?

In order to get a good score in oral reading what must you do?

You can find out your own *memory reading* score. How many words in the poems you have memorized this period? What is your memory reading score?

SIXTH PERIOD[1]

"King Cotton" in Dixie's Land [S]

This story tells about two children from the North who spent their summer vacation on their Uncle John's cotton plantation in Dixie's Land. They had a fine time, and learned a good deal about cotton. Read silently, and find out what they learned.

After you have completed your silent reading, find one or more paragraphs that you think are especially good for oral reading, and prepare to read them to the class.

The story is in three parts. See if you can give a good name to each part.

I. ―――――――――

It was a warm, sunny day in the last of June. Gordon and his sister Louise had just come from the North to spend their vacation with their Uncle John in Dixie's Land.* Uncle John lived on a large farm, or plantation as people in the South would say.

"I am going to the field to-day, children," said Uncle John. "Would you like to go with me?"

It was always such a pleasure to be with Uncle John that the children were delighted. Besides, they had never lived in the country, and the broad, beautiful fields made them feel like birds let out of a cage. They wanted to run and jump and sing all the time.

―――――

[1] TO THE TEACHER: During this period, review and strengthen the pronunciation and dictionary drills of all the preceding periods. By the end of the year, fourth-grade pupils should be master of the diacritical marks of both the vowels and the consonants. Give phrase drills as needed from blackboard or flash cards, gradually increasing the length of the word groups. Let the pupils practice marking phrases in given paragraphs or whole lessons.

Gordon said he believed wings were beginning to grow on his feet.

Uncle John knew just how they felt. He took the children by the hand, one on each side of him.

"Let's have a run to the field," he said.

And away they went!

When they stopped, they were standing by a large field of yellow blossoms about as large as morning glories. Acres and acres of these blossoms stretched out before them.

"Oh, what beautiful flowers!" exclaimed Louise.

"What are they, Uncle John?" asked Gordon.

"This is a field of cotton in blossom," said Uncle John, as he picked a few blossoms. "Does it look like any flower you know?"

In school the children had been studying about flowers and flower families.

"It is something like the mallow that we have at home," said Louise.

"It looks to me like first cousin to the hollyhock," said Gordon.

"Fine!" said Uncle John. "The cotton plant belongs to the mallow family, the same as the hollyhock. Some cotton blossoms are creamy white. These soon turn pink, and as the flower fades, it turns quite purple. Some kinds of cotton bear brownish-red blossoms. Other kinds have rose-colored blossoms. The petals fall very quickly, lasting only from one to three days."

"Oh, Gordon," said Louise, "let's press one of these flowers for our Nature Portfolio."

"I was just thinking about that, myself," said Gordon. "And wouldn't it be fine to mount a number of Southern wild flowers, to show the boys and girls in school next fall!"

"That is just what we will do!" agreed Louise.

Gordon and Louise visited the cotton fields often after this. As soon as the pretty petals were gone, they noticed that a little green pod started to grow. Uncle John told them that this pod was called the boll.* When the bolls were about as large as hen's eggs, they began to turn brown.

Early in September the field of flowers had changed to a field of snow, —not real snow such as covers the ground up North in the winter, but snowy clusters of soft white cotton. The bolls had burst, and each one was a big fluffy ball of ripe cotton. Uncle John said a field of cotton was the most beautiful sight in the world. And the children thought so, too.

A cotton boll in blossom

II.

"When the cotton bolls burst open, it is time to begin picking," Uncle John said. So the next morning about twenty pickers—men, women, and children—came to help him. Gordon and Louise wanted to help too. It was such a novelty* to them to gather real cotton. Each picker fastened a bag to his shoulders. The men had very large sacks, some of them yards long. The children used smaller sacks. Off they all

started down the rows of cotton. Uncle John went by the side of Gordon and Louise, to show them how.

"Try to get all the cotton out of a boll at one time," he said. "Be careful not to get bits of leaves and broken bolls mixed up with the cotton. It should be picked as clean as possible. Don't pick bolls that are not really ripe, for that cotton will not take dye well. If you ever find white specks in colored cotton cloth, you may know that the cotton used was not ripe."

Gordon and Louise wanted to do their work well. And they worked hard. But the pickers who were used to it were soon away ahead of them. They could clear the pod with one movement of the hand. By the time Gordon and Louise had their little sacks half full, the sun was getting very warm.

"Maybe you had better stop now," said Uncle John. "You are not used to our Southern sun as the rest of these folks are."

But Gordon and Louise did not want to be quitters, so they begged to fill their sacks first. They did so, and a good job it was—just as clean as one could wish.

A little later in the day they visited the field again, to watch the pickers. It was a funny sight. Just quietly picking cotton gets monotonous* after a while. So the pickers were trying to cheer one another by singing as they swayed* their bodies to the time of their music. In fact, working in the cotton fields is so much a part of the life in the South that it has found its way into many of the songs of Dixie's Land.

"Old Black Joe" starts with:

"Gone are the days when my heart was young and gay;
Gone are my friends from the cotton fields away."

Gordon and Louise learned to sing some of Dixie's pretty songs.

The cotton bolls do not all ripen at once. So there are several "pickings." In fact, the cotton is not *all* picked until November or even later. Many of the schools close during picking time, for the children must help earn money in the cotton fields.

III. ───────────────

In each boll of cotton there are a number of hard seeds about as large as a small bean. The cotton clings to these seeds so tightly that it is hard to pull it away. Years ago this was all done by hand. But in the year 1792, Mr. Eli Whitney invented a machine to do this work. It is called the cotton gin.

The cotton gin can clean more cotton in one day than a man could clean in many months by hand. After the seeds are taken out, the cotton is packed and tied up in large bales, and sent away to be woven into different kinds of cotton cloth, such as gingham, calico, muslin, lawn, duck, and sheeting. Cotton thread and cotton batting are also made from cotton.

Our great-great-grandmothers made the cotton into threads with their spinning wheels. Then they wove these threads into cloth on their hand looms. Now, large machines do this work, and of course much faster than the spinning wheel and hand loom could do it.

Out of every three pounds of cotton that are picked, two pounds are cotton seeds. Some of these are kept to be planted the next year. For a long time the rest of the seeds were thrown away or burned. But now every part of the seed is used.

The seeds are ground in a mill. The oil that is pressed out is called cottonseed oil. This is used in salads and in cooking. It is also used in the making of soap and substitutes* for butter.

After the oil is pressed out, a cotton meal is left. Some of this is used as food for cattle. Some is used to fertilize the cotton fields. The hulls of the seeds are often mixed with the meal and used as fuel. So you see "King Cotton" is a very good friend.

Comprehension Test. Complete these sentences:
1. Cotton blossoms are a ——— color.
2. The cotton blossom belongs to the ——— family.
3. The cotton pod is called ———.
4. ——— cotton does not take dye well.
5. The machine that takes the seeds from the cotton is called ———.
6. It was invented in the year ——— by ———.
7. Cotton seeds are good for ——— and ———.
8. Three kinds of cloth that are made from cotton are ———, ———, ———.
9. Long ago cotton was made into threads with ———, and these threads were woven into cloth on ———.
10. Now all this work is done by ———.

The states in the South where cotton grows are:

Virginia	Alabama	Arkansas
North Carolina	Mississippi	Tennessee
South Carolina	Louisiana	Missouri
Georgia	Texas	Oklahoma
Florida		

These states are called the cotton belt of the United States. Find the cotton belt on the map.

Some cotton grows also in California.

Cotton also grows in Egypt, India, Cuba, China, Japan, and some parts of Europe and South America.

A Bird's Nest [129]

As you read this poem, see what lessons you can find that these "little brown-winged birds" teach us. Can you guess the name of these birds? Is there any line in this poem that you cannot read at a glance? Which?

1. Over my shaded doorway,
    Two little brown-winged birds
 Have chosen to fashion their dwelling,
    And utter their loving words.
 All day they are going and coming,
    On errands frequent* and fleet,*
 And warbling, over and over,
    "Sweetest, sweet, sweet, oh sweet!"

2. Their necks are changeful and shining,
    Their eyes are like living gems,*
 And all day long they are busy
    Gathering straws and stems,
 Lint and feathers and grasses,
    And half forgetting to eat,
 Yet never failing to warble,
    "Sweetest, sweet, sweet, oh sweet!"

3. What if the sky *is* clouded?
   What if the rain comes down?
They are all dressed to *meet* it,
   In waterproof suits of brown.
They never seem discouraged,
   Nor murmur at storm or heat,
But say, whatever the weather,
   "Sweetest, sweet, sweet, oh sweet!"
            —*Florence Percy.*

A Camping Trip (S)

As you read this story, find out how sheep are sheared and how the wool is prepared to be woven into cloth. Find out also who was the first man that kept sheep, and how long ago. Where in the Bible is wool told about, and what was it used for?

After reading silently, practice reading paragraphs 2, 3, 5, 7, 16, 17, and 18 orally.

1. It was in California, and we were going up into the Coast Range Mountains on a camping trip. The party was made up of a wagonload of happy children and a few grown-ups.

Two strong farm horses hitched to a big wagon stood at the door. The boys had filled the wagon box nearly half full of nice clean straw, which they covered with blankets. This was for the children to sit on. The grown-ups, one of them, sat on the seat with the driver. The others thought it would be more fun to sit in the box on the straw with the children.

Besides the children, there was a tent, a big roll of blankets, a few dishes, and plenty of good things to eat—quite a load. But at last everything was ready. Dad was the driver.

2. "Get-up, Nell! Get-up, Jim!" he called to the horses.

"Good-by, Tom!" came a chorus of children's voices to the man who stayed at home to look after things. "Good-by, Tom! Good-by! Good-by!"

Away down the lane we went, the children's happy laughter floating out on the fresh morning air.

And what a ride we had! It was in April when, in California, every spring flower is at its best. The fields were carpeted with them, and the air was filled with their fragrance.

3. Late in the afternoon, we found ourselves at a sheep ranch* about halfway up the foothills. We had intended to go to the top before camping. But the horses were getting tired, and the mountain road was not very good, so we decided to stop here for the night.

The man who keeps sheep on a sheep ranch is called a sheep ranger.*

"Do you mind if we camp here for the night?" dad asked the ranger.

"Not a bit of it. Just make yourselves at home," said the sheep ranger pleasantly.

4. So out we all climbed. Dad and one of the boys pitched the tent. The rest of the children gathered sticks for a camp fire, while the grown-ups brought something to eat from the box of food. It seemed al-

most no time until a fine hot supper was spread on the green grass. How good everything tasted! And how we did eat!

5. While we were eating, the sheep ranger came to our camp. He looked as if he would like to add some pleasure to our good time.

"We are shearing the sheep this evening," he said. "Would you like to come down to the pen and see how we do it?"

"Oh, thank you! thank you! That would be a great treat," chorused half a dozen voices.

6. So, as soon as supper was over, we all went down to the pen. The sheep had been driven in, and several men were already at work. A man would take a sheep and lay its head on his knee. Then up and down the sheep he carefully passed a tool that was run by a machine. It acted something like a

lawn mower. In about five minutes the fleece fell from the sheep. But the wool was so matted that it did not fall apart. It seemed like a real coat of wool. Each fleecy coat was rolled up and tied with a string.

7. After the sheep were sheared, they looked small and oh, so naked! They really didn't look much like sheep at all, except their heads. Even the little lambs did not know their own mothers. They went around crying, "Baa! Baa! Baa-aa!"

8. When the work of shearing was past, the men put all the fleeces into big sacks. These were piled up in a shed. Later they were weighed and hauled away to be sold.

The children watched the shearing for some time. Then we thanked the ranger again and went back to our camp.

9. The camp fire was low, but the children had gathered a good supply of wood, and we soon had a bright blaze. As we sat around the fire, we talked about wool.

"What do the men who buy the wool do with it?" asked one.

"They sell it to some big factory where it is made into woolen cloth," said dad, who seemed to know almost everything. "First it is sorted. The fine wool is put in one pile, and the coarse into another.

10. "You saw how dirty the wool was as it came from the sheep to-night. It was full of dust, and burs, and oil from the sheep's body. Before it can be made into cloth, it must be cleaned. So after it is sorted in the factory it is put into a tank full of soap-

suds. Here it is boiled until the dirt is all out. Then it is put through rollers to press the water out. After that it is spread out to dry. Soon it is a great heap of soft, fluffy white fleece.

11. "Some of the wool is then put into other tanks that are full of dye water. After it is dyed, it is dried again.

12. "It is next put through what is called a carding machine. Here it is pulled out into rolls ready for spinning. Spinning is pulling it out and twisting it into long threads, or yarn. This yarn is wound on reels. It is now ready to be woven into cloth.

13. "The wool that grows on the backs of sheep may be made into dresses, coats, stockings, sweaters, carpets, blankets, mittens, and many other very useful things."

14. "When were the first garments made from wool?" asked Stanley, the oldest boy.

"Probably no one knows," said dad. "But in the book of Proverbs, Solomon tells us about a woman who used wool and clothed her household. Who can find the verse in the Bible?"

15. The children got the Bible, which had been put carefully in with the things they had brought from home. They soon found the place and read:

" 'She seeketh wool, and flax, and worketh willingly with her hands.' 'She is not afraid of the snow for her household: for all her household are clothed with scarlet.' "

16. "This woman lived about three thousand years ago. But nearly five hundred years before that,

the women spun goats' hair into woolen cloth. Read Exodus 35:26," said dad.

The verse was quickly found, and Henry read: " 'And all the women whose heart stirred them up in wisdom spun goats' hair.' "

"Do you remember what they did with the goats' hair after it was spun?"

"Oh, I know!" said Mabel, who was in the fourth grade in school. "They made one of the coverings of the tabernacle."

"Good!" said dad.

17. "I shouldn't be surprised if woolen cloth was made even before that. Who was the first man that kept sheep? Can you find that in the Bible?"

"I know that. Let me tell, daddy," said little Hazel, who was in the third grade in school. "It was Abel, and it is told in the fourth chapter of Genesis." She soon found the verse and read clearly: " 'Abel was a keeper of sheep, but Cain was a tiller of the ground.' Genesis 4:2."

18. "Fine!" said dad. "Now what do you suppose he did with all that wool? Who knows but that his mother spun the wool and made clothing for her children? What was her name?"

"Eve! Eve!" they all said at once.

"And how long ago was that?" asked dad.

"That was when the earth was first created, nearly six thousand years ago," they answered.

19. It was now time to go to bed. We all knelt around the warm camp fire, while dad thanked our heavenly Father for His care during the day, and

claimed the promise, "The angel of the Lord encampeth round about them that fear Him, and delivereth them."

20. Our father and the two boys slept in the wagon box under the shining stars, while the rest of us spread our blankets on a big bed of straw in the tent. Soon we were all fast asleep.

21. After breakfast the next morning we climbed to the top of the mountain. The valley below was hidden by a dense rolling fog, but the mountain was lighted up by the warm sunshine. We were above the clouds! On the mountain, we found many strange and beautiful flowers. We ate our dinner by a clear little mountain stream. We visited some geysers,* and saw the water spout into the air. We heard the songs of strange birds. And when we returned to camp that evening, we were tired enough to sleep soundly through another night.

The next day we drove home. All agreed that we had had a most delightful trip.

Speed and Comprehension Test. Write in a column the numbers of the paragraphs that tell: (See how many you can find in five minutes.)

Ready for the trip
Sheep shearing
Carding the wool
On the mountain top
The wool cleaned
Dyeing the wool
The wool sorted

The ride to the mountains
Woolen cloth 3,000 years ago
Goats' hair cloth
Our first camp supper
The first sheep ranger
Welcome to the sheep ranch
Evening prayer at camp

Which of these birds is the swallow? Which is the bluejay? the wren? the robin?

Poor Robin ^(o)

1. "Oh, what *is* the matter with Robin,
      What makes her cry round here all day?
   I think she must be in great trouble,"
      Said Swallow to little Blue Jay.

2. "*I* know why the Robin is crying,"
      Said Wren, with a sob in her breast.
   "A naughty, bold robber has stolen
      Three little blue eggs from her nest.

3. "He carried them home in his pocket;
      I *saw* him from up in a tree.
   Ah me! how my little heart fluttered
      For fear he would come and rob *me*."

4. "Oh, what little boy was so wicked?"
      Said Swallow, beginning to cry.

"I wouldn't be *guilty* of robbing
    A dear little bird's nest, not *I!*"

5. "*Nor I*," said the birds in a chorus;
    "A cruel and mischievous* boy!
I pity his father and mother;
    He surely can't give them much joy.

6. "He surely forgot what a pleasure
    The dear little robins all bring
In early springtime and in summer
    By the beautiful songs that they sing.

7. "He surely forgot that the rule is,
    To do as you would be done by;
He surely forgot that from heaven,
    There looks down an all-seeing Eye."

—*Author Unknown.*

1. Who is the "bold robber" spoken of in stanza 2?
2. What season of the year is it? Why do you think so?
3. What rule is meant in stanza 7? Find it in the Bible, and read it. Luke 6:31.
4. Who is the "all-seeing Eye"?

The Mysterious Singer (O)

How many birds are named in this story? Which of these birds do you know by their song or call? Find pictures of as many of them as you can.

The Carter house stood in a large garden. The garden was full of trees, and the trees were full of birds.

"Do you hear that bobolink?" said Carrie one day.

"I hear a robin," said Fannie.

"And I hear a bluebird," said Ruth.

"And I'm sure it is a thrush," said Will.

"Oh no! it is an oriole," said Harry.

"I can't tell what it is," said Mary, "but it is a sweet singer. Let's ask Aunt Lucy."

"I think it is a catbird," said Aunt Lucy when the children ran to her chair on the porch, and asked her about the mysterious bird in the garden.

"A catbird!" cried all the children in one breath.

"We will go out and find the bird," said Aunt Lucy. "There he is, on the highest branch of that tree. He is after cherries."

"Isn't he pretty! How slender he is! But I didn't know a catbird could sing," said Mary.

"Climb up and pick some cherries, Harry," said Aunt Lucy, "and see what the pretty fellow will do."

Harry climbed the tree, and down came the sweet singer, scolding and crying out very much like a cat.

"It *is* a catbird!" they all said. Then Aunt Lucy told them about the catbird. She told them that the catbird can imitate the songs of other birds. Sometimes he sings a song that is made up of the notes of other birds, and finishes it with a sweet, clear whistle of his own. He is a shy bird, and loves a leafy thicket, where he can be heard but not easily seen.

"He is welcome to my share of the cherries, if he will only keep on singing like that," said Ruth, clapping her hands.

—*Little Men and Women.*

Taught by a Dream ^(S)

This is a wonderful story of how God brings His truth to persons who study the Bible. As you read it, find out what the dream was, and how it came true. It happened in Austria. Find Austria on the map. Vienna is the capital of Austria. Find it also.

God is working in the dark places of earth to-day. In a part of Austria* where the second coming of Christ had never been preached, a company of seventy Sabbath keepers were found. They had never heard of Adventists.* The man who led them to God had been wounded in the war, and was taken to a hospital. Here, for the first time, he saw a New Testament. He wanted to buy it, but the nurses would not sell it. He found an old shopkeeper in the city who helped him to get one. Afterwards he got an entire Bible.

This man read the Bible faithfully. He learned that the seventh day of the week is the true Sabbath. He learned that Jesus is soon coming in the clouds of heaven. He learned that a tithe of all we have belongs to God. He learned that the dead will be raised when Jesus comes. He learned that Christ is now examining the lives of people from records in the books in the most holy place in the heavenly sanctuary. He learned about healthful living. He learned almost every part of the special truth for these last days.

On May 27, 1925, this man dreamed that just two years later, on the 27th of May, 1927, some one would come and tell him and his people that there were others in the world who believed the same truth that he had found.

"We will test it," his friends said. "We have two years to try it out. We will wait patiently, and if on the 27th of May in 1927, your dream comes true, we will know that these truths are of God."

On the 27th day of May, 1927, a young lady canvasser came into that part of Austria. She called at this man's house, and showed a book that taught the third angel's message. The man saw at once that this was the fulfillment of his dream. He called all his people together.

"Do you keep the Sabbath?" he asked the young lady. "Do you believe that Jesus is soon coming? Do you believe that a tithe is the Lord's? Do you believe that the dead will be raised by Jesus when He comes?"

To each question she answered, "I do believe."

Then he said, "Two years ago, God showed me that on this very day some one would come and tell us that there is a people somewhere in the world who believe as we do. Now tell us, are there any people of our kind anywhere? Are there any in Vienna?"

"They are found in all the earth, and there are many in Vienna," the canvasser replied.

This greatly strengthened them in their faith. They sent to Vienna for the president of the conference. He found seventy people thoroughly instructed in the Bible. They had learned many parts of it by heart. The brother had been very conscientious* in his work. A church of thirty-seven was formed.

Who Stole the Bird's Nest? (334)

As you read this poem, try to make your voice sound like the animals who talk.

Find out, as you read, who stole the nest, and from what bird it was stolen.

How many birds are named in this poem? Which of these do you know?

---

1. "To-whit, to-whit, to-whee!
   Will you listen to me?
   Who stole four eggs I laid,
   And the nice nest I made?"

   "Not I," said the cow; "moo-oo!
   Such a thing I'd never do.
   I gave you a wisp* of hay,
   But didn't take your nest away.
   Not I," said the cow; "moo-oo!
   Such a thing I'd never do!"

2. "Bobolink! bobolink!
   Now, what do you think?
   Who stole a nest away
   From the plum tree to-day?"

   "Not I," said the dog; "bowwow!
   I wouldn't be so mean, anyhow.
   I gave hairs the nest to make,
   But the nest I did not take.
   Not I," said the dog; "bowwow!
   I wouldn't be so mean, anyhow!"

3. "Coo-ooo! coo-ooo! coo-ooo!
Let me speak a word or two:
Who stole that pretty nest
From little yellow breast?"

"Not I," said the sheep; "oh no!
I wouldn't treat a poor bird so.
I gave wool the nest to line,
But the nest was none of mine.
Baa! baa!" said the sheep; "oh no!
I wouldn't treat a poor bird so!"

4. "Caw, caw!" cried the crow;
"I should like to know
What thief took away
A bird's nest to-day."

"Cluck, cluck!" said the hen;
"Don't ask me again;
Why, I haven't a chick
Would do such a trick!
We each gave her a feather,
And she wove them together.
I'd scorn* to intrude*
On her and her brood.*
Cluck, cluck!" said the hen;
"Don't ask me again."

5. *"Chir-a-whir! chir-a-whir!*
We'll make a great stir,
And find out his name,
And all cry, 'For shame!'"

6. "I would not rob a bird,"
   Said little Mary Green;
   "I think I never heard
   Of anything so mean."

   "It is very cruel, too,"
   Said little Alice Neal;
   "I wonder if he knew
   How sad the bird would feel!"

7. A little boy hung down his head,
   And went and hid behind the bed;
   For *he* stole that pretty nest,
   From poor little yellow breast;
   And he felt so full of shame,
   He didn't like to tell his name.
   —*Lydia Maria Child.*

A Lesson Father Taught Me ^(S)

In this story, Edgar A. Guest tells you how his father once taught him a good lesson. Read silently, and find out what the lesson was. How long does it take you to find out? Think whether *you* have learned this same lesson. After you have done your silent reading, practice reading paragraphs 2 and 3 orally.

---

1. Once when I was a little chap,* I had a train of cars, of which I was very fond. I thought more of it than of any other toy I had. A playmate who had come into the house wanted to play with it. I refused him. What if he should break my toy? My father, who was reading in the next room, heard me tell the boy he could not have the train and track. He called me to him.

2. "What does Bobby want?" he asked.

"He wants to play with my train of cars," I said. "He'll break it, and I don't want him to have it."

"Get it out," said my father quietly. "Let him play with it."

3. I did as I was told, for I had been taught to obey. I thought my father was unjust, and I know I did his bidding very unwillingly. As I had feared, the boy broke my toy. It was a sobbing, heartsick little fellow that my father called to him a second time.

"What are you crying about?" he asked.

"Bobby broke my train. I knew he would if I let him have it," I said, sobbing.

Father put down his newspaper and smiled. Then he took me on his knee.

"You're not hurt at all," he said very gently. "Bobby didn't kick you, or give you a black eye, or anything like that. Your fingers aren't cut, and your legs are all right. I've looked you all over, and I can't find anything has happened that should make you cry."

4. Then he talked it all over with me.

"Toys are made to give little boys *pleasure*," he said. "A toy that no one ever uses is a *wasted* toy. If toys were never *broken*, never *scratched* and *soiled*, it would be a sign that no one ever had any *fun* out of them. Now you had a train, and Bobby wanted to play with it. If you had refused him that pleasure, you would have been selfish. I am sorry that Bobby broke it, but you shouldn't cry about it, for we can get more trains. It is easier to mend broken toys than it is to make an unselfish little boy out of a selfish one."

5. But I still felt that I had been wronged in some way. Later I came to learn that it was this spirit of my father's which helped him to face losses without whimpering.* I owe to him the knowledge that in the mere having of things there is no great happiness, and that there is no great sorrow in the loss of them. He taught me to use freely the things I had, especially if in the use of them I could bring joy to others.

6. Since then I have had the average man's run of hard luck. I have seen my precious little toys go

all to smash. I have been given the worst of it at times. But so long as my losses have been material* only, I have tried not to "cry" over them. My father had taught me that they were not *worth* it.

When Shall I Be a Man? (282)

1. "When shall I be a man?" he said,
   As I was putting him to bed.
   "How many years will have to be
   Before Time makes a man of me?
   And will I be a man when I
   Am grown up big?" I heaved a sigh,
   Because it called for careful thought
   To give the answer that he sought.

2. And so I set him on my knee,
   And said to him: "A man you'll be
   When you have learned that honor brings
   More joy than all the crowns of kings;
   That it is better to be true
   To all who know and trust in you
   Than all the gold of earth to gain
   If winning it shall leave a stain.

3. "When you can fight for victory sweet,
   Yet bravely swallow down defeat,
   And cling to hope and keep the right,
   Nor use deceit instead of might;
   When you are kind and brave and clean,
   And fair to all, and never mean;

When there is good in all you plan,
That day, my boy, you'll be a *man*.

4. "Some of us learn this truth too late—
That years alone can't make us great,
That many who are threescore* ten
Have fallen short of being men,
Because in selfishness they fought
And toiled without refining* thought;
And whether wrong or whether right
They lived but for their own delight.

5. "When you have learned that you must hold
Your honor dearer far than gold;
That no ill-gotten wealth or fame
Can pay you for your tarnished* name;
And when in all you say or do,
Of others you're considerate,* too,
Content to do the best you can,
By *such* a creed,* you'll be a *man*."

—*Edgar A. Guest.*

Appreciation Study

Stanza 1. Read the question the little boy asked his father. What did the father have to do before he could answer the question?

Stanza 2. What brings more joy than to wear a king's crown? What is better than all the gold of earth?

Stanza 3. How many things are named in stanza 3 that make a man?

Stanza 4. How many years are "threescore ten"? Why are some men this old not real men?

Stanza 5. What is meant by a "tarnished name"? What is it to be "considerate of others"?

DICTIONARY EXERCISE

Copy these words in their places in your word book:

warble	ball	bobolink	mallow
frequent	fleet	brood	gems
novelty	oriole	swallow	thrush
gingham	canvasser	creed	threescore

Pronounce these words according to their markings:

mys-tē′ri-ous	săne′tu-a-ry	Vĭ-ĕn′na
ō′ri-ole	dĭe′tion-a-ry	re-fīn′ing
mĭs′chĭe-vous	mĭs′sion-a-ry	tär′nished
Ăd′vent-ist	con-sci-ĕn′tious	Czech′ (Chĕck) o-
Ạus′trĭ-a	ful-fĭll′mĕnt	Slo-vä′ki-a

A Bible in the Fiery Furnace (S)

This story happened in Czecho-Slovakia. Find this country on the map. It tells not only how God saved the Bible from being burned, but it tells how He changed the heart of a wicked man. Read until you can tell this story.

Czecho-Slovakia* is one of the countries of Europe. It lies east of Germany. It is only about one third as large as the state of California. But there are nearly three times as many people living there as are living in California.

Some of God's own jewels live in Czecho-Slovakia. Many of them have suffered for His truth. But God remembers each one of them. He sees their troubles, and sympathizes with them.

Not long ago, a woman and her daughter living in Czecho-Slovakia heard the message that Jesus is soon coming. They were very happy. They longed to be ready to meet Him, so they began to obey all His commandments.

They loved to study the Bible. They loved to read good books that helped them to understand the teachings of God's word. They loved to read the papers that tell how wonderfully a knowledge of the Bible is going all over the world. They loved to visit with others who wished to obey God.

The husband and father was angry because his wife and daughter believed God's message. He did not want them to keep holy the Sabbath day as God commands. He did not want them to study the Bible, or to read about the work of God in other lands. He did not want them to visit with others of like faith.

One afternoon, when some of the mother's friends were visiting at their home, the husband took the Bible, a copy of the New Testament, a book which told about the second coming of Jesus, and some religious papers. And what do you think that angry man did? He put them into the kitchen stove to burn them. When he saw the fire burning brightly, he was happy. Poor man! He surely did not know how basely he had insulted the One whose written word he had cast into the fire!

His wife and daughter were deeply grieved. When could they ever get another Bible? Would they ever again be allowed to read the books and papers that tell about God's truth and His great work? Even if they *could* buy other books, would they be able to *keep* them from being destroyed? Sad and almost discouraged, they sat down and wept.

Supper time came. The mother opened the stove to start the fire again. She began to take out the ashes. She struck something hard. What was it? She looked closely. Oh, joy! Here in the ashes she found her precious Bible and New Testament! Like the three men who were cast into the fiery furnace, these books were not burned at all! All the other books and papers were burned to ashes, but the Bible was not burned. Surely God had taken care of His word!

That husband is no longer angry with his wife. When church time comes, he says, "It is time for you to go now." No doubt God wants to help this father. He wants to show him that there is a God in heaven. He wants him to know that God has power to work on earth. God will yet do great things for him, if he will listen to that "still small voice."

The Way to Try (S)

This story tells two ways of saying "I'll try." Read until you can tell what both ways are. Which way is the real "I'll try"? Think of something *you* have to do, and then tell *how* you will "try."

A long, shrill whistle sounded outside the house, followed by two more of shorter length.

"That's Jasper Heath. He wants me to play handball, mother," explained Paul Winter, jumping up from the sofa where he had been reading a book. "May I go?"

"Put your book on the table, dear," reminded Mrs. Winter, nodding "Yes" to his request.

Paul gathered it up from under the sofa, and throwing it on the table, began looking for his cap. Finally he found it on the piano. Next—the handball.

"Mother, where is it? Jasper won't wait."

"Then maybe with a few disappointments, you will learn to put things away, son. What did you tell me the last time I asked you to be more orderly?"

"I said I'd try," hurriedly called back Paul, having found the ball under the radiator,* where it had rolled when he was playing with the cat.

It was an hour later that Mr. Winter came in.

"Letty," he said to his wife, "I don't know what to do. I must get a message to the city. The man I want to reach has no telephone, and I can't leave the office long enough to make the trip."

Mr. Winter lived in a small town, and his office was in his own yard.

"Why not send Paul?"

"But could he make such a trip?"

"Yes, indeed. I know where he is, and I will call him."

Much relieved, the father went back to his office. Paul was not far away, and came at once at his mother's call.

"Do you think you could go to the city with a message? Your father needs a trusty boy to deliver it promptly."

"Certainly, mother. If I hurry, I can get that five-o'clock car," he added after looking at a time-table. "May I have your commutation* ticket?"

His mother handed him the ticket, and he ran to his father's office for directions.

The errand was not a simple one. The address was hard to find, and since Paul seldom went to the city alone, it was only by asking questions of the right persons that he finally succeeded. But the errand was properly done, and Paul was at home in good time, much to his father's satisfaction.

"Paul, son," said his mother that night as he was going to bed, "the only 'I'll try' that counts is the 'certainly' kind. Suppose that when I asked you if you could go to the city for father, you had said merely, 'I'll try,' and then had done nothing more about it. But you said, 'Certainly.' Then you looked up the time the train leaves, got the ticket from me, went to father for instructions, boarded the train, and did the business in proper style."

"I see the point, mother," laughed Paul. "Certainly, sure thing. Everything in its place. You'll see, mother," he promised, kissing her good night. Mothers do not expect miracles, but Paul did improve.

—Viola Woodville (adapted).

How Birds Learn to Sing [91]

1. How do birds first learn to sing?
   From the whistling wind so fleet,*
   From the waving of the wheat,
   From the rustling of the leaves,
   From the raindrop on the eaves,
   From the children's laughter sweet,
   From the plash when brooklets meet.

2. Little birds begin their trill
   As they gayly float at will
   In the gladness of the sky,
   When the clouds are white and high;
   In the beauty of the day,
   Speeding on their sunny way,
   Light of heart and fleet of wing—
   That's how birds first learn to sing.
   —*Mary Mapes Dodge.*

A Modern Raven [S]

The most wonderful answer to prayer that I ever saw was that of a poor Mohammedan* widow, who, with her children, was starving.

I had closed the White Memorial Hospital in Pasrur,* India, for two months. One day, I decided to open it, and, taking with me my assistant, a young Indian girl, we drove out in the evening to put the hospital and dispensary* in order. As my decision was made suddenly, I took with me only a small five-cent loaf of bread and some butter. The next morning at five o'clock, we ate most of the bread and butter.

We were so anxious to open to patients the next day that we worked on till two o'clock that afternoon, forgetting our need of food. Then, becoming weak and faint, I sent the assistant to prepare some Indian bread and greens for herself, telling her I would take what was left of the bread and butter we had in the morning.

Later, I drew a small table to the edge of the veranda, and sat down to my bread and butter. My Indian assistant drew a native bedstead close to the veranda, with her bread and greens on a brass plate, and also made ready to eat.

She had just seated herself, but had not yet touched her food, when a big black mountain crow, or raven,* flopped down on her. He took one side of the bread in one claw and the opposite side in the other claw. Then he carefully brought his feet together and took up the vegetables.

It is not uncommon for crows to steal food from our plates when we sit outside, but they generally fly into a tree near by and caw and brag. This bird acted differently, and although both of us were most indignant, we watched him with interest. Up into the clear sky he went, over the hospital, across the city, on, on, till only a speck, when he seemed to sink and vanish.* I shared my bread and butter with my assistant, and we finished the work. Then we opened up to patients the next day.

I cannot recall whether it was one or two days later that we saw a poor, weak woman coming in the gate, carrying a baby in her left arm, and a child of two or more on her right hip. Two other children came trailing after her, snatching at her clothes whenever they could to help themselves along. She staggered to the veranda and sank exhausted* to the floor. We revived* her, and asked from what she suffered.

"I am a Mohammedan widow," she said. "My husband died six months ago, and left me with these four children. My children and I have been starving. For three days we had nothing to eat. I prayed, oh, how I prayed to Mohammed;* but Mohammed never cares for women and children. Then I prayed to the gods of the Hindus,* but they, too, never care for women and children. Then I threw myself on the ground and clasped my hands as the Christians do, and I cried, 'O God of the Christians, send food to us, that my children may not die.'

"While praying, a crow dropped down and swept my head with its wings and flew away. I lifted my head and looked. There before me lay a beautiful piece of bread and some vegetables. I took the food, and my children and I ate.

"Some of the village women came past me as we ate, and asked me where I got the food. I told them the crow had brought it. 'That is not a poor man's food,' they said. 'That has come from some one of the better class.'

" 'I know the tender-hearted doctor who has a hospital at Pasrur,' one woman said. 'I think if you go to her, she will take you in and care for you.' I started at once. Sometimes we got a ride, sometimes we walked, but we are here."

My assistant thanked God that she had been counted worthy to give her dinner to answer this woman's prayer. It was her food, without a doubt, that the crow had carried to the starving widow and her children.

—*Maria White, M. D., in the United Presbyterian (adapted).*

Comprehension Test

1. Do you know any story in the Bible where God sent a raven to some one with food? 1 Kings 17:1-6 tells.

2. How does this story show the truth found in Hebrews 13:8?

3. Find on the map the country where these things took place.

4. How did this crow act differently from most crows?

5. Where did he take the stolen food?

Silent Reading Test

The reading for this lesson is the twelfth silent reading rate and comprehension test. It is found in your "Reading Tests and Scores" pad.

The Missionary Pumpkin ^(o)

Have you ever had a missionary garden? How much money did it bring you for missions? Why not try again this spring? See if you can learn from Caleb in this story how to have a better missionary garden than you ever had before. Try it, boys and girls.

I.

Caleb sat in church listening to a man who was telling of the heathen in far-away lands. How his heart swelled as he heard of little ones, like himself, who were neglected and abused because those who *should* have been kind to them had never heard of the Saviour, who loves children!

They were talking about raising money to send men to tell these poor people the story of God's Son, and how He came to save sinners.

Caleb lived with his grandmother who was very old and quite deaf. And even if she could have heard him tell of what was on his heart, he knew very well she had no money to give him.

"Why are *we* so much better off than *they?*" the speaker asked. "We cannot tell why the Lord has chosen that *we*, instead of *they*, should be born to this blessed knowledge. How can we ever expect His favor unless we do our best to send the glad tidings* to our poor brethren who sit in darkness?"

How, indeed! The thought fell like a weight on Caleb's heart. Some of the men in church got up and told what they would give—a great, *great deal*, it seemed to Caleb. Then the plate was passed to those who could not give so much.

"I have nothing except this pumpkin seed," said Caleb, showing one to his teacher, who sat near him. "It's a good kind to plant. Do you suppose the heathen like pumpkin pies?"

With a smile, Miss Lane took the small hand that held the pumpkin seed. "I haven't a *doubt* of it, especially if they are *boys*. But why don't you plant it *yourself?*" she said. "Then you could sell the pumpkins you raise, and give the money."

"It would be so *long to wait*," said Caleb.

"But it would be so much *more to give*."

II.

That settled it. Caleb put the seed back into his pocket. That same evening Caleb sought out what he thought was the best spot in his grandmother's untidy back yard in which to soften the earth and intrust his treasure to it. Then he went away to the woods for brush to shelter it.

He rejoiced in the earliest shoot. He removed everything in the way of the vine as it set out on its travels. *That* corner of the yard was "swept and garnished,"* for a *missionary* pumpkin must grow in a clean place. And before long, as there was no telling which way that dainty green plant would choose, Caleb cleaned the *whole* space as it had never been cleaned before. Blossoms full of the sunshine's gold came, and then the green promise of good things to come.

Miss Lane came one day to see his vine.

"The Lord's servants are helping in your work, Caleb. He sends His sun and wind and rain to do their best for you. I think they must almost know that you are preparing a gift *for Him*—as everything is, you know, which we do for the least of those He loves."

Caleb stopped playing truant,* and saying ugly words because his grandmother could not *hear* them. Such things would not do for a boy who was raising an offering for the Lord, for one who hoped to pass on His blessing to those who stood in great need.

III. ───────────────

"You have a fine vine there, Caleb," said Mr. Ward, his neighbor, looking over the fence one morning. Caleb's heart swelled with pride as he looked at the half-dozen green balls, which were growing larger every day.

"But if *I* were *you*, I'd pull off all but *one*."

Caleb stared in terror at such an idea!

"Yes, I *would!* Then *that* one would get all the strength of the vine. It would grow to be a *monster*. You could sell the seeds alone for more than all the others would bring."

It brought a pang to Caleb's heart to do it, but he was willing to take advice, and soon had his reward in the rapid growth of his one pumpkin. Lovingly he watched it. It seemed to him that with each day he could see new growth. Joyfully did he greet the first tinge of yellow.

"I tell you, Caleb," said Mr. Ward, looking earnestly at the great pumpkin in its full ripeness, "that pumpkin must go to the county fair. It will take *first premium,** I'm sure.*"

"Oh, *my!*"

"And it will be *yours* just the same *afterwards.*"

Caleb's eyes shone.

"I'll get it there for you."

IV.

Anxious eyes followed the big pumpkin as it went away in Mr. Ward's wagon. Caleb missed it sadly. He felt lonely at this sudden ending of his summer's care. The last day of the fair, he walked five miles to see it again, and to hear if it had won a premium.

There it was, in all its glory, standing among *other* big pumpkins, by *far* the largest among them. And *there,* tied around its great stem, was the *blue ribbon!*

"You've *got* it, Caleb, just as I *told* you!" said Mr. Ward, crowding up to him. "Now, you want to sell the pumpkin, don't you?"

"Yes," said Caleb.

It was a little hard to part with it, but it *belonged* to the *heathen*, and *not* to *himself*. A few minutes later, Mr. Ward was standing up beside the pumpkin, calling attention to it.

"Gentlemen, this pumpkin is for sale. I needn't *tell* you it is the biggest one you ever saw in your lives, for you can *see that* for *yourselves*. I needn't tell you it will make the finest pies you ever tasted, for you know it *without* telling. But there's *one* thing about it you *don't* know. It is a *missionary* pumpkin, and the *very best* quality of the Lord's sunshine has gone into it. What am I offered? One dollar? Thank you—that might be a good bid for a *small* pumpkin, but not for a *giant* like *this*. Why, there isn't a lady *here* that hasn't been just *aching* to try her hands at making pies out of this pumpkin. Two? Three? Why, gentlemen, in lands thousands of miles away men have been raising stuff to put into those pies, trying their very best to make them good enough, and hardly reaching it. Sugar and spices such as never grew before—four dollars? Thank you, sir,—a good bid for a *common, everyday* pumpkin, but not for a *missionary* pumpkin. Five? I can almost fancy"—the orator* dropped his light tone and spoke earnestly—"little ones away across the ocean listening to hear how far our thought of them can go down into our pockets. Six? Seven? Yes, they're beginning to believe we're thinking of them—nine! How much more, gentlemen? Make it an *even ten* for them. Going! Going! Am I offered the ten? Going! *Ten!* Going at ten dollars! Going—*gone*, at ten dollars!"

"Where's the man who raised it?" came from the crowd that had gathered near.

"Here he is!"

Caleb had remained close at Mr. Ward's feet, gazing with eager, shining eyes. With a quick movement he was lifted, and stood beside Mr. Ward.

There was a moment's silence, and then a *shout* as the morsel of a boy looked shyly about him, at *first, half frightened, then,* meeting only kindly faces, breaking into a *smile.* Many who looked knew him and the small hardships and neglect that belong to the life of an orphan boy. Smiling glances deepened into *sympathy,* and he bashfully hung his head as the crowd heartily cheered the little missionary.

"Caleb, here is your missionary money," said Mr. Ward to him, after the excitement had quieted down. "It isn't *many* of us that have *such* a sum to give."

—*Herald.*

Comprehension Test

1. What is meant by "the glad tidings" and "our poor brethren who sit in darkness" in Part I?

2. Did Caleb belong to a rich or a poor family? How do you know?

3. Was he a good or a bad boy? Why? What shows that he was really kind at heart?

4. What effect did this missionary work have upon the back yard at Caleb's home? What effect did it have upon Caleb's actions and words? Why?

5. How did Caleb obey this Bible instruction: "Whatsoever thy hand findeth to do, do it with thy might"?

6. What "servants" did the Lord send to help Caleb?

7. What kind of man do you think Mr. Ward was?
8. What did "the blue ribbon" show?
9. Why did Caleb live with his grandmother?
10. Think of a good name for each of the four parts of this story. Discuss in class the names that each pupil has, and tell which you think are the best.

Temperance ⁽¹³⁴⁾

This lesson is taken from the Bible. It tells what comes to anyone who uses intoxicating* wine. Read and reread these verses until you find *eleven* things that wine does to those who drink it.

1. Wine is a mocker, strong drink is raging:*
And whosoever is deceived thereby is not wise.
He that loveth pleasure shall be a poor man:
He that loveth wine and oil shall not be rich.

2. Be not among winebibbers;*
Among riotous* eaters of flesh:
For the drunkard and the glutton* shall come to poverty:
And drowsiness* shall clothe a man with rags.

3. Who hath woe? who hath sorrow? who hath contentions?*
Who hath babbling*? who hath wounds without cause?
Who hath redness of eyes?
They that tarry long at the wine;
They that go to seek mixed wine.

4. Look not thou upon the wine when it is red,
   When it giveth his color in the cup,
   When it moveth itself aright.
   At the last it biteth like a serpent,
   And stingeth like an adder.*

   —*Selections from the Bible.*

Where to Drink (98)

These stanzas tell the best place to get a drink. Where is it?

1. Where the dew is cool and sweet,
       In the dingles* hiding,
   And the brook, on happy feet,
       Through the meadows gliding,
   There my brimming cup I'll fill
   From the clear and sparkling rill.*

2. Not for me the ruby* wine
       In the goblet gleaming;
   Death is in its hue divine;
       Sorrow in its beaming;
   But my brimming cup I'll fill
   From the clear and sparkling rill.

3. Not for me the drunkard's cup;
       Want and woe it bringeth,
   Bitter tears have filled it up,
       Anguish* from it springeth;
   But my brimming cup I fill
   From the clear and sparkling rill.

   —*Author Unknown.*

What to Drink ⁽¹³⁵⁾

1. The lily drinks the sunlight;
   The primrose drinks the dew;
 The cowslip sips the running brook;
   The hyacinth, heaven's blue;
 The peaches quaff* the dawn light;
   The pears, the autumn noon;
 The apple blossoms drink the rain,
   And the first warm air of June.

2. The wild flower and the violet
   Draw in the April breeze;
 And the sun and rain and hurricane*
   Are the tipple* of the trees;
 But not a bud or greenling,*
   From the hyssop* on the wall
 To the cedars* of Mount Lebanon,
   Is steeped in alcohol.

3. From all earth's emerald* basin,
   From the blue sky's sapphire*
     bowl,
 No living thing of root or wing
   Partakes that daily dole.*
 I'll quaff the lily's nectar;*
   I'll sip the cowslip's cup;
 I'll drink the shower, the sun,
     the breeze,
   But ne'er a poisoned drop.
         —*Author Unknown.*

Appreciation Study

1. What flowers are named in this poem? What does each one drink?
2. What do the trees drink? the peaches? the pears?
3. What is the "earth's emerald basin"? the "sky's sapphire bowl"? the "poisoned drop"?
4. Where is Mount Lebanon?
5. What does the Bible say about "the cedars of Mount Lebanon"? 1 Kings 5:1-6.

Horace Mann (S)

Find three things in this story that Horace Mann did for the children of the United States. Can you find something that he did that helps *you*? He spent his childhood in Massachusetts. Can you find this state on the map?

See how far you can read in three minutes.

1. No one has done more for the school children of America than Horace Mann. When Horace was a little boy, he did not have good schools to go to. He did not have a happy childhood. Perhaps that is why he tried so hard when he became a man to make the schools a happy place for children.

2. His parents lived in Massachusetts.* They were very poor. They had to work hard to get food for their family. Horace began to work on the farm earlier than he could remember. He had to go barefoot in the stony fields when he was plowing or hoeing or pulling up weeds. Even in the winter time, he often went barefoot in a cold room helping to braid straw for baskets and bonnets. This was how he earned money to buy a few schoolbooks.

3. Horace went to school only a few weeks during the winter. It was a poor school. The teacher did not love the children. He did not know how to make the lessons interesting. He seemed to think that children were made to be punished. Still, Horace was so anxious to learn that he was always sorry when school closed.

4. No matter how hard it was to get an education, Horace would not give up. At last a teacher who came to the town where Horace went to school became interested in this boy. He said he would get Horace ready for college. It usually takes years to prepare for college. But Horace studied so hard that he was ready in six months after this teacher came. When he finished college, he was at the head of his class.

5. God used Horace Mann to do a great work for children. Horace Mann believed that the way to make the world better was to make the schools better. And he believed that the way to make the schools better was to have better teachers. He went to many places, talking his ideas.

6. After a while, he was given twenty thousand dollars to build a school where teachers could be trained. This was the first normal* school in America. He told the teachers that the schoolroom should be a happy place, and not a place to punish children. He told the parents that children should not be kept out of school to work. After that, more children began to come to school. He did much to have a library

in each school. He did everything he could think of to make good schools and to help the children.

7. One of the last sayings of Horace Mann was: "Be ashamed to die until you have won some victory for humanity."* By that he meant that no one was ready to die until he had helped some one else to live a better life.

8. Whenever we think of Horace Mann, we should remember that even though our parents are poor, and many times we may have to work when we would like to play, if we are truly unselfish, we may still become useful men and women, and God will use us to help others.

Comprehension Test. Answer these questions by "Yes" or "No":
1. Did Horace Mann have a happy childhood?
2. Did he attend a good school when he was a child?
3. Did this discourage him?
4. Did he go to college?
5. Is his life an encouragement to poor children?
6. Did he build the first school in America for training teachers?
7. Were his parents rich?
8. Did he help to make the schools better?

Speed Test. See how quickly you can find and write the paragraph numbers that tell:
How Horace Mann earned money to buy books
How God used him when he became a man
One of his last sayings
The help his life should be to us
The school he went to when he was a boy
Building the first normal school
Getting ready for college

The Way for Billy and Me [103]

Each of these stanzas has a picture. Try to *see* it, and *tell* what you see. In which picture would you prefer to be? Why?

1. Where the pools are bright and deep,
   Where the gray trout lies asleep,
   Up the river and o'er the lea,*
   That's the way for *Billy* and *me*.

2. Where the blackbird sings the latest,
   Where the hawthorn blooms the sweetest,
   Where the nestlings* chirp and flee,
   That's the way for *Billy* and *me*.

3. Where the mowers* mow the cleanest,
   Where the hay lies thick and greenest;
   There to trace the homeward bee,
   That's the way for *Billy* and *me*.

4. Where the hazel* bank is steepest,
   Where the shadow falls the deepest,
   Where the clustering nuts fall free,
   That's the way for *Billy* and *me*.

—*James Hogg.*

The D. D. Class [O]

As you read this story find out what "D. D." stands for, how the "D. D. Class" came to be formed, and what the "D. D.'s" did during the quarter.

"Where's Helen Babson?" asked Hilda Ames, president of the newly organized junior class of the Sabbath school.

"Helen Babson?" repeated Margery Tilton. "Why, her mother is sick, and Helen can't leave her."

"My mother is not well, either. I wonder if I should have left *her*," thought Hilda to herself. But what she said aloud was, "This is the third class meeting she has missed."

"Why not go over there for our meeting?" suggested Amy Grant. "We might meet around at our homes as well as in our classroom. Then all our mothers could see what we are doing."

"You go and ask Helen if we may come over," directed Hilda, without waiting for a formal vote.

Marian was back from the telephone almost directly.

"She says come right over. Her mother will enjoy it almost as much as she will."

They found Mrs. Babson in a reclining chair, a rose-colored shawl lending a bit of its glow to her pale cheeks. She was so interested in their work, and asked so many questions, that it was some time before they could settle down to a formal class meeting.

"We must come to order." Again Hilda tapped with her pencil. "We must select our name and our work to-day. Suggestions are in order, but please don't all talk at once."

There was little danger of that. Helen's devotion to her mother, the little quiet attentions she showed her from time to time, reminded the girls that in each home represented there was another mother. Were they as thoughtful of their mothers as they might be?

"Let's take our own mothers and other mothers for our class work," exclaimed Amy Grant. "There's Mrs. Carlson, so lonely without Muriel; and Mrs. Endrith, all alone, now Eric has gone. And, of course, we might—"

"Be more thoughtful of our *own* mothers," added Marian. "I left mine all alone this evening." Marian's lips almost quivered as she remembered the half longing in her mother's voice as she asked if Marian could not stay at home sometimes.

"That would be a delightful work, and I am sure your mothers would appreciate it," smiled Mrs. Babson. "But would it be the kind of Sabbath school work you are expected to do?"

"They have a class of young mothers, with a teacher and a class of young girls to help. I don't see why we can't take our own mothers, and work that into Sabbath school."

"My mother can't go, because she can't get the children ready. I have to leave a half hour early because I lead the prayer band. Well, they can easily find another leader for that, and I'll bring my mother every Sabbath. I think that will be really-truly home missionary work."

"Let's call ourselves the D. D. Class, and have the rest of the school guessing," laughed Margery.

"D. D.—that's good," commented Hilda. "Will some one make that a motion?"

The D. D. Class they were from that hour. They began planning what they could do for mothers in general. They could not make public their little plans for their own mothers. But one thing they did decide to do—Monday evening each week they would give to their mothers, for then all mothers were more tired than usual. That evening they would get and clear away the supper. Each girl would spend her whole time giving pleasure to her mother, and treating her as an honored guest.

They asked for the planning of Mother's Day, in the month of May. At that time they arranged a picnic for fathers and mothers. They tried to be to each mother what Helen was to hers, and they did what they could for other lonely mothers.

The task they had selected gave the girls great pleasure, although it kept them at home rather more than usual. Class meetings were held at the homes, with the mother of the home as a special guest of honor. Each mother's or father's birthday was remembered by the entire class as well as by the daughter in the home. They had their picnic, and they had a reception* for their fathers and mothers, to which a few lonely adopted fathers and mothers were invited, as were also the church pastor and Sabbath school superintendent and their wives.

It was a very simple report that the D. D. Class

made at the end of the quarter,—a perfect record of attendance, daily lesson study, liberal offerings to missions, and the statement that they had done their best to live up to their class name. That was all they reported.

"Living up to their name means something," remarked the superintendent. "How many of you have guessed what 'D. D.' stands for? 'Devoted Daughters.' And a score or more of homes can testify to the excellent work they have done. Why cannot every girl be a 'D. D.,' every boy a 'D. S.'?"

—Adapted.

The Spider and the Fly [277]

1. "Will you walk into my parlor?"
    Said the spider to the fly;
    " 'Tis the prettiest little parlor
        That ever you did spy.*
    The way into my parlor
        Is up a winding stair,
    And I have many curious things
        To show when you are there."

2. "Oh, no, no!" said the little fly,
        "To ask me is in vain;
    For who goes up your winding stair
        Can ne'er come down again."

3. "I'm sure you must be weary, dear,
        With soaring up so high;

    Will you rest upon my little bed?"
        Said the spider to the fly.

4. "There are pretty curtains drawn around,
      The sheets are fine and thin;
   And if you like to rest awhile,
      I'll snugly tuck you in."

5. "Oh, no, *no!*" said the little fly,
      "For I've often heard it said,
   They never, never wake again
      Who sleep upon your bed."

6. Said the cunning spider to the fly,
      "Dear friend, what can I do
   To prove the warm affection
      I've always felt for you?
   I have within my pantry
      Good store of all that's nice;
   I'm sure you're very welcome—
      Will you please to take a slice?"

7. "Oh, *no, no!*" said the little fly,
      "Kind sir, that cannot be;
   I've *heard* what's in your pantry,
      And I do not wish to *see*."

8. "Sweet creature," said the spider,
      "You're witty* and you're wise.
   How handsome are your gauzy* wings!
      How brilliant are your eyes!
   I have a little looking-glass
      Upon my parlor shelf;

> If you'll step in one moment, dear,
> You shall behold yourself."

9. "I thank you, gentle sir," she said,
   "For what you're pleased to say,
   And bidding you good-morning now,
   I'll call another day."

—*Mary Howitt.*

Appreciation Study

1. What is the spider's "parlor"? its "winding stair"? the "fine, thin sheets"?
2. How many ways did the spider try to coax the fly to come in?

The spider finally destroys every fly it can catch in its web. It is like our great enemy, Satan, who tries every way he can to get us into his net so that he can destroy us.

Cornelia's Jewels ^(S)

This is a beautiful story of the olden days of Rome. It tells about a lady, named Cornelia, who had some jewels of which she was very proud. Read, and find out what her jewels were and why she was proud of them. Find Rome on the map.

1. Once there lived in the city of Rome a noble woman whose name was Cornelia.* This was more than one hundred years before Jesus was born. Cornelia had two fine boys. The name of the older boy was Tiberius* Gracchus.* The younger boy's name was Caius* Gracchus. Their father, whose name was also Tiberius Gracchus, was one of the leading

men in Rome. When the boys were quite young, their father died.

2. The father's death was a terrible blow to Cornelia. But she was brave, as well as beautiful and cultured.* In those days, the noble ladies of Rome wore rich dresses and costly jewels. Cornelia's fortune was not large, but she was a sensible woman. She willingly went without jewels and costly garments. She would rather spend her money to educate her children. She made up her mind that her sons should have the best education that Rome could give. She wanted them to become useful men.

3. Cornelia had many friends. She loved to have them visit her. Even kings often sat at her table. She was a charming hostess,* and her friends were happy to be her guests. She did not talk about her sorrows. Her wonderful cheerfulness and gentle courtesy made her greatly beloved by all.

4. One bright morning, a lady friend came to visit Cornelia. She was richly dressed. She wore beautiful pearls and flashing diamonds. Cornelia was simply dressed in a plain white robe. No rings or chains glittered on her hands or about her neck. Instead of flashing jewels in her hair, her long, soft brown braids crowned her head. She took her friend to walk among the flowers and trees in her beautiful garden.

5. Tiberius and Caius were standing in the vine-covered summer house. They were looking at their mother and her friend.

"Isn't our mother's friend a handsome lady?" said Caius to Tiberius. "She looks like a queen."

"She is not so beautiful as *our mother*," replied Tiberius, who was nine years older than his little brother. "She has a fine dress, but her face is not so noble and kind as our mother's is. It is our mother who is like a queen."

"You are right," answered the younger boy. "There is no woman in Rome so much like a queen as our mother."

6. Soon Cornelia came down the garden path to speak to the boys. She looked into her sons' proud eyes with a loving smile.

"Boys," she said, "I have something to tell you."

They bowed before her as Roman lads were taught to do.

"What is it, mother?" they asked.

"When you return from school to-day, you are to dine with us here in the garden."

Again they bowed as politely as if she had really been a queen. Then they left the garden, and went to school.

7. While they were gone, the lady opened a wonderful casket of jewels which she had brought to show her friend. She carefully picked up first one shining jewel and then another. She showed Cornelia their rich colors. She told her of their great value. There were diamonds, and pearls, and rubies, and many others. They were indeed beautiful gems.

At last she looked up at Cornelia, and said, "Is it true, Cornelia, that you have no jewels? Is it true, as I have heard, that you are too poor to own them?"

8. Just then, Tiberius and Caius came in from school.

"No, I am not poor," answered the fond mother, as she drew her two boys to her side. *"Here* are *my* jewels! They are worth more to me than all the costly gems you have shown me."

9. Tiberius and Caius Gracchus grew to be great men in Rome. They stood for what they thought was right. They tried to get laws that would help the poor. Tiberius helped the common people to get comfortable homes. Caius helped them to get food at small cost. They both lost their lives working to make Rome a free country. And that is why the world still likes to hear the story of "The Gracchi," and of Cornelia's jewels.

Comprehension Test. What shows that Cornelia was a sensible woman? What shows that she was a wise mother? What shows that her sons had been well trained?

After reading this story only *once,* see how many of these sentences you can complete correctly from memory. If you fail on any of them, read the story a second time, or until you can do all.

1. Cornelia lived in the city of ———.
2. Her sons' names were —— ——— and —— ———.
3. Cornelia wanted her sons to have a ——— ———.
4. She often had ——— at her table.
5. Cornelia had no —— or —— or other costly jewels.
6. She said her ——— were her jewels.
7. When her sons became men, they helped the ——— people.
8. They both lost their lives trying to make ——— a ——— country.

Vacation ⁽²⁵⁴⁾

1. I have closed my books and hidden my slate,
   And thrown my satchel across the gate.
   My school is out for a season of rest,
   And now for the schoolroom I love the best!

2. My *schoolroom* lies on the meadow wide,
   Where under the clover the sunbeams hide,
   Where the long vines cling to the mossy bars,
   And the daisies twinkle like fallen stars;

3. Where clusters of buttercups gild the scene,
   Like showers of gold dust thrown over the green,
   And the wind's flying footsteps are traced, as they pass,
   By the dance of the sorrel* and dip of the grass.

4. My *lessons* are written in clouds and in trees.
   And no one whispers, except the breeze
   That sometimes blows, from a secret place,
   A stray, sweet blossom against my face.

5. My *school bell* rings in the rippling stream
   Which hides itself, like a schoolgirl's dream,
   Under the shadow and out of sight,
   But laughing still for its own delight.

6. My *schoolmates* there are the birds and the bees,
   And the saucy squirrel, less wise than these,
   For he only learns, in all the weeks,
   How many chestnuts will fill his cheeks.

7. My *teacher* is patient, and never yet
   A lesson of hers did I once forget;
   For wonderful love do her lips impart,
   And all her lessons are learned by heart.

8. Oh, come! Oh, come! or we shall be late,
   And autumn will fasten the golden gate.
   Of all the schoolrooms in east or west,
   The schoolroom of nature I love the best.
   —*Katherine Lee Bates.*

Reading Tests and Scores for the Sixth Period

Silent Reading. Have you reached your goal of ability to read 140 words a minute? Perhaps you have gone beyond it. Some children in the fourth grade can read 180 words or even more in a minute, and know what they read, too. But if you can read 140 words, you have done well. You deserve a grade of 100, provided your comprehension score and your memory tests are perfect.

Oral Reading. How many stories from your reader have you prepared and read to others this year? Can you read with good expression? Can you read distinctly and correctly? Can you read by phrases, and look off your book often without losing your place? If so, you deserve a good grade in oral reading.

For your oral test at this time you may choose any (O) story in your fourth grade reader.

Memory Reading. Have you learned perfectly at least six poems this year averaging at least 300 words each or their equivalent, so that you can recite them *now?* If you have, you should have a grade of 100 in memory reading.

Fourth Grade Dictionary Teacher

(Only the meanings that apply in this reader are given here.)

A

ăb′bĕȳ, a place of worship.
a-bīdĕ′, dwell.
a-bŏm-ĭ-nā′tion, a very great hatred.
ab-stāin′, keep away from.
ăd′der, a kind of poisonous snake.
ad-drĕss′, a speech.
ad-jŭst′ed, put in place.
a-dŏpt′, to take as one's own.
Ăd′vent-ist, one who believes in the personal second coming of Jesus.
af-fĕc′tion-ate, showing a feeling of love.
ăf′flu-ent, abundant.
Airĕ′dālĕ, a dog of the terrier kind, known to be very fond of children.
a-kĭn′, very much like.
al′der, a kind of tree whose blossoms are in long tassels.
Al-lē′gra, a girl's name which means happy.
an′chŏr, a heavy iron instrument fastened to a boat which when thrown into the water sinks to the bottom and holds the boat from drifting.
ăn′guish, very deep sorrow and trouble.
ănt′lerṣ, branching horns.
ăn′vil, an iron block on which metal in a blacksmith shop is hammered.

ap-prĕn′tĭçĕ, one who works with some one to learn a trade.
Ăr′ab, a native of Arabia.
Ăr-a-bĕl′la, a girl's name.
A-rā′bi-an, belonging to Arabia.
ärch′er, one who can shoot well with a bow and arrow.
Ăr-mē′ni-a, a small country in western Asia in which Mt. Ararat is located.
Är′mis-tĭçĕ, agreement of peace between the countries at the close of the World War. The Armistice was signed Nov. 11, 1918.
ar-rīv′al, coming.
är′tist, one who draws or paints beautiful pictures.
as-sĭst′ant, helper.
a-strāy′, out of the way.
at-tăckĕd′, tried to injure.
ăt′tĭc, a room just under the roof of a house.
Aŭs′trĭ-a, a country in Europe.

B

băb′bling, foolish talking.
băg′pipe, a musical instrument having a windbag from which air is forced into pipes.
ban-dĭt′tĭ, highway robbers; more than one bandit.

băn′ish, drive away; make one forget.
băr′ri-er, anything that hinders.
Bar-thŏl′o-mew, a man's name.
bāy, a reddish color; sometimes a horse of this color.
bēa′con, a guiding light.
be-get′, bring to life; produce.
be-gṳile′, to cause the time to pass pleasantly.
bĕl′lōws, an instrument for blowing fires.
be-rēaved′, robbed by death.
bĕv′ies, flocks.
Bĭng′en, a town in Germany.
bĭrd′ling, a young bird.
bĭsh′op, a church officer.
bless′ed, giving joy.
blŭs′ter-ing, windy and noisy.
bōll, the pod of a cotton plant.
brawn′y̆, having large, strong muscles.
bree*ch*′ing, the part of a horse's harness that passes around his thighs.
brībed, to offer a gift of money, or something else of value, to lead one to do wrong.
brĭde′grōōm, a man about to be married, or one newly married.
brĭnk, edge.
brĭs′tle, stand out.
brōōd, a family of young birds.
bŭck′ler, a kind of shield.
Bṳd′dhist, one who worships a religious teacher named Buddha.

Bûr′roughs, the name of America's greatest naturalist.

C

căb′i-net-mak-er, one who makes furniture.
căb′i-net shop, a place where fine furniture is made.
Cā′ius, a boy's name.
eăm′brĭe, a kind of cotton cloth.
Cām′brĭdge, a city in Massachusetts.
căn′ni-bal-ĭsm, a practice among cannibals who eat human flesh.
căn′ni-bals, savages who kill and eat human beings.
eā′per-ing, playfully running about.
căp′i-tal, money.
căr′a-mel, a kind of candy.
ca-rĕss′es, pettings; expressions of love.
căt′kins, flowers that hang in long tassels like those on a willow or birch.
căt′a-mount, wild cat.
eăv′ern, cave.
çē′dar, a large, strong evergreen tree.
Cēy-lŏn′, an island south of India.
*ch*ăff, the husk that comes from grain when it is threshed.
*ch*ärge, a duty to look after and perform.
*ch*ăr′i-ty, help to those in need.
*ch*ăt′tel, property.
*ch*ĕr′ish, keep in mind.

çĭr-eū-lā′tion, moving around and returning to the starting point. The air and our blood circulate.

elēạr′ings, open places where the trees have been cut down in a forest.

coat of māil′, a war coat made of small pieces of metal joined together.

cŏl′o-ny, people from their native country who settle in another land but who still belong to the parent country; the country thus settled.

cŏl′pōr-tĕụr, one who sells religious books from house to house.

com-mū′ni-ty, the people living near together.

com-mū-tā′tion, a low-priced ticket given to one who travels from day to day over the same road.

cȯm-pärt′ment, a section of an English train.

cȯm′pass, an instrument with a balanced needle that always points toward the north.

eŏm′pound, an inclosed place where mission houses are built.

cŏn′fi-dĕnçẹ, trust.

con-nǿis-sẹụr′, a critical judge of fine art.

cŏn′science (shĕns), that part of our mind that tells us what is wrong.

cŏn′se-crātẹ, to set apart to a sacred use.

cŏn′se-quĕnç-es, results.

con-sĭd′er, think about earnestly.

con-sĭd′er-ate, thoughtful of others.

con-si-ĕn′tious, careful to do right.

Con-stan-tĭ-nō′ple, a city in Turkey, Europe.

con-tĕn′tionṣ, quarrels.

cŏn′tĭ-nent, one of the six large bodies of land on the earth.

con-tra-dĭe′tion, a denial of some statement or fact.

con-trăet′, become smaller.

eōō′lĭẹ, a native workingman of India.

eōōn, a small animal of North America having a valuable fur.

Cŏr-nē′li-a, a woman's name.

côr′net, a kind of horn used as a musical instrument.

eôr′po-ral, an officer of the lowest grade.

cŏs′tūmẹ, style of dress.

cräft, a small ocean boat.

crēẹd, a statement of one's religious belief.

erĕst, top of a mountain.

erouch′ing, bending low, as if about to leap.

erup′per (or crŭp′per), the leather loop in a horse's harness that passes under his tail.

eŭl′prit, one guilty of a fault.

cŭl′tūrẹd, well educated and courteous.

ẹzär, the ruler of Russia.

Czech′ (chẹẹk) o-Slŏ-vä′kĭ-a, a small country east of Germany.

D

de-clâre', tell about.
de-creed', said in a determined way.
ded-i-cā'tion, setting something apart to a special work.
de-ject'ed, discouraged; cast down.
dĕll, a small valley.
de-plōred', grieved about.
dĕs'o-late, lonely.
de-spŏnd', be discouraged.
de-spŏn'dent, discouraged.
dew'y, full of dew; covered with dew.
dī'a-dem, crown.
din'gle, a narrow hollow between hills.
dis-cŏv'er-y, when first found.
dis-heart'ened, discouraged.
dis-pĕn'sa-ry, a place where medicines are given out.
Dixie, or Dix'ie's Land, a name given to the Southern States in the United States during the Civil War. The name came from a Northern negro song which expressed the supposed troubles of the slaves of a man named Dixie. Originally written *Dixie's Land*.
dōle, a small quantity.
dōle'ful, dismal; gloomy.
dōle'ful-ly, very sadly.
do-mĕs'tic, belonging to the house or home.
do-mĭn'ion (yon), rule.

dŏm'ĭ-no, a set of dotted pieces of bone or wood for playing a game called dominoes.
dŏve'cŏt, a small house for doves.
drought, dry weather.
drow'si-ness, oversleeping; laziness.
dūke, an English nobleman.
dŭn'geon, a dark inner prison.
dŭsk, nearly dark.
dўs-pĕp'sĭ-a, disease of the stomach.

E

ea'sel, a support for holding a picture or blackboard.
ĕb'on, dark colored like ebony.
ef-fāçe', destroy; blot out.
e-lĕe-trĭç'i-ty, a substance that gives light, heat, and power.
ĕm'er-ald, a green color.
e-mō'tion, deep feeling.
Em'press Jo'se-phine, wife of the French emperor Napoleon Bonaparte.
ĕn'tered, went into.
en-ter-tāin'mĕnt, a pleasant time given to others.
en-tiçed', attracted; drew toward itself.
ĕn'try, a small room into which one comes from the outdoors.
es-sayed', tried.
es-tēemed', thought about kindly and with respect.
Eu(ū)'rope, one of the six great continents.

e-văn'ġel-ist, preacher.
ex (ĕḡz) -ḥaust'ed, without strength.
ĕx'īlḙ, rudely compelled to leave one's country.
ex-pănds̠', becomes larger.

F

făc'to-ry, a building where things are made by machinery.
Fäh'ren-hḙit, name of the man who first used mercury in a thermometer.
făn'çy, thought.
Făr'rar, name of an English clergyman and author.
Fĕb'ru̠-a-ry, the second month in the year.
fī'ber, cloth.
Fï-jï'an, a native of Fiji.
flăx, a plant from which linen thread is made.
fleeç'y̆, soft like fleece.
flēḙt, swift.
flĭnt'y, very hard like flint rock.
flŭr'ry, nervous hurry.
fŏd'der, food for horses and cattle.
fō'lĭ-age, leaves growing on a tree or plant.
förġḙ, or fôrġḙ, an open fire where a blacksmith heats metal to hammer it into shape.
fŏr'ḙïġn, belonging to another country.
fôrt'night, fourteen nights or two weeks.
fôr'tress, a place where one is protected from an enemy.

fôr'tūnḙ, wealth.
fowl'er, one who catches and kills wild fowls or birds for sport.
frē'quĕnt, often.
frŏl'ickḙd, played freely and joyfully.
fū'ri-ḙus-ly, madly.

G

găn'der, a male goose.
ġär'nishḙd, made beautiful.
ġau̠z'y̆, thin and nearly transparent.
ġĕms̠, jewels; sparkling stones.
Ḡĕss'ler, a man's name.
ġḙy̆'sēr, a boiling spring that throws up hot water or mud.
ḡïll, that through which a fish or polliwog breathes.
ġĭl'ly-flow'er (July-flower), the common stock.
ġïrths, bands by which the saddle is fastened on a horse.
glādḙ, open place in the woods.
glee, joy.
glĕn, a narrow valley.
glōōm, partial darkness.
glŭt'ton, one who eats too much.
gŏb'bler, a male turkey.
Gold'en Gate, the narrow neck of water that joins San Francisco Harbor to the Pacific Ocean.
ḡōrḙ, a three-sided piece of cloth sewed into a garment to make it wider.

25   385

Grăc′chus, a man's name.
grāve, sober.
green′ling, a small green plant.
grĭm, stern looking.
guīle, deceit.

H

hab-i-tā′tion, dwelling place.
half-wit′ted, having little sense.
hăn′dĭ-work, something made by hand.
hăp′ly, perhaps; it might happen.
här′bor, a quiet place in the ocean near the shore where ships rest.
hâre′bell, a bell-shaped flower.
här′mo-ny, unity and peace.
hay′mow, a place in a barn where hay is stored.
hā′zel, a shrub that bears clusters of small nuts.
hĕad′stall, that part of the halter that goes around a horse's head.
hęarth, fireplace.
hearth′stone, fireplace; sometimes means home.
heed, give attention to.
hĕm′ĭ-*sph***ēre,** half of the earth's sphere, or ball.
hĕr′e-tic, one whose religious opinions differ from the faith of his church.
hē′ro, one famous for courage.
hĕṣ′i-ta-ting-ly, slowly and not seeming to feel sure.

Hī-a-wa′tha, name of an Indian boy whom the Indians believed was sent among them to clear their rivers, forests, and fishing grounds, and teach them the arts of peace.
Hĭn′dus̩, natives of Hindustan, a country in Asia. The god worshiped by the Hindus as Creator is called Bräh′ma.
hip-pō-pŏt′a-mus, a large animal living in the water.
hōst′ĕss, a lady who entertains company.
hou̯nds̩, hunting dogs.
hŏv′els̩, huts or cabins.
hūge, very large.
hū-măn′i-ty, the people living on the earth.
hŭr′ri-cane, a hard windstorm.
hy̆p′o-crītes, people who are not so good as they pretend to be.
hy̆s′sŏp, an herb belonging to the mint family.

I

i′çĭ-eles̩, sticks of ice hanging from the edge of a roof or other edge.
ī′dol, something worshiped.
im-prĕss′īve, having deep effect.
In̩′ca̍, a tribe of South American Indians.
in-cli-nā′tion, that which one desires to do.
in-dŭs′trĭ-ŏu̯s, not idle.
in-tĕl′li-ġençe, power to understand and learn.

in-tŏl'er-a-ble, not to be put up with.
in-tŏx'i-cāt-ing, producing drunkenness.
in-trṳdę', go in without being invited.
in'va-lid, a person in poor health.
I-tăl'ian (yan), belonging to Italy.

J

jū'bi-lee, a time of special joy.
jŭṉ'ḡlę, dense trees, brush, and grass growing in hot countries.
jus'tĭçę, fairness.

K

keen, sharp and cold.
kĕn'nel, a small house for a dog.
kĕr'o-sēnę, an oil that comes from soft coal.
king'dȯm, a country ruled by a king.
knight (night), a title given to a person because he has won some great honor. He has the word Sir put before his name.
Kĭm'ber-lęy̆, a city in South Africa where there are rich diamond mines.

L

Lär'eȯm, the name of an American poet.
läṳnchęd, the sliding of a new ship into the water.

lāvę, bathe.
lays, songs.
lēạ, meadow.
leaf'let, a small leaf.
lĕc'tūr-er, one who gives public addresses.
lēı̆'ṣūrę, spare time.
light'some, cheerful.
lĭn'seed, the seed of the flax plant from which an oil is made.
lĭt'er-a-ry, those who love learning and are learned.
lōōm, a machine for weaving.
Lǿŭgh'bo-rōŭgh, a man's name.
Lōẉ'ell, a city in Massachusetts where much cotton cloth is made.
lŭḡ'ḡāḡę, baggage of a traveler.

M

măg-a-zīnę', a small paper-bound book published regularly.
man'tlę, a loose cape.
Mas-sa-chū'setts, a State in the eastern part of the United States.
mȧs'tiff, an English watchdog.
ma-tē'ri-al, that which has to do with our bodily wants.
Mẹ'lĭ, a Fijian man's name.
mēr'eū-ry, quicksilver.
mĭl-dēw̄, a plant disease.
mĭn'er-al măt'ter, a part of the food that builds bone and teeth; the hard part of the bones and teeth.

mĭs′*chĭ∉*-v∅ŭs, full of mischief; doing harmful things.

Mis-sis-sĭp′pĭ, one of the largest rivers of North America. The name means *Father of Waters.*

mŏb, a disorderly crowd.

mŏc′ca-sin, a low shoe made of deerskin.

Mo-hăm′mĕd, a false prophet who once lived in Arabia, and who was thought by his followers to be greater than Christ.

Mo-hăm′me-dan, one who worships a man named Mohammed.

mŏn′ĭ-tor, one appointed to look after others.

mo-nŏt′o-n∅ŭs, tiresome because of its sameness.

môr′al, a lesson of truth or right.

Mouse T*ow*′er, a tower on an island in the Rhine River where, according to a German story, a bishop was once eaten by mice because of his cruelty to the poor.

mōẃ′ers, those who cut the fields of ripe grain or grass.

mū-ri-ăt′ic, an acid made from sea salt.

mûrk′y, dark; gloomy.

mûr′mŭr∉d, spoke in a low, soft tone.

mūṣ∉, think in an absent-minded way.

mŭs-tache (tȧsh)′, hair worn on a man's upper lip; a man who wears a mustache.

mys-tē′ri-∅ŭs, not easy to understand.

mўs′ter-y, something that cannot be explained.

N

Na-pō′le-on Bo′na-part∉, a French general and emperor.

năt′u-ral-ist, one who knows a great deal about nature.

nā′vў, ships of war belonging to a country.

nĕc′tar, the honey of flowers.

ne̸i̸g̸h̸, the cry of a horse.

ne̸i̸g̸h̸′bor-ing, near by.

nest′lings, young birds before they leave the nest.

Nēw′found-land, a shaggy-haired, intelligent dog whose native home was Newfoundland.

nĭm′bl∉, quick and active.

n*oi*′some, destructive.

nôr′mal, a school where teachers are trained.

nŏs′trĭlṣ, passages in the nose.

nŏv′el-ty, something new and unusual.

nûrs′er-y, a room for young children; a place where young plants are grown.

O

ŏc-cā′sion-al-ly, once in a while.

ŏc-cū-pā′tion, that which one does as a business.

ōd∉, a short song.

ŏft, often.
o-mĭs′sion, a neglect to do something.
op-por-tū′ni-tĭe̸ṣ, when everything seems favorable.
op-por-tū′ni-ty, having great advantage.
op-prĕssé̸d′, cruelly treated.
o-rāt′ing, making a forceful speech.
ôr′a-tor, a public speaker to whom people like to listen.
or-dāiné̸d′, made and set apart for some special use.
O′Ré̸il′ly, a man's name.
ō′rĭ-ōle̸, a bird with black and yellow feathers.
or′na-mĕnt, fancy decoration.

P

pāle̸ṣ, pointed sticks made into a fence.
păn′thêr, a wild animal belonging to the cat family.
Päs′rŭr, a place in India.
pȧs′tor, a minister who has charge of a church.
pa-trĭ-ŏt′ic, loving one's country.
Penn-sȳl-vā′ni-a, a State in the eastern part of the United States.
pêr′fūme̸, a sweet-smelling scent.
per-se-eū′tion, illtreatment because of one's religion.
per-sē-vēre̸′, never giving up.
per-sĭst′ed, kept on in the same way.
per-spi-rā′tion, sweat.

pĕs′tĭ-lĕnçe̸, a disease that attacks many people at the same time; a plague.
pĕt′tĭ-coat, an underskirt.
pet′tish-ly, fretfully.
Phĭl-a-dĕl′phĭ-a, a large city in Pennsylvania.
pḯēr, a landing place reaching into the sea from the shore; a wharf.
plāgṷé̸, a disease that attacks many people at the same time; a pestilence.
plŭck′ing, picking the feathers from a dead bird's body.
plṷme̸, anything like a fluffy feather.
pŏl′i-çȳ, rule to go by.
pōr′ing, studying with close attention.
pōr′ter, a man on a train or boat who carries parcels and does other work to help passengers.
pŏv′er-ty, being very poor.
Pow-ha-tăn′, a tribe of Indians named after their chief.
prāḯ′rḯe̸, a large tract of land without trees.
prē′mĭ-um, prize.
prĕṣ′ent-ly, in a short time.
prīme̸, youth; when at its best.
prē′tĕnse̸, make believe.
pre-vāil′, win out.
preyé̸d, seized for food.
prĭn′çĕss, the daughter of a king or queen.
Prĭs-çĭl′la, the name of Longfellow's great-great-great-grandmother.

prō′tē-in, a part of the food that builds muscle.
Prŭs′sia, a country in Europe northeast from Germany.
pŭne′tū-al, on time.
pŭne-tū-ăl′i-ty, being on time.
pûr-sūe′, keep on seeking; follow after.

Q
quăff, drink a great deal.
quāint, odd; old-fashioned.

R
rā′dĭ-ance, brightness.
rā′dĭ-ā-tor, coils of pipes that contain steam, hot air, or hot water for heating a room.
rāġ′ing, acting with rage or anger; causing one to act madly or with rage.
rāid, a rush upon a place to conquer it.
rănch, a farm.
rän′ġĕr, a man who takes care of a ranch.
Rä′tū, a Fijian chief.
rā′ven, a large, glossy black bird of the crow family.
rēared, raised from a small beginning.
re-çĕp′tion, a social gathering of friends.
re-fīne′, separate gold from other material by melting.
re-fīn′ing, noble.
re-fôrm′, a bad habit left off for a good one.
ref′ūġe, a place of safety.
re-grĕt′, think of with sorrow; unwilling to take things as they are.

re-hĕarse′, repeat; tell.
reigned, ruled.
re-lăx′, become loose.
re-lĭēf′, freedom from care.
re-pōse′, rest.
re-ṣŏlved′, made up one's mind.
rĕv′er-ent, showing respect for sacred things.
re-vīved′, refreshed and strengthened.
rĭġ′ging, the ropes fastened to the masts and sails of a vessel.
rĭll, small stream of water.
rī′o-tøŭs, disorderly and without reasonable limit.
rĭv′en, torn.
rĭv′ū-let, a very small river or stream of water.
rōġue, a sly, mischievous person; sometimes used playfully for one who is full of fun.
rōv′er, wanderer.
rōv′ing, wandering about.
ru′bў, red in color.
rŭf′fian (yan), a low, base fellow.

S
sāġ′ĕṣ, wise men.
sap(săf)′phīre, a precious stone of a sky-blue color.
saw′horse, a wooden rack on which boards or logs are placed for sawing.
saw′yer, one who saws wood.
sēāled, climbed over.
seôrn, despise.
scȳthe, a curved cutting instrument used for mowing grass, etc.

390

sĕl′dŏm, not often.
self-săc′rĭ-fīç-ing, denying one's self that which is naturally pleasant.
Se-rär′pī, name of an Armenian girl.
sĕx′tŏn, a man whose duty it is to toll the bell for a funeral.
shăb′bў, a worn condition of clothes.
shēęn, brightness.
ship′shape, in good order.
shrou̇d′ed, wrapped in a shroud or gloomy covering.
shŭt′tlę, an instrument on which the thread is wound for weaving.
shȳ′ly, timidly as if afraid.
sin′ew(ū)-y, strong and with large muscles.
sleet, a rain with snow or hail.
slŏv′en-ly, without neatness or order.
smĕlt′er, a place where metal is melted.
smith′ў, a blacksmith shop.
snârę, a trap for catching an animal.
sŏr′rel, a reddish brown or yellowish color; a small herb having an acid taste.
sŏv′er-ęīgn, a British gold coin worth about five dollars.
spȳ, see something that was hidden.
squīrę, a title for a man who is justice of the peace.
stăḡ, a male deer.

stạll, a place in a stable where a horse is kept and fed.
stĭr′rŭp, an iron hoop hung from a saddle in which a horseman sets his foot when he mounts or rides.
stū′dĭ-ō, the room where an artist draws.
sŭb′stĭ-tūtę, that which is put in the place of the real thing.
sŭlk′ў, a light, two-wheeled carriage with a seat for only one person.
sŭm′mit, the highest point of a hill or mountain.
sûr′ly, ill-natured.
Swĭss, belonging to Switzerland.
Swĭt′zer-land, a small country in central Europe.

T

tăb′er-nă-elę, dwelling place.
tăl′lōw, the melted fat of oxen and sheep.
tär′nĭshęd, spoiled by wrongdoing.
tăt-tōō′, to mark the skin with a needle and rub stain or dye into the wounds so the pattern can never be removed.
tĕm′per-a-tūrę, degree of heat.
tĕm′pest, storm.
thĕr-mŏm′e-ter, an instrument that measures heat.
thrall, slavery.
threạd′lets, fine threads.
three′scōrę, three times twenty.
thrōnę, a king's chair.

tīde, the rising and falling of the water in the sea.
Tī-bē′rĭ-us, a boy's name.
tī′dings, news.
tĭm′brĕl, a kind of drum.
tĭm′ĭd, bashful, afraid.
tĭp′plė, habit of drinking often.
Tĭ-tĭ-cä′ca, a lake in Peru, South America.
Tōk′yō, or Tō′kĭō, the capital city of Japan.
tŏr′rent, a downpour of rain.
trĕas′ū-rў, a place where money is kept.
trī′fling, of little importance.
trĭ′ō, a group of three people.
trī-ŭm′phant, rejoicing for victory.
tru̇′ant, one who runs away from duty.
tûr′ret, a small tower that turns around.
tў′rant, a cruel ruler.

U

un-çēas′ing-ly, without stopping.
un-heed′ed, without being noticed.
un-tū′torėd, not taught.

V

Vä̇al, a river in South Africa that flows into the Orange River.
vālė, land between hills

văl′lėў, land between hills.
văn′ish, go from sight.
vȧst, large.
Vĕn-ė-zue(zwē)′la, a country in the northern part of South America.
vĕs′ti-būlė, a small room or hall at the entrance into a house.
vĕt′er-an, a person of long experience.
Vĭ-ĕn′na, the capital city of Austria.
vī′ta-mĭn, an important food element found especially in vegetables, fruit, and milk.

W

West-mĭn′stėr Ăb′bėў, the name of one of the large church buildings in London where many famous people are buried.
wharf, a place built on the shore so that boats can load and unload.
whĭm′per-ing, whining.
wine′bĭb-ber, one who drinks much wine or other strong drink.
wĭsp, small bundle.
wĭt′ness, see.
wĭt′tў, able to say wise things in a funny way.
wōld, open country without woods.

Graph of Pupil's Weekly Silent Reading Rate

Fourth Grade, 19...... Name..

PERIOD	I	II	III	IV	V	VI
160						
155						
150						
145						
140						
135						
130						
125						
120						
115						
110						
105						
100						
95						
90						
85						
80						
75						

These blank graphs provide for those who may use the book in successive years.

Graph of Pupil's Weekly Silent Reading Rate
Fourth Grade, 19...... Name..

PERIOD	I	II	III	IV	V	VI
160						
155						
150						
145						
140						
135						
130						
125						
120						
115						
110						
105						
100						
95						
90						
85						
80						
75						

These blank graphs provide for those who may use the book in successive years.

Graph of Pupil's Weekly Silent Reading Rate

Fourth Grade, 19...... Name..

PERIOD	I	II	III	IV	V	VI
160						
155						
150						
145						
140						
135						
130						
125						
120						
115						
110						
105						
100						
95						
90						
85						
80						
75						

These blank graphs provide for those who may use the book in successive years.

Graph of Pupil's Weekly Silent Reading Rate

Fourth Grade, 19...... Name..

PERIOD	I	II	III	IV	V	VI
160						
155						
150						
145						
140						
135						
130						
125						
120						
115						
110						
105						
100						
95						
90						
85						
80						
75						

These blank graphs provide for those who may use the book in successive years.

We invite you to view the complete
selection of titles we publish at:
www.TEACHServices.com

scan with your mobile
device to go directly
to our website

Please write or email us your praises, reactions, or
thoughts about this or any other book we publish at:

www.TEACHServices.com • (800) 367-1844

11 Quartermaster Circle
Fort Oglethorpe, GA 30742

Info@TEACHServices.com

TEACH Services, Inc., titles may be purchased in bulk
for educational, business, fund-raising, or sales
promotional use. For information, please e-mail:

BulkSales@TEACHServices.com

Finally if you are interested in seeing
your own book in print, please contact us at

publishing@TEACHServices.com

We would be happy to review your manuscript for free.